The Effects of Compulsory Competitive Tendering and European Law on Local Authorities

STUDIES IN LAW

*A series of publications issued
by the Centre of European Law,
King's College London*

General Editor
Mads Andenas

Editorial Board
Walter Baron van Gerven
Francis Jacobs QC
C. G. J. Morse

Volume 6

The aim of this series is to publish studies in the broad area of European Community Law and Comparative European Law. Each publication will provide an important and original contribution to the development of legal scholarship in its field and will be of interest to the legal practitioner, academic, government and Community official.

The titles published in this series are listed at the end of this volume.

CENTRE FOR EUROPEAN LAW
KING'S COLLEGE LONDON

The Effects of Compulsory Competitive Tendering and European Law on Local Authorities

Philip Gosling

KLUWER LAW INTERNATIONAL
THE HAGUE · LONDON · BOSTON

Published by Kluwer Law International
P.O. Box 85889
2508 CN The Hague, The Netherlands

Sold and distributed in the USA and Canada by
Kluwer Law International
675 Massachusetts Avenue
Cambridge, MA 02139, USA

Sold and distributed in all other countries by
Kluwer Law International
Distribution Centre
P.O. Box 322
3300 AH Dordrecht, The Netherlands

A C.I.P. Catalogue record for this book is available from the Library of Congress

Printed on acid-free paper

ISBN: 90-411-9825-3

© 2001 Kluwer Law International

Kluwer Law International incorporates the publishing programmes of Graham & Trotman Ltd, Kluwer Law and Taxation Publishers and Martinus Nijhoff Publishers.

This publication is protected by international copyright law.
All rights reserved. No part of this publication may be reproduced, stored in a retrieval system, or transmitted in any form or by any means, electronic, mechanical, photocopying, recording or otherwise, without the prior permission of the publisher.

Printed and bound in Great Britain by Antony Rowe Ltd

Table of Contents

Abstract   vii

Part One: The Legal Framework of Compulsory Competitive Tendering

Chapter One
Blue-Collar CCT under the Local Government Act 1988   3

1.1 Background   3
1.2 Defined Authorities and Defined Activities   5
1.3 The Competitive Tendering Rules   16
1.4 Accounting, Financial and Disclosure of Information Requirements   23
1.5 Enforcement Provisions   27

Chapter Two
CCT for Professional Services   37

2.1 Background and Development of Professional Services CCT   37
2.2 The Defined Activities   44
2.3 Accounting Provisions – the Statement of Support Service Costs   47
2.4 New Rules for Competitive Tendering   49
2.5 Summary   59

Chapter Three
CCT for Construction and Maintenance Work under the Local Government, Planning and Land Act 1980   61

3.1 Activities covered by the Act   61
3.2 The CCT Requirements   65
3.3 Requirements for Accounts, Financial Returns and Disclosure of Information   70
3.4 The Enforcement Provisions   73

Part Two: Legal and Practical Issues raised by CCT

Chapter Four
EC Public Procurement Law and its Implications for CCT   77

4.1 Background   77
4.2 The Overlapping Scope of the EC and CCT Regimes   80
4.3 The EC Rules and their Interaction with CCT   84
4.4 Summary   101

Chapter Five
The Limitation of Local Discretion in the Contract Tendering Process   103

5.1 Background   103

5.2 Restricting Contract Compliance Policies: the Prohibition of
    Non-Commercial Considerations under Part II of the LGA 1988   105
5.3 An Overview of Anti-Competitive Conduct   112
5.4 Examples of Anti-Competitive Conduct in the Tendering Process 119
5.5 Summary   133

CHAPTER SIX
TUPE and its Implications for CCT   135

6.1 The Acquired Rights Directive and its Implementation by TUPE   135
6.2 Identifying a TUPE Situation   138
6.3 The Consequences of TUPE   153
6.4 Summary   164

PART THREE: CASE STUDIES

CHAPTER SEVEN
A Case Study: Resbrough Borough Council   167

7.1 Local Authority Profile   167
7.2 The Results of CCT   168
7.3 Management of Service Provision under CCT   177
7.4 Case Studies of CCT Tenders   192
7.5 Summary and Conclusions   210

CHAPTER EIGHT
A Case Study: Greenbrough Borough Council   213

8.1 Profile of Greenbrough   213
8.2 The Results of CCT   213
8.3 Managing Service Delivery under CCT   219
8.4 Case Studies of CCT Tenders   239
8.5 Summary and Conclusions   259

PART FOUR: SUMMARY AND CONCLUSIONS

CHAPTER NINE
Summary and Conclusions   265

APPENDICES AND BIBLIOGRAPHY

Appendix 1: Research Methodology for Case Studies   275

Appendix 2: Recent Developments   277

BIBLIOGRAPHY   285

INDEX   289

Abstract

This book is the outcome of doctoral research into the effects of compulsory competitive tendering (CCT) on two English local authorities. CCT was a statutory procurement regime introduced from 1980 onwards by Conservative governments with the purpose of improving efficiency and value for money in local government and creating a competitive market for the provision of local services. Local authorities and certain other public bodies were permitted to carry out certain activities directly (that is through their own employees), only if they could do so competitively. This had to be demonstrated by compliance with a statutory competitive tendering procedure regulated by the Secretary of State. Although abolished from 2 January 2000 and replaced by a duty of best value regime under the Local Government Act 1999, CCT has had a significant and continuing impact on local authorities.

This book is organised into four parts and examines the CCT legislation, the principal legal and practical issues that it has raised (particularly through its inter-action with aspects of European Law), and the effects it has had on the two local authorities selected for study. Part One consists of three chapters and considers the particular CCT rules that were established for local authority manual and managerial work ('blue-collar CCT'), professional services work ('white-collar CCT'), and construction and maintenance work. Part Two considers in three chapters the inter-action of CCT with European Union public procurement law, the impingement of CCT on local authority discretion in contract tendering processes, and the implications for CCT of the European Acquired Rights Directive and the Transfer of Undertakings (Protection of Employment) Regulations 1981. The case studies of the local authorities are presented as two chapters in Part Three. Each considers the results of CCT and the effect on the authority's approach to service provision, organisational structure and general culture. A summary and the conclusions of the research are presented in Part Four.

The book is based on case study research conducted in the period up to the May 1997 general election. A separate annex provides information and analysis of post-1997 developments.

Part One

The Legal Framework of Compulsory Competitive Tendering

Chapter 1
Blue-Collar CCT under the Local Government Act 1988

Chapter 2
CCT for Professional Services

Chapter 3
CCT for Construction and Maintenance Work under the Local Government Planning and Land Act 1980

Chapter One

Blue-Collar CCT under the Local Government Act 1988

Contents

1.1 Background
1.2 Defined Authorities and Defined Activities
1.3 The Competitive Tendering Rules
1.4 Accounting, Financial and Disclosure of Information Requirements
1.5 Enforcement Provisions

Compulsory Competitive Tendering was a statutory procurement regime introduced from 1980 onwards by Conservative governments with the purpose of improving efficiency and value for money in local government and later of creating a competitive market for the provision of local services. In the formal language of statute, the purpose of compulsory competitive tendering was to ensure that local authorities (and other public authorities) only carried out certain work if they could do so competitively.[1] The development and key features of CCT are outlined in the first three chapters of this book. They will show that CCT was a detailed legal regime encompassing competitive tendering, accounting and financial requirements supported by strong enforcement powers wielded by the Secretary of State. This first Chapter will examine the CCT provisions as they related to local authority blue-collar services. Subsequent chapters will consider the CCT provisions that related to local authority professional services (Chapter 2) and construction and maintenance work (Chapter 3).

1.1 Background

The principle of CCT was first introduced in Part III of the Local Government, Planning and Land Act 1980 (LGPLA) 1980, which required local authorities to establish trading accounts for construction and maintenance work undertaken by their Direct Labour Organisations (DLOs) and to subject certain amounts of such work to competitive tender. This was intended to improve the efficiency of local authority DLOs and is considered further in Chapter 3. At first, the government showed little enthusiasm for extending the principle further.

What drove the extension of local competitive tendering forward were the actions of a few radical Conservative councils in the early 1980s, who began to voluntarily contract out the provision of local services. Local circumstances rather than any central ideology (that came later) lay behind their actions.

---

1 Long Title to the Local Government Act 1988.

One common factor was the need to escape obstruction to changes in working methods from public sector trade unions.[2] Spurred on by this grassroots pressure, the government exhorted councils to voluntarily contract out services. There was initial interest but in the end little take-up.[3] Disappointed, the government was drawn towards the use of compulsion, influenced by its experiences with contracting out in the National Health Service and other privatisations, and by pressure from Conservative councillors from the activist councils, some of whom had become MPs after the 1983 general election. A Department of the Environment (DOE) Consultation Paper "Competition in the provision of local services" was released early in 1985. Consultations and the imminence of a general election delayed the necessary legislation, but the policy became part of the 1987 election manifesto and following the government's reelection in June 1987 it was made the central part of a new Local Government Bill.

The Secretary of State for the Environment, Nicholas Ridley, outlined the government's aims in the following terms:[4]

> "The Bill represents a further significant step in two of the Government's major objectives – introducing greater competition and securing greater value for money...
> ...The free operation of the market is the best way of delivering greater choice, higher productivity and better quality services at lower prices...
> ...The Bill requires compulsory competitive tendering not compulsory contracting out or compulsory privatisation. Those that fear contracting out frequently say that it will lead to poorer services. This is utter nonsense. The Bill requires local authorities to specify the standard of service that they require, whether that service is provided in-house or by contractors. For some authorities even that process will be a new departure. Up till now few have attempted the essential management task of saying precisely what outputs they are aiming for..."

The Opposition concentrated its attack on what it viewed as the centralising tendencies of the Bill:[5]

> 'It is significant that the first Bill to be produced for a Second Reading debate by the government demonstrates the enduring determination of Ministers, and of especially this Secretary of State and this Prime Minister, to go on diminishing the role of democratically elected local government."

The Local Government Act of 1988 (LGA 1988) became the statutory basis of CCT for most local authority services. While the 1980 Act still governed local authority construction and maintenance work, its provisions were

---

2 K. Ascher "The Politics of Privatisation" is a good history of this early period.
3 See Ascher (footnote 1) and Local Government Chronicle – Privatisation Surveys 1983–87.
4 Hansard, House of Commons, 6 July 1987, Vol. 119, cols. 79–82.
5 Dr Cunningham, Hansard, 6 July 1987, Vol. 119, col. 87.

considerably amended and brought into line with its successor.[6] The present Chapter will concentrate on the LGA 1988. The Chapters that follow will consider the modified CCT regime created for professional services (Chapter 2) and the rules of the 1980 Act governing construction and maintenance work (Chapter 3).

1.2   Defined Authorities and Defined Activities

CCT applied to those "defined authorities" listed in section 1(1) of the LGA 1988. The list included all principal local authorities in England, Wales and Scotland, as well as the smaller parish and community councils. Also covered were joint committees established by two or more defined authorities for the discharge of any of their functions under section 101 of the Local Government Act 1972 (in Scotland, the Local Government (Scotland) Act 1973 applied). In that situation the joint committee was itself a defined authority. The list went on to include other public authorities such as police authorities, urban development corporations, and certain fire, civil defence, and transport authorities that were established following the abolition of metropolitan county councils and the Greater London Council in the Local Government Act 1985.

The provisions of the Act were later on extended to Northern Ireland, so local authorities and other public bodies in the province also became defined authorities for these purposes.[7]

CCT applied where a defined authority wished to carry out a "defined activity" using its own employees. Defined activities were those activities listed in section 2(2) as interpreted by reference to Schedule 1 of the Act. The final list of defined activities (as of May 1997) is set out below:

- collection of refuse
- cleaning of buildings
- other cleaning (otherwise known as street cleansing)
- catering for the purposes of schools and welfare
- other catering
- managing sports and leisure facilities
- maintenance of ground
- supervision of parking
- repair and maintenance of vehicles
- management of vehicles
- housing management
- security work
- legal services
- construction and property services
- financial services

---

6   Schedule 6, Local Government Act 1988
7   S.I. 1992 No. 810 (N.I. 6).

- information technology services
- personnel services

Where a defined authority decided that it would like to continue to undertake work falling within any defined activity, it had to ensure that its in-house workforce had faced competition by a date specified by the Secretary of State in regulations. The primary legislation left defined authorities with a wide discretion over how defined activity work was presented for competition. Therefore work within a defined activity could be let as a single contract or as multiple contracts. In the latter case, the splitting of work could be on the basis of, for example, function, geography or financial threshold. However the exercise of this discretion was controllable by the courts if it was ultra vires and by the Secretary of State if it was intended or likely to restrict, distort or prevent competition (see later). The primary legislation explicitly clarified the extent of this discretion in two ways. Firstly, it recognised that some work might be capable of falling within more than one defined activity (DOE guidance gave as an example the removal of litter from flower beds, which could fall, either under other cleaning or ground maintenance).[8] Section 2(5) allowed an authority to place such work where it considered most suitable. In such a situation, the defined authority had to ensure that the combined work was subjected to competition by the earlier of any dates specified in competition regulations made by the Secretary of State (see later). A related problem concerned the treatment of non-defined activity work that was closely connected to the carrying out of defined activity work. Section 2(7) permitted a defined authority to treat such work as part of the defined activity work if the authority decided that it could not be carried out efficiently separately from the defined activity work.

1.2.1   The original seven defined activities

The Act originally extended to just seven defined activities, characterised by the manual and operational nature of the work involved (hence the references in this area to blue-collar CCT).

Refuse collection[9]

This covered the collection of household waste and commercial waste (as defined by section 45 of the Environmental Protection Act 1990).

Building cleaning[10]

The defined activity covered the interior cleaning of buildings and the cleaning of both sides of windows. The cleaning of dwellings (homes),

---

8   DOE Circular 19/88.
9   Section 2(2)(a) and Schedule 1(1).
10 Section 2(2)(b) and Schedule 1(2).

residential establishments established under social welfare legislation, and certain police buildings, was not included in the definition.

Other cleaning (usually known as street cleansing)[11]

This was defined, in exclusive terms, as removing litter from any land, emptying litter bins, street cleaning, emptying gullies, and cleaning traffic signs and street name plates. The definition of litter did not include larger environmental nuisances such as abandoned cars or scrap metal; local authorities could remove these as they saw fit.

Schools/welfare catering[12]

Schools catering encompassed the provision of ingredients for, preparing, delivering and serving of school meals. It also included the provision of refreshments in schools. Special schools and boarding schools run by the local education authority, and where meals were prepared on-site were exempted. Welfare catering covered the provision of ingredients for, preparing and delivering of meals for consumption in residential establishments and day centres (and also the provision of refreshments). However, the serving of meals was exempt because this was often carried out by volunteers or wardens based on-site. The provision of ingredients and preparation of "meals-on-wheels" was another part of the defined activity. The delivery and serving of meals-on-wheels was exempt.

Other catering[13]

This covered any other catering services (eg – staff canteens at the Town Hall, catering outlets serving the public at council-owned arts centres, libraries, leisure centres etc.) but not those carried out at further education institutions.

Ground maintenance[14]

The defined activity included the cutting and tending of grass, planting and tending of trees, hedges, shrubs, flowers and other plants, and controlling weeds. Landscaping work and the initial seeding or turfing of ground was not included, nor work conducted primarily for research or to secure the survival of any type of plant.

---

11   Section 2(2)(c) and Schedule 1(3).
12   Section 2(2)(d) and Schedule 1(4).
13   Section 2(2)(e) and Schedule 1(5).
14   Section 2(2)(f) and Schedule 1(6).

Repair and maintenance of vehicles[15]

The definition covered repair and maintenance to any motor vehicle or trailer except a police vehicle. It did not extend to situations where the need for repairs had been occasioned by accident damage.

In each case the extent of the work covered by the defined activity was fully defined in Schedule 1 of the Act. Unlike some of the subsequent defined activities, every activity that was included in the defined activity was subject to the compulsory competition rules.

1.2.2   The power to create new defined activities

Section 2(3) conferred on the Secretary of State the power to add new defined activities to the original list by statutory instrument. This power was made subject to a duty to consult with local government representatives under section 2(4).[16] The necessary statutory instrument then had to receive an affirmative vote in each House of Parliament.[17] The scope of section 2(3) was subsequently widened by the LGA 1992[18] to cover provisions contained in any definition paragraph in Schedule 1 of the Act, which created exclusions for particular activities within any defined activity.

Initially, there were some concerns about the lawfulness of using section 2(3) to make defined activities of services that were markedly different in character to the original seven. When the legislation was going through its second reading in the House of Commons, the Secretary of State said that the power would certainly not be used in the case of core services such as policing, teaching and planning control. However the addition of sport and leisure management to the list of defined activities was under consideration at that time, and this was clearly a different type of service to the original seven blue-collar services, in that it involved essentially managerial work. Despite this difference, the DOE experienced no legal problems when it was shortly afterwards made into a defined activity.[19] This was also the case with the introduction of all subsequent defined activities, whether blue-collar, managerial or professional in character. In practice therefore, section 2(3) proved flexible enough to make any service into a defined activity.

---

15   Section 2(2)(g) and Schedule 1(7).
16   The Secretary of State must consult with "such representatives of local government as appear to him to be appropriate". The duty to consult means a duty to allow adequate time for responses to be made and considered: see *R v Secretary of State for Social Services ex p Association of Metropolitan Authorities* [1986] 1 All ER 164.
17   Section 15(1)
18   Section 11 and Schedule 1(10) LGA 1992. Commencement Order: S.I. 1994 No. 1445 (C.25).
19   S.I. 1989 No. 2488.

When a section 2(3) order was made, the Act permitted certain consequential amendments to be made to the primary legislation. Section 15(7) provided that orders, regulations, specifications or directions made under the CCT provisions of the Act "may include such supplementary, incidental, consequential or transitional provisions as appear to the Secretary of State to be necessary or expedient". But section 15(8) went further than this by providing that:

> "...an order under section 2(3) above may include provision amending or adapting any provision of this Act for the purpose of interpreting any paragraph added by the order or for the purposes of commencement or otherwise..."

Together, these provisions gave the Secretary of State a notable power to amend parts of the Act by secondary legislation. They were used to modify parts of the CCT regime in relation to housing management and the professional service defined activities, as will be seen below and in the next Chapter.[20]

1.2.3 The new defined activities

The services described below were made into defined activities after 1989 by the Secretary of State under the powers in section 2(3) of the Act. Unlike the original seven defined activities, they show a diverse range of characteristics incorporating manual, managerial and professional tasks. Each new activity was added onto section 2(2) with an accompanying definition paragraph being inserted into Schedule 1.

Managing sports and leisure facilities[21]

The activity covered the management of a wide range of facilities, which were comprehensively listed in the section 2(3) order: swimming pools; skating rinks; gymnasia; tennis, squash and badminton courts; pitches for team games; athletics grounds; tracks and centres for bicycles (whether motorised or not); golf courses; putting greens; bowling greens; bowling centres; bowling alleys; riding centres; courses for horse racing; artificial ski slopes; centres for flying, ballooning, and parachuting; and finally, centres for boating or water sports on inland and coastal waters. The accompanying DOE guidance stated that the term "facility" included associated ancillary areas connected with its use, such as changing rooms.[22] However this would not appear to cover the corridors and other areas of a building.

---

20 The principal modifications have been in relation to section 2(6) ("the cut-off exemption"), the definition of functional work in section 3(4) and the implementation dates for the works contract provisions in section 4.
21 Section 2(2)(ee) and Schedule 1(8): created by S.I. 1989 No. 2488.
22 DOE Circular 9/92.

The term "managing" was defined "without prejudice to the generality of the term" to include the following activities: arranging for supervision or instruction in the recreational activities provided; catering; hiring out equipment; marketing and promoting the facility; taking bookings; collecting and accounting for fees and charges; the physical security of the premises; and the cleaning and maintenance of the facility, other than the external parts of buildings. It also included assuming responsibility for heating, lighting and other service charges relating to the facility.

There was an exemption for the management of facilities provided:

- on premises not predominantly used for sport or physical recreation (eg – village halls and community centres).
- on premises occupied by educational institutions (local authority maintained schools or colleges of further or higher education).

Another exemption covered "dual use" facilities, shared between educational institutions and the surrounding community. To qualify the facility must have been provided for recreational, social and physical training by a local educational authority under section 53 of the Education Act 1944 (or Scottish equivalent), and educational institutions must have had exclusive use of the facility for over 600 hours in the preceding financial year. Where there were two or more facilities on the same site, then educational institutions must have had exclusive use of at least half of the individual facilities provided, for an aggregate period of over 600 hours in the preceding financial year, in order to claim the exemption.

Housing management[23]

The defined activity covered a number of particular tasks concerning the local authority as landlord in relation to its individual weekly tenants. The specified tasks, in general terms, involved the assessment and reporting of situations (back to the local authority), the implementation of decisions taken by the local authority pursuant to its statutory functions, and various other administrative tasks. The list included:

- handling applications for housing once a property was allocated.
- keeping tenants informed of the terms of their tenancies and enforcing these terms.
- collecting rent and service charges.
- arranging for the vacation of a property on termination of a tenancy.
- inspecting and assessing vacant property in readiness for the next letting.
- taking steps to prevent vandalism and squatting on vacant property.
- removing unlawful occupants.

---

23 Section 2(2)(h) and Schedule 1(9): created by S.I. 1994 No. 1671.

- in relation to the common parts of local authority housing, assessing its condition and also maintaining, repairing, cleaning (including de-infestation) and clearing such parts as necessary, ensuring that any necessary work is carried out and reporting back to the local authority as landlord.
- in relation to local authority housing, carrying out surveys and inspections on the state of occupation and repair of properties, and assessing requests for repairs, ensuring that any necessary work is carried out and reporting back to the local authority as landlord.
- assessing claims for compensation and applications for payment made by tenants of the local authority.
- operating reception and security services provided at the entrance to local authority housing.
- taking action to control disturbances and to resolve disputes between occupants.

Supervision of parking[24]

Under the Road Traffic Act 1991, local authorities were empowered to regulate on-street parking (where authorised by the Secretary of State for Transport) and to set penalty fines with a view to covering the costs of supervision. The defined activity covered the following tasks: giving penalty charge notices; fixing or removing immobilisation devices (or authorising the same); removing or arranging the removal of vehicles through the use of parking attendants; and the custody, release or disposal of removed vehicles.

Security work[25]

The defined activity applied to land occupied by a defined authority or in which it had an interest, excepting museums, libraries, art galleries and police establishments. It covered the operation of security controls over persons entering, leaving or moving between different parts of land (except where the land in question is a dwelling or a residential establishment),[26] and the operation of security patrols.

Management of vehicles[27]

The defined activity covered the following tasks, except in relation to police and fire authority vehicles:

- arranging for motor vehicles to be available to meet the requirements of a defined authority;

---

24 Section 2(2)(ff) and Schedule 1(6A): created by S.I. 1994 No. 2884.
25 Section 2(2)(i) and Schedule 1(10): created by S.I. 1994 No. 2884.
26 That forms a part of housing management work.
27 Section 2(2)(gg) and Schedule 1(7A): created by S.I. 1994 No. 2884.

- ensuring that those vehicles satisfied the statutory provisions relating to registration, licencing, safety and insurance, and ensuring that the drivers of those vehicles were duly licenced;
- making arrangements for the fueling, cleaning, repairing and maintaining of the vehicles.

White-collar services

The government also made legal services, construction and property services, financial services, information technology services, and personnel services into defined activities. These services were the subject of separate and extensive consultation processes. The whole area became known collectively as white-collar CCT. White-collar CCT was based on the blue-collar CCT regime described elsewhere in this Chapter but modified in many important respects to meet the different circumstances. For this reason, the white-collar CCT regime is considered separately in Chapter 2.

1.2.4 Exemptions

The Act made provision for three categories of exempted work. Firstly, many types of activities were excluded from the definitions provided for each defined activity in Schedule 1 of the Act. Secondly, the Act also provided specific exemptions for emergency work, and work incidental to defined activities. Finally, the Act empowered the Secretary of State to create exemptions by regulation.

Emergency work

Emergency work was exempted under section 2(8). It was defined as work "calculated to avert, alleviate or eradicate the effects or potential effects of an emergency or disaster (actual or potential) involving or likely to involve danger to life or health or serious damage to or destruction of property".

Incidental work

Section 2(6) exempted incidental work, which was defined as:

> "Work which is carried out by a defined authority through an employee and which would (apart from this subsection) fall within a defined activity shall not do so if it is incidental to the greater part of the work he is employed to do and the greater part does not constitute a defined activity".

Sometimes known as the "cut-off" exemption, it was applicable in situations where an identifiable employee was carrying out a mix of defined activity work and non-defined activity work. The question was whether the latter constituted the greater part of his work, to which the former was merely incidental. If so, then the employee's work could be exempted from competition.

Clearly, there would often be room for argument as to whether a part of an employee's work was incidental or not. Dictionary definitions of "incidental" include "being likely to ensue as a chance or minor consequence"[28] or "casual, not essential".[29] On this basis it should have been relevant for an authority to consider things such as an employee's job description, criteria by which an employee came to be accepted into its employment, or the amount of time spent on an activity. Naturally, these considerations could yield conflicting answers and so the authority would have to be careful not abuse its discretion. A wholesale reorganisation of job descriptions and practices to maximise the potential scope of the exemption would have probably been unreasonable in law and also anti-competitive behaviour under section 7(7) of the Act (see later).

Section 2(6) was amended in relation to the later defined activities of housing management and the professional services. This was done under the power to consequentially amend the primary legislation in relation to new defined activities provided by section 15(8). The new definition used a percentage figure based on time spent by an employee doing work in the relevant defined activity. In the case of housing management work the cut-off point was set at 25% for full-time employees (defined as those working over 30 hours per week) and 50% for part-timers. In the other cases it was set at 50%.

Work exempted by orders under section 2(9)

The Secretary of State was empowered to create particular exemptions by means of an order under section 2(9). This could be done by statutory instrument subject to annulment in pursuance of a resolution of either House of Parliament.[30] The power was very flexible and in particular section 15(5) allowed such orders to make different provision for different cases or descriptions of case (whether for different areas, different authorities or types of authority, different activities etc.). Up to the end of March 1996 forty-nine orders had been made under section 2(9).[31] They ranged from the general to the particular. Most related to specific problems or special local difficulties with the CCT process: for example, allowing a local authority to delay the onset of CCT for a particular defined activity or even at a named facility.[32] The most significant of the section 2(9) exemptions are considered below.

---

28   Merriam Webster Collegiate Dictionary, Tenth Edition.
29   The Concise Oxford Dictionary.
30   Section 15(2).
31   Encyclopedia of Local Government Law at 3-784.
32   Following the change of government in the May 1997 general election, CCT is likely to be superceded by a general duty on local authorities to achieve best value in the provision of local services. It is likely that local authorities that have prepared approved schemes for "best value" will be granted general exemption from CCT by way of section 2(9) orders.

Chapter One

(i) The de minimis exemption[33]

An exemption was provided for work within any one defined activity, where the estimated gross cost (based on the cost in the previous financial year) was no more than £100,000. Local authorities were allowed to deduct the cost of work performed by subcontractors,[34] the cost of work exempted under other exemptions, and those client-side costs which would be incurred irrespective of whether the work was won by outside contractors or retained in-house. Where the estimated cost exceeded £100,000 then the whole of the activity had to be subjected to CCT, not just the excess balance.[35] The value of this exemption declined in real terms after 1988 because it was not adjusted to take account of inflation. The £100,000 limit applied to all the blue-collar and other non-professional defined activities except for housing management for which it was £500,000.[36] The remaining white-collar activities were treated on a different basis (see Chapter 2).

(ii) The tied accommodation exemption

This covered work within a defined activity carried out by an employee who is required to live in particular accommodation for the better performance of his duties. Its purpose was to protect those employees living in tied accommodation who might otherwise through CCT lose not only their jobs but also their homes. A straightforward example would be a residential school caretaker who carried out all the building cleaning work on that site.[37]

(iii) The repair/maintenance of a motor vehicle or trailer used only for fire service functions by a defined authority.[38]

(iv) Work carried out (and wholly or partly paid for) under an agreement between the local authority and the Training Commission or the Secretary of State, pursuant to the terms of the Employment and Training Act 1973.[39]

(v) The Small Schools Exemption[40]

This exemption permitted small, locally managed schools to carry out up to

---

33 S.I. 1988 No. 1372.
34 This would otherwise have to be counted as functional work because of section 3(4).
35 DOE Circular 19/88 at paragraph 18.
36 See S.I. 1994 No. 2296. From 1998 onwards the de minimis exemption for housing management work is intended to be based on the size of a local authority's housing stock: up to 4000 houses will meet the exemption in 1998: see S.I. 1997 No. 176.
37 S.I. 1988 No. 1372.
38 ibid.
39 ibid.
40 S.I. 1992 No. 1626.

117 hours per week of building cleaning and ground maintenance work without having to go through CCT. The origin of the small schools exemption provides an interesting example of how the CCT regime had to be amended to allow other pieces of local government legislation to work effectively. The Local Management of Schools (LMS) provisions of the Education Reform Act 1988 required local education authorities to prepare plans for delegating much of the control of school budgets to school governing bodies. This was to be phased in over the years to 1994. The consequence was that control over those defined activities affecting education (such as catering, ground maintenance and building cleaning) would pass from local authorities to the school governing bodies. The governing body of a school would therefore assume client-side responsibilities when the existing arrangements for those services expired and CCT became due. At that point it would face three courses of action:

- it could continue to rely on the local education authority to make arrangements to do the work (and so surrender back client-side responsibilities under CCT), or
- it could set up its own school based DSO to tender for the work (and deal with CCT itself), or
- it could go straight to private contractors (in which case CCT would not apply).

The government recognised that this would place an administrative burden on small schools, and proposed an exemption, in relation to ground maintenance and building cleaning work only, in a joint DOE/DES Circular in February 1992. The government considered but ultimately rejected defining the exemption by reference to types of school, or to pupil numbers. In the first place, while small schools were most likely to be primary schools, the fact remained that there were small schools of every type. As for pupil numbers, these were liable to fluctuate year on year so making it uncertain whether the exemption would be applicable. The favoured option was to base the small schools exemption on estimated staffing requirements for carrying out defined activities.

To qualify for the exemption a school had to satisfy three conditions. The first was that building cleaning and ground maintenance work were being carried out on school premises controlled by a governing body with a delegated budget under LMS. The second was that the local authority estimated the staffing requirement for both defined activities in the coming financial year as not exceeding the equivalent of three full time employees. The third was that the estimate of staffing requirements was made having regard to the advice of the school governing body and the experience of previous years. For the purposes of the exemption, a full time employee was treated as one who worked a 39 hour week,[41] so three full time equivalents (regardless of the

---

41 A "full time employee" is one whose working week does not exceed the standard working week for a full time employee specified by the National Joint Council for Local Authorities' Services (Workers).

number actually employed) equated to 117 hours per week. For these purposes the tied accommodation and incidental work exemptions were not applicable (so the hours worked by a resident caretaker had to be counted).

1.3 The Competitive Tendering Rules

The LGA 1988 envisaged that defined authorities would carry out defined activity work either under works contracts or as functional work. It set out different competitive tendering rules for each of these situations.

1.3.1 The definition of works contracts and functional work

Section 3 of the Act defined both of these terms. Section 3(2) defined a "works contract" as a contract constituting or including an agreement that provided for the carrying out of work by a defined authority. In other words, this covered the situation where a defined authority was carrying out work under contract for another legal person. There were two exceptions. Section 3(3) provided an exception in the case of agreements to discharge the functions of a Minister of the Crown, another defined authority or a sewerage undertaker. This covered a range of joint arrangements, such as those made under section 101 of the LGA 1972 whereby a local authority can delegate the performance of its functions to another local authority. They are known as agency agreements. Under these, while the first local authority remains ultimately responsible for the work in question, the delegatee local authority will have wide powers to decide how the work is carried out. In particular, it will be responsible for fulfilling the client-side responsibilities such as specifying, procuring and monitoring the work. In this situation the work would be treated as the functional work of the delegatee authority. Work undertaken as sub-contractor to another authority's DSO would also be treated as functional work by virtue of section 3(4)(b) (see below).

It is important to note that while section 3(2) defines a contract for the purposes of CCT, it does not itself provide authority for a local authority to enter into a contract. It does not protect it from the operation of the ultra vires rule. The local authority will need quite separate statutory authority for its actions. Section 1 of the Local Authority (Goods and Services) Act 1970 is often cited in this context. It permits a local authority to enter into an agreement with another public body for the following purposes: the supply of goods and materials, the provision of administrative, professional or technical services, the use of any plant, vehicle or apparatus, or the carrying out of works of maintenance. The extent to which this provision authorises cross-boundary tendering or "municipal trading" (local authorities tendering to carry out work for other authorities) has been the focus of much controversy since the passing of the LGA 1988. The Audit Commission has attempted to nip the development of municipal trading in the bud, by advising its auditors that the power contained in section 1 of the 1970 Act is very limited.[42] Its position, based on counsel's opinion, is that authorities cannot trade for the purpose of making a profit or to provide or maintain employment, and that any cross-boundary agreements should do no more than utilise any surplus capacity left over from the fulfillment of functions in their own area. The DOE has more recently indicated that, while the power in question is indeed limited, this is too strict an interpretation.[43] The question has yet to come before the courts and so remains unresolved.

Any work that could not be brought within the definition of a works contract was, by virtue of section 3(4), functional work. Essentially, this covered work undertaken by an authority's own employees pursuant to its functions, and because they are excepted from the definition of works contracts by section 3(3), work carried out under agency agreements.[44] By virtue of section 3(4)(b), work carried out by subcontractors, that is dependant upon, or incidental or preparatory to other functional work, was treated as functional work as well. Clearly most of the work carried out by a local authority would be functional work.[45]

1.3.2   Statutory provisions for works contracts

The CCT provisions for works contracts were contained in section 4, and applied to the local authority that was bidding to carry out the work (the bidding authority). It had to satisfy two conditions before entering into a works contract. These conditions applied to all works contracts entered into after 1 April 1989 in the case of the original seven defined activities, and from a date specified in regulations in the case of subsequent defined activities.[46]

The first condition

This could be satisfied in either of two ways. Firstly, the bidding authority could win the contract in a tendering exercise involving at least three other

---

42   "Cross-Boundary Tendering – Local Authorities Doing Work for One Another" Audit Commission Technical Release 23/90.
43   DOE Letter to local authorities – 7 December 1995. A fuller discussion of this area can be found in Cirell and Bennett "Compulsory Competitive Tendering: Law and Practice".
44   The House of Lords considered the meaning of a local authority's functions in *Hazell v Hammersmith LBC* [1992] 2 AC 1; Lord Templeman said that "functions embraces all the duties and powers of a local authority; the sum total of all the activities Parliament has entrusted to it".
45   The relations between a local authority and its Direct Service Organisation(s) for the carrying out of functional work are often expressed in the language of contract law. While this may serve for the purposes of convenience, the relationship between them is not contractual because a DSO has no separate legal identity.
46   Provision is made in the relevant section 2(3) Orders.

persons willing to carry out the work and who were not other defined authorities. The alternative was that before entering into the contract the other party had published a notice inviting tenders for the work in one local newspaper and a relevant trade journal.

The second condition

The second condition, contained in section 4(5), was what became known as the prohibition of anti-competitive behaviour. It was that "the other party, in entering into the contract and in doing anything else (whether or not required by this Part) in connection with the contract before entering into it, did not act in a manner having the effect or intended or likely to have the effect of restricting, distorting or preventing competition".

Both conditions related to the conduct of the defined authority that was commissioning the work, over which the bidding authority could be expected to have little control. However, under section 4(6) the conditions would be satisfied so long as the bidding authority were not aware of any failure to fulfill either condition before entering into the contract.[47]

1.3.3   Statutory requirements for functional work

Local authority functional work became subject to CCT on or after a date specified in regulations issued by the Secretary of State under section 6(3). This meant that an authority could only carry out work through its DSO on or after the specified date if it had won the right to do so under the CCT rules. It followed that where CCT had resulted in an outside contractor being awarded the work, the contract had to be up and running by the specified date. Of course, it was open to authorities to bring in CCT by an earlier date if they wished.

The principal regulations made under section 6(3) were the 1988 Competition Regulations.[48] When the Act was passed, Ministers were worried on two counts. The first was that local authorities would be overwhelmed by the work involved in preparing services for competition. The second was that the letting of a number of contracts to competition at one time risked flooding the market and overwhelming the private sector's chances of realistically competing. To avoid these pitfalls the Regulations provided for CCT to be phased-in over six dates between 1 August 1989 and 1 January 1992.[49] To achieve this, local authorities were divided into six groups, each group containing a varied assortment of local authorities (by type and geographic area) and following an independent timetable. The

---

47   Originally this referred to the time when it was proposed to enter into the contract but this period was later extended by section 11 LGA 1992. Contrast with the equivalent provisions for works contracts under the LGPLA 1980 (at 3.2.2).
48   S.I. 1988 No. 1371.
49   These dates were 1.8.89, 1.1.90, 1.8.90, 1.1.91, 1.8.91 and 1.1.92.

first day of August and January would see each group being brought within the CCT regime in respect of a different defined activity. The exception was ground maintenance, which was to be phased-in across the country in minimum tranches of 20% per annum from 1 January 1990 to 1 January 1994.

Separate competition regulations were later issued alongside each of the new defined activities created under section 2(3).[50] In the case of housing management, the relevant regulations provided that only a "specified proportion" of the defined activity had to be subject to CCT.[51] This was calculated according to the formula T − (A + B), where "T" represented the total value of work (including overheads), "A" represented the value of a competition-free allowance, and "B" represented the value of work voluntarily contracted out before September 1994. This approach was very similar to that pursued in relation to the professional services, which are considered in Chapter 2. The competition-free allowance represented by "A" was 5% and most local authorities were given a 2–3 years transition period before competition was fully applied.

Regulations under section 6(3) have been used for other purposes, including delaying the onset of competition. The principal example of this concerned the defined activity of other cleaning (street cleansing), which had to accommodate local authorities' obligations under the Environmental Protection Act 1990 to "ensure that land is, so far as practicable, kept clear of litter and refuse". Under that Act, the Secretary of State issued a code of practice, which detailed the standards to be kept in clearing streets and land of litter. Because this was published halfway through the initial CCT implementation period many local authorities found themselves in the situation of having to revise their detailed specifications for other cleaning work during the tendering process. They succeeded in persuading the DOE to amend the 1988 Competition Regulations, allowing them extra time to do this. Those that had been due to commence CCT contracts by 1 January 1991 and 1 August 1991 were consequently given a period of grace, with the start dates being delayed until 1 August 1991 and 1 January 1992 respectively.[52]

Section 6(1) stated that a defined authority must not carry out functional work unless each of the six conditions specified in section 7 had been fulfilled (subject to any relevant additional requirements imposed by the Secretary of State through section 8).

---

50 S.I. 1990 No. 1564 (management of sports/leisure facilities phased-in: 35% by 1.8.92; 70% by 1.1.93; 100% after 1.1.93); S.I. 1994 No. 3165 (supervision of parking, management of vehicles, security work, from 1.1.96 depending on status under local government reorganisation). For white-collar defined activities see Chapter 2.
51 S.I. 1994 No. 2297.
52 S.I. 1990 No. 2082; see also an article by Cirell and Bennett in Solicitors Journal Vol. 135 No. 14 (12 April 1991). The concession was less generous than it appears because the starting dates for other activities were unchanged.

CHAPTER ONE

The First Condition

This was contained in section 7(1) and (2). Before carrying out the work in question, the defined authority must have published an advertising notice in at least one local newspaper and a relevant trade journal, containing:

(i) a brief description of the work;
(ii) a statement that a detailed specification of the work would be available for inspection free of charge at a place, a time and for a period stated in the notice;
(iii) a statement that copies of the detailed specification could be purchased for a specified charge;
(iv) a stated period within which persons might notify the authority of their interest in carrying out the work; and,
(v) a statement of the authority's intention to invite tenders to carry out the work in accordance with the third condition.

The requirement to prepare a detailed specification was originally intended to assist potential tenderers by putting them on an equal footing with the in-house teams who may have been carrying out the work for years. It was also seen as a tool to improve the management, and through that the quality of services, by forcing authorities to think strategically about what they wanted to achieve.[53] Later, as part of the Citizens' Charter programme its purpose was broadened further.[54] Section 10 of the LGA 1992 required the service specification (or a summary of it) to be available for public inspection and copying throughout the life of a contract. This was intended to enable local recipients of services to check that they were receiving the standards of service to which they were entitled.

The second condition

The second condition contained a number of requirements that amplified the first. Section 7(3)(a) and (b) required that the periods, place, time and charge specified in the notice were reasonable, and that the detailed specification actually was made available in accordance with the notice. Finally, section 7(3)(c) stated that the detailed specification should contain a statement of the period during which the work was to be carried out (ie: the length of the contract). The Secretary of State exercised powers under section 8(1) to issue regulations specifying maximum and minimum contract periods for contracts concerning each of the defined activities. The specified contract periods post-1995 for England are shown in the Table below.[55] The maximum periods

---

53 DOE Circular 19/88.
54 Cm 1599 (1991).
55 S.I. 1995 No. 2484 (replacing S.I. 1988 No. 1373). A number of regulations have been made under section 8(1): see Encyclopedia of Local Government Law at 3-796.

Specified Contract Periods (Years): 1995 Regulations (England)

Defined activity	Education related	Non education related
Refuse collection	6–10	6–10
Building cleaning	3–4	4–6
Other cleaning	5–10	5–10
Schools/welfare catering	4–5	4–6

were generally extended compared to the previous regulations of 1988 in order to allow greater flexibility. Shorter minima and maxima were specified for work wholly or mainly relating to educational functions.

The third condition

The third condition was contained in section 7(4) and (5), and set out requirements relating to the handling of invitations to tender. These had to be made between three and six months after the authority had complied with the first condition. At least three persons who were not defined authorities had to be invited. If less than four such persons had expressed an interest, each of them had to be invited. This was an absolute requirement, unaffected by the authority's opinion on the suitability of any person to be invited to tender. There were no such requirements in relation to inviting other defined authorities to tender. Any or none might be invited, at the authority's discretion.

The Secretary of State had reserve powers under section 8(2) to prescribe the contents of any invitations (such as the time and method of responding) and the manner in which an authority handled any responses. This power was used to impose further time limits (see below).

The fourth condition

This came under section 7(6), which required that "before carrying out the work the authority, through their direct labour organisation or a similar organisation, prepared a written bid indicating their wish to carry out the work". This was to ensure that the price and other details of an in-house bid could be compared on the same basis with tenders submitted by other persons. Again, powers were reserved to the Secretary of State under section 8(3) and (4) to prescribe various matters relating to the in-house bid by regulations. No such regulations were ever made.

The fifth condition

This prohibited authorities from engaging in what became known as anti-competitive behaviour and was set out in section 7(7):

"The fifth condition is that the authority, in reaching the decision that they should carry out the work and in doing anything else (whether or not required by this Part) in connection with the work before reaching the decision, did not act in a manner having the effect or intended or likely to have the effect of restricting, distorting or preventing competition."

The Act does not give any further indication of the type of behaviour that would be considered anti-competitive, and no power to define it by regulation was supplied.[56] This omission caused problems for the Secretary of State until it was rectified by section 9 of the LGA 1992. This was the most important and far reaching of all the conditions. Its influence on CCT is considered in Chapter 5.

The sixth condition

Finally, section 7(8) required that in carrying out the work the authority comply with the detailed specification for it. This provision was intended to stop local authorities setting unduly onerous requirements in the detailed specification with the intention of driving away competitors, and then letting the DSO carry out the work on an amended and far less rigorous basis. Some concerns were raised about this requirement, on the basis that a strict adherence to the terms of the specification would be unworkable in practice. Circumstances will inevitably change over the course of a contract lasting several years. In practice, the inclusion of an appropriately drafted variation clause in the specification should overcome such difficulties.[57]

Time limits for CCT procedures

The Secretary of State used the reserve powers under section 8 to introduce additional time limits. In the 1993 Competition Regulations,[58] the time limits used by the EC public procurement rules were applied to cover all CCT tenders. This meant that local authorities had to allow a minimum of 37 days to receive expressions of interest in response to the initial advertisement of the work and then a minimum of 40 days for the submission of

---

56 The Secretary of State could make regulations under section 8(5) empowering him to require local authorities to submit a report appraising responses to invitations to tender and in-house bids in terms of any prescribed matters under section 8(2), (3) or (4). This power was never used because no matters had ever been prescribed under the other sub-sections, and because it proved easier to proceed using informal correspondence and sections 13 and 14 (see 1.5).
57 See Cirell and Bennett "Compulsory Competitive Tendering: Law and Practice".
58 S.I. 1993 No. 848.

tenders.[59] The 1993 Regulations were also used to impose further time limits that were not derived from the EC rules. One was a requirement to announce the award of the contract within 90 days (120 days in the case of housing management) of the closing date for the receipt of tenders.[60] The other was for the commencement of work under the contract within 30 to 120 days of the announcement of an award.[61]

Competition provisions for local authority companies

Local authorities have powers to establish or participate in companies for the performance of their functions. Local authority companies are not defined authorities and so they are not covered by the CCT rules. To prevent local authorities evading CCT by reconstituting their DSOs as local authority companies, the government introduced a further competition requirement. Section 33 of the LGA 1988 requires that before entering into a contract with an associated company to carry out a defined activity, a local authority take reasonable steps to ensure competition. What constitutes "reasonable steps" is not defined, but it would mean at the least that alternate bids were considered. A company can become associated with a local authority in two ways:

- if, by virtue of a decision of the authority, the authority, a member or officer, or any nominee is a member either of the company itself, or its subsidiary or holding company; or,
- if the company is controlled or subject to the influence of the local authority, or the authority has a minority interest in the company within the meaning of Part V of the Local Government and Housing Act 1989.[62]

1.4   Accounting, Financial and Disclosure of Information Requirements

The LGA 1988 imposed a number of other duties on defined authorities carrying out defined activity work. These included duties to keep separate trading accounts and to achieve financial objectives for each defined activity. There were further duties to report on the work, and to disclose certain information relating to contracting matters to any interested persons.

These requirements closely tied-in with the competition requirements

---

59 ibid: Regulation 2.
60 ibid: Regulation 5(1)(b) and (2).
61 ibid: Regulation 3.
62 Part V of the LGHA 1989 establishes a framework for the regulation of local authority interests in companies. The precise controls are contained in the Local Authorities (Companies) Order 1995: S.I. 1995 No. 849. See also Elizabeth Yates "Local Authorities and Outside Organisations": Sweet & Maxwell: 1996.

considered earlier and they ensured that defined authorities carried out work that they had won in competition in a proper commercial manner. For example, were a local authority to submit a loss-leading bid to retain work in-house, this ruse would soon be revealed by a "loss" on the trading account and a consequent failure to meet the financial objective set for the work. In that situation the Secretary of State would have been able to take enforcement action under sections 13 and 14 (see 1.5 below). The requirements on local authorities to disclose certain information about DSO operations and the contracting process, served a related purpose in promoting accountability to what was (perhaps optimistically) hoped would be an active local citizenry. However this "openness" only extended to DSOs; never to outside contractors that may have won the right to carry out services.

1.4.1   Accounting for DSO work

Section 9 required defined authorities to keep separate accounts for all of the work that they carried out under each defined activity. These were commonly known as "trading accounts". The purpose was to ring-fence the DSO's performance in carrying out each defined activity so that its financial performance could be assessed against any financial objective set for it by the Secretary of State under section 10 (see below).

Only three types of item could be entered in a DSO trading account. In the case of a works contract, a defined authority was required to credit the price specified in the contract (or ascertained under it). Functional work had either to be debited or credited to the account in the manner that best reflected the terms of the DSO bid. This phraseology reflected the fact that a DSO bid might take different forms, either a requirement to be paid to undertake the work (credit entry), or alternatively, of a payment by the organisation to the authority for the right to undertake the work (debit entry). The Secretary of State had the power to specify in writing further items to be entered in an account and/or the method of calculating the amount of any item. This could be used if he suspected that items of account were being either omitted or miscalculated. No other items were permitted to be credited to a trading account. These provisions prevented an authority from boosting the apparent performance of its DSO by crediting income to the account from unrelated activities (so called cross-subsidisation).[63]

---

63   However because both functional work and works contracts could be entered in a trading account, it was possible for an authority to support the performance of its functional work through profits made on cross-boundary contracts. Section 9(7) was added at the Bill's committee stage in the House of Commons to ensure that an authority did not have to account a second time for works contracts because of section 2(2) of the Local Authorities (Goods and Services) Act 1970.

1.4.2   Financial objectives

The requirement to keep trading accounts for each defined activity was the basis on which the Secretary of State could specify the achievement of financial objectives for defined activity work under section 10. The key provision was section 10(2), which required that an authority secured in its revenue for the work concerned, the achievement of any financial objective specified by the Secretary of State for the financial year in question.

This power was first used in the 1988 Financial Objectives Specifications, which required authorities to show a 5% rate of return on capital employed in carrying out each defined activity.[64] This essentially repeated the target set for construction and maintenance work under the LGPLA 1980. An exception was made in the case of building cleaning. Building cleaning does not require much in the way of capital employed, and so the financial objective was simply a requirement to break-even.

The 1988 Specifications also differed from the LGPLA 1980 regime in that assets owned by an authority only counted as capital employed where the invitation to tender required contractors to bid on the basis of providing the relevant assets themselves.[65] This was to ensure the equal treatment of outside contractors and DSOs. In some circumstances, an authority might decide to retain ownership of capital assets (such as depots and motor vehicles) but promise to make them available (free) to whoever won the tender. In that case nobody bidding for the contract would have to include the cost of providing those assets in the price of their bid. Clearly then, if the DSO won, it would be inappropriate to make the assets count as capital employed for these purposes.

The 1988 Specifications had a loophole. Where authorities could structure their operations so that they had no capital employed (eg – by leasing assets), no financial objective was applicable (except in the case of building cleaning work). The loophole was closed in 1991 by amending specifications, which required DSOs to break-even notwithstanding the absence of capital employed. They also subjected the new defined activity of sports and leisure management to a simple break-even objective, as for building cleaning work.

All of the previous financial objective specifications under both the LGPLA 1980 and the LGA 1988 were replaced by the Financial Objectives Specifications 1994.[66] This reflected a wider change in the treatment of fixed assets in government accounting. The new financial objective for all defined activities was to break-even after taking into account a capital financing charge of 6%.

---

[64] Financial Objectives (England) Specifications 1988: Annex to DOE Circular 19/88.
[65] It is the norm for building/repair contractors to provide their own assets.
[66] Annexes A and B to DOE Circular 12/94.

1.4.3 Requirements to disclose information about DSOs and other contracting matters

Defined authorities were required by section 11 to prepare a report each year about their operations in each defined activity where the right to do so had been won under CCT. Section 11 specified the information that the report had to contain and gave the Secretary of State powers to require further information to be included and to specify the form in which the information was presented.[67] In particular, it stipulated that the report had to contain a summary of the trading account and a statement showing whether or not any financial objective specified under section 10 had been met.

Section 11 reports had to be prepared no later than 30 September of the following financial year. Copies were to be sent to the local authority's auditor and the Secretary of State no later than 31 October of the following financial year. The purpose of sending a copy to the auditor was so he could certify that the authority had met its financial objectives under section 10 by means of a written opinion sent to the authority and to the Secretary of State. Reports also had to be publicised in accordance with section 12 of the Act; in particular they were to be available for inspection and copying by any person for a reasonable charge.

Section 12 further required defined authorities to make available to any person who requested it, certain information about the contracting process where its DSO had won the right to carry out defined activity work under CCT. On request and at any time (no time limits being stipulated) a written statement had to be supplied to the person showing:

- the authority's decision to carry out the work
- the "financial provisions" shown in each tender submitted in response to the authority's invitation to tender, and
- the "financial provisions" of the (winning) in-house bid.

The precise meaning of "financial provisions" was not made clear in the Act or by subsequent DOE guidance. The phrase was given a broad interpretation by Andrew Sparke,[68] who argued that:

> "[t]he width of the wording used in section 12 means that where a tender is other than a fixed sum for a set volume of work, the full schedules of rates for different types of work will have to be released."

---

67 For example, the Secretary of State wrote to the local government associations in October 1992, asking that local authorities supply to the DOE on a voluntary basis a wide range of information. This request was met; if it had not been met, the Secretary of State could have used his powers under section 11 to require it.

68 Andrew Sparke "The Compulsory Competitive Tendering Guide" Second Edition: Chapter 6 and p. 48–50.

Sparke went on to argue that this gave contractors a formidable advantage over DSOs, especially where a complaint of anti-competitive conduct had been made. He continued:

> "Armed with full and current details of the pricing strategy employed by the DSO, which must bid to recover its costs and overheads in full, an external contractor will be ideally placed to win if a subsequent complaint results in an instruction to the council from the Secretary of State to retender the service".

But such a wide interpretation would have had undesirable consequences. Companies would have been free to go on fishing trips for useful information. For the price of posting a letter to any local authority whose DSO had won defined activity work in competition, all would have been revealed, not only DSO prices but also the prices and pricing strategies of firms that had submitted tenders. This would have caused problems for many private firms who would have found commercial information submitted in confidence for the purposes of a tender falling, albeit anonymously, into the hands of commercial rivals.

This matter never came before the courts, but the wide interpretation of section 12 was probably unsound. If CCT was intended to provide a level playing field for competition between DSOs and outside contractors, the unacceptability of permitting the revelation of commercially sensitive information in the case of outside firms should have equally applied in the case of DSO commercial secrets. Cirell and Bennett suggested the adoption of a minimal interpretation, limited to disclosure of the total contract price over the whole contract period.[69]

1.5 The Enforcement Provisions

Sections 13 and 14 of the Act gave the Secretary of State powers to ensure that defined authorities followed the rules for CCT. These provisions applied without prejudice to any other remedy available to a person in law for contravention of CCT.[70]

1.5.1 The legal provisions

The Secretary of State had the power to serve a notice under section 13 where it appeared to him that in a financial year a defined authority had acted in any of the following ways:

---

69 Cirell and Bennett "Compulsory Competitive Tendering. Law and Practice": pages A42–43.
70 Section 16(2). Other remedies might include actions for judicial review of an authority's decisions, action under EC public procurement law, civil action for breach of contract etc.

- entering (as the bidding authority) into a works contract contrary to the conditions set down in section 4;
- either carrying out functional work contrary to the conditions set down in section 7, or reaching a decision to carry out functional work in circumstances where that decision, if implemented, would have the same effect;
- failing to keep trading accounts in respect of any defined activity as required by section 9;
- failing to achieve the financial objective set in respect of any defined activity by section 10;
- failing to prepare an annual report in respect of any defined activity in accordance with section 11.

A notice under section 13 had to follow a certain format. The Secretary of State had to inform the authority that it appeared to him that in a particular financial year it had acted in one of the ways set out above. The work concerned was to be identified in the notice together with the reasons for the Secretary of State's view. The notice then had to specify a time within which the authority was required to provide a written response. This could be either in the form of a reasoned denial of the alleged contravention or alternatively an admission combined with reasons why the Secretary of State should not exercise his powers under section 14.

Section 13(5) gave the Secretary of State the flexibility to serve different notices in respect of the same financial year and the same work, which could refer to the same alleged contravention or different ones.

The power to issue directions to a defined authority under section 14 only came into play where the time specified in the section 13 notice had passed (whether or not there had been a written response), and the Secretary of State remained of the view that the alleged contravention had taken place. Through a section 14 direction, the Secretary of State could order a defined authority to do any of the following:

- cease carrying out all or part of the work within the defined activity ("a barring order");
- continue carrying out all or part of the work within the defined activity, but subject to conditions (a "conditions order").

The lawfulness of certain conditions was the subject of legal dispute in the *Knowsley* case.[71] To put this and related matters beyond doubt, the government used the LGA 1992 to amend section 14 by the addition of sections 14A, 14B and 14C.[72] Section 14A allowed the Secretary of State to impose conditions requiring that he be satisfied as to matters specified in the direction, or that his consent be granted for the carrying out of work. By virtue of section 14B, a direction could also provide that a condition take effect

---

71 See footnote 75 below.
72 Inserted by LGA 1992 s.11, Sched.1, para.14.

Anti-competitive behaviour: statutory action[74]

Category	1997	1996	1995	1994	1993	1992
Compaints	–	89	66	100	157	–
Notices	7	19	12	20	20	13
Directions	5	10	7	9	13	8

instead of any other requirement contained in Part 1 of the Act. Finally, section 14C gave legal status to variations of a direction agreed between the Secretary of State and the defined authority.

The Secretary of State had the power at any time to issue new directions to replace previous directions. A new direction could withdraw a prohibition contained in the previous direction entirely, downgrade an absolute prohibition to a conditional one in respect of the same work, or retain the terms of the prohibition contained in a previous direction but apply it to only part of the work formerly covered.

In practice the two statutory stages of enforcement action were invariably preceded by informal correspondence between local authorities and the DOE. A rare description of this exists in relation to the refuse collection contract that was awarded by Wolverhampton MBC to its DSO in May 1989. The DOE, acting on complaints raised by a contractor and opposition councillors, questioned the merits of a number of adjustments made by the council to the price of outside tenders in the course of the financial evaluation. Several letters were exchanged in the following months and a meeting between council officers and DOE officials was held at the DOE building in London. The differences could not be resolved and the DOE issued a section 13 notice in January 1990. Further discussions followed until in July 1990 the DOE informed the council that it would not be taking any further action.[73]

It would appear that the majority of complaints were resolved through these informal consultations. This is illustrated by the Table above, which shows the incidence of complaints to notices and directions in relation to alleged anti-competitive conduct over the period 1992–1997.

1.5.2 The attitude of the courts to the enforcement powers

The Secretary of State's powers under sections 13 and 14 came before the courts in a number of applications for judicial review. The cases showed that the courts were unwilling to interfere with any proper exercise of discretionary power by the Secretary of State. This left the Secretary of State in a powerful position to police infringements of the CCT regime.

---

73 "Preparing the Winning Bid. A Handbook for Competitive Tendering" edited by M. T. Lyon and A. Johnson (Charles Knight Publishing) (1992).
74 Source: CCT and Local Government – Annual Reports 1993–97 (DOE).

CHAPTER ONE

The Secretary of State as arbiter of breaches of the Act

The leading case on the use of the Secretary of State's discretionary power is *R v Secretary of State for the Environment ex parte Knowsley MBC and others*.[75] This case went up to the Court of Appeal and is also of interest for its consideration of tender evaluation (for which see Chapter 5). The local authorities in question (the others were Leicester and York) had gone through CCT in relation to their refuse collection services. Knowsley had invited tenders for a 5-year contract to carry out the work in accordance with CCT. After receiving tenders from the DSO and an external contractor, Knowsley awarded the contract to the DSO. The losing contractor complained to the DOE because its tender had been £354,000 cheaper. The DOE pursued inquiries. Knowsley explained that in the course of evaluating the tenders, it had deducted a number of costs from the price of the DSO bid in order to reflect the full cost of awarding work to an outside contractor. The DOE accepted the validity of some of these deductions but not others. Eventually the Secretary of State served a section 13 notice stating that it appeared to him there had been anti-competitive behaviour (rejection of a lower priced tender without good reason) contrary to the fifth condition of section 7 of the LGA 1988. Knowsley's reply failed to satisfy the Secretary of State, who proceeded to issue a section 14 direction, ordering Knowsley to retender the work in question, and to obtain the Secretary of State's consent before awarding the work again to its DSO. A similar factual background pertained in the cases of the other local authorities. They all challenged the directions given by the Secretary of State by way of judicial review.

Knowsley's case was that it had acted in good faith and had considered its fiduciary duty to its local taxpayers. In these circumstances the Secretary of State was only entitled to find a breach of the fifth condition of section 7 (anti-competitive behaviour) if the authority had acted unreasonably according to the usual public law principles. This argument was rejected in the High Court. The structure of the Act meant that it was for the Secretary of State to decide whether or not the six conditions set out in section 7 had been fulfilled. For example, The Times report of the judgement by Popplewell J in the High Court says:

> "There could be no doubt that the Secretary of State was the judge as to whether or not the conditions had been fulfilled and so, under section 13, whether to issue a notice. Section 14 depended on section 13 so as to make the Secretary of State the judge under that section too. Whether the fifth condition under section 7 had been fulfilled was a matter for him alone."

Knowsley did not contest that particular point on appeal, but still contended that the Secretary of State had misdirected himself in his judgement that a

---

75 The Times, 28 May 1991 (High Court); The Independent, 25 September 1991 (Court of Appeal). Transcript available on LEXIS.

number of the deductions from the price of the DSO bid made by Knowsley were unlawful.

In the Court of Appeal, Ralph Gibson LJ considered the legal principles underlying the exercise of discretion by the Secretary of State. The usual rule was that the Secretary of State's decision could only be challenged on public law principles, that is if his decision was illegal, irrational or procedurally improper.[76] He went on to consider how this applied in the context of the LGA 1988:

> "... it is not open to the Secretary of State to say: 'It appears to me that the authority has acted in a manner having the effect of distorting competition' unless that which appears to him to have been the relevant act of the local authority is capable of being regarded as distorting etc competition, and whether it is so capable is a matter of law for the court."
>
> *There must therefore be before the Secretary of State, if the section 13 powers are to arise, material upon which he could reasonably conclude that the local authority were in breach* [my italics]. Having regard to the difference in the apparent bid and tender costs, it could not have been, and has not been, suggested that the Secretary of State did not act lawfully in serving the section 13 notices. It then became the obligation of the authority by their written response under section 13 (3)(a) to state that they had not acted in breach of the conditions and to "justify" the statement if they chose to proceed under that alternative. The structure thus provides that it is for the local authority to put before the Secretary of State the material to justify their assertion and it is for the Secretary of State to decide whether it does.
>
> It is the duty then of the Secretary of State to consider the material and to decide whether or not, having regard to it, it still appears to him that the authority have acted in breach of the condition. At this stage also, although the Secretary of State may decide that on any relevant factual issue he is not satisfied that the justification put forward has been made out, the statute still in my judgement requires that, having resolved any such factual issues, *the Secretary of State should only regard acts of the authority for the purpose of Condition 5 in section 7(7), as acts "having the effect of distorting etc competition" if there is material upon which he can reasonably so conclude* [my italics]."

On this basis, most of the points of appeal in *Knowsley* were decided in favour of the Secretary of State, and the section 14 direction was upheld, as it was in the appeal by Leicester CC.

Clearly, this ruling left the Secretary of State in a position of great strength. As long as there was material before him, on the basis of which he could reasonably conclude that there had been a breach of the Act, the courts would not interfere. This was followed in subsequent cases such as *R v*

---

76 Council of Civil Service Unions v Minister for the Civil Service [1985] AC 374.

Secretary of State ex parte Lakeland DC.[77] The case involved another challenge under judicial review to a section 14 direction. The Secretary of State considered that the authority, the Lakeland DC, had acted anti-competitively in the manner in which it required external tenderers to supply an indemnity against the possible effects of the application of the TUPE Regulations (see Chapters 5 and 6). Giving his judgement, Tucker J said:

> "I am guided in my approach to this case by the principles which I distil from (the Court of Appeal decision in *Knowsley*). These principles seem to be as follows. First it is not for the court to referee a mere disagreement between the Applicant and the Secretary of State. Second, the Secretary of State is the arbiter of whether the fifth condition has been complied with. Thirdly, the words 'it appears' in the section provide for a subjective test.
>
> Accordingly the application can only succeed if the Applicant demonstrates that there was no material before the Secretary of State upon which he could reasonably conclude that the applicant was in breach of the fifth condition. Therefore the issue in this application is: was the material available to the Secretary of State when he issued the Direction, pursuant to section 14 of the LGA 1988, such that it could reasonably have appeared to him that the applicant had failed to comply with the fifth condition specified in section 7 of the 1988 Act? In my opinion there was such material. The Secretary of State acted reasonably in issuing the Direction. Accordingly the application is refused."

However a judicial review action against a section 14 direction did succeed in the case of *Ettrick and Lauderdale DC v Secretary of State for Scotland*.[78] The events leading up to the decision were as follows. The council had put its ground maintenance work out to tender in accordance with CCT and received two tenders from the DSO and a private contractor, Brophy plc. The work had been tendered in the form of a bill of quantities broken down into 13 separate items. Each item of work had to be individually priced, and the council reserved the right to accept a tender in whole or in part. Brophy appear to have misunderstood the contract documentation, and to have submitted an integrated bid, broken down into prices for each of the 13 items, but intended to stand together as a whole. For item 1 "grass cutting" Brophy's tender was £120,000 lower than the DSO. For the remaining items the DSO was cheaper by £107,000 in total. The council decided to accept Brophy's tender with regard to item 1, and the DSO's for items 2–13. Brophy asked for permission to adjust its price for item 1 work and when permission was refused withdrew its tender claiming (with a supportive counsel's opinion) that no contract had ever existed between them and the council. The council then asked the DSO to undertake the item 1 work as well. In the meantime, Brophy complained about its treatment to the Secretary of State.

---

77 Unreported hearing: 2 April 1996: transcript available on LEXIS.
78 Unreported hearing: 25 May 1994: transcript available on LEXIS.

After an exchange of correspondence, the Secretary of State issued a section 13 notice alleging that the council had engaged in anti-competitive behaviour, which was followed later by a section 14 direction. Both were based on the grounds that there was no contract and that the council had behaved unreasonably in not allowing Brophy to adjust its price for item 1 following its decision to accept only a part of the tender.

In considering the council's application for judicial review, the court examined first the contract documentation and held that the council had the right to accept tenders in whole or in part and that there was a binding contract between the council and Brophy. Therefore the Secretary of State had misdirected himself in law when he issued a section 13 notice predicated on there not being a binding contract. The same misdirection flawed the subsequent section 14 direction.

The Secretary of State's discretionary power over sanctions

The courts took a similar approach to the exercise of sanctions under section 14 of the Act. In *Knowsley* the court had to consider the lawfulness of a condition that after retendering the work in accordance with section 7, the council obtain the Secretary of State's consent before awarding the work again to the DSO. The reason given for imposing this condition was that it would give the Secretary of State the opportunity to satisfy himself that the council had complied with the statutory requirements the second time around. It was not to impose any further requirement on the council. In the High Court, Popplewell J had some sympathy with this approach but held that the only sanction that the Act provided for a breach of section 7 was contained in sections 13 and 14. The consent requirement was therefore struck out. This point was reversed on appeal. Although the consent condition was imperfectly worded, the Secretary of State could be held to his explanation of its purpose, and as such the condition was in that context a lawful one. The Court therefore exercised its discretion to reinstate the condition. It was to put these matters beyond doubt, that the government amended section 14 by adding sections 14A–C in the LGA 1992 (see above).

In *R v Secretary of State ex parte Haringey LBC*[79] the council rejected cheaper tenders to carry out refuse collection work in favour of letting the work to its DSO. The DSO bid was priced at around £17.8 million compared to bids of £13.3 million and £15 million from the other tenderers. The Secretary of State served a section 13 notice alleging anti-competitive conduct. The grounds stated in the notice were that the council had given excessive and unjustified weight to technical reservations about the outside tenders while giving insufficient weight to similar reservations concerning the DSO and also to the potential savings offered by the outside bids. After considering the council's response, the Secretary of State decided to serve a section 14 direction in terms that the council should cease to have the power

---

79 Unreported hearing: 2 February 1994: transcript available on LEXIS.

to carry out refuse collection from a specified date. This is known as a barring order (as opposed to a conditions order).

The council challenged the direction by way of judicial review. The Divisional Court held that, on the evidence before the Secretary of State, he was entitled to issue a direction but he had acted unlawfully in deciding to make the direction in the form of a barring order as opposed to a conditions order. The scope of the Secretary of State's powers was a matter of law. Because the making of a barring order under section 14 was more serious and carried severer consequences than a conditions order, it required greater justification. There was no evidence that the Secretary of State had considered the form of conditions that might have been attached to the direction and whether the making of a conditions order might have been more appropriate in the circumstances. There was also evidence that the barring order had been made as a deterrent to other local authorities. This, the court said "did not justify an excessive sanction".

The Court of Appeal rejected this approach and restored the barring order. On the deterrence point, the Court said that the Act placed no express limits on the exercise of discretion by the Secretary of State. All that the general law required was that the Secretary of State exercised his discretion rationally and so as to promote the policy and objectives of the Act (as construed by the court). The policy of the Act, as stated in the long title, was to secure that local authorities undertook certain activities only if they could do so competitively.

> "An intention to demonstrate to the country at large, and to those entrusted with the making of decisions on behalf of authorities in the tendering process under the 1988 Act, that action by the Authority which is clearly in favour of the Authority's DSO and is in breach of the fifth condition, may be met with the imposition of a barring order, seems to me to be an intention to promote the policy and the objects of the Local Government Act 1988."

The Court also rejected the argument that the Secretary of State should have given consideration to what particular form of conditions might have been imposed in the circumstances. The point was of "no significance". The arguments for and against the imposition of a barring order had been considered by the Secretary of State, and his reasoning was not unlawful.

Conclusion

In its own way the *Haringey* decision is perhaps more indicative of the British courts' hands-off approach to CCT issues than is *Knowsley*. In the latter case, it is hard to see how the Court of Appeal could have come to any other decision than the one it did: *Knowsley* was wholly in line with long established case law. The same cannot be said in *Haringey*. The Divisional Court had shown that there was scope for judicial creativity that was still consistent with the usual principles of judicial review. There was even perhaps the scope to import and press into service the European legal principle of proportionality, had the court been so minded.[80] Instead the Court of Appeal chose to give the benefit of any legal leeway to the Secretary of State. To do so might have been perfectly justifiable. CCT was a confrontational and politically charged legal regime, and the court may well have taken the view that this was an arena into which judges should tread with extreme caution. Nevertheless that they took this line was their own choice and illustrates the caution with which the courts approach decisions by the executive.

---

80 A general principle of EC law applied by the ECJ in cases such as *Internationale Handelsgesellschaft* Case 11/70 [1970] ECR 1125: the means used by a public authority to achieve an objective should be no more than that which would be appropriate and necessary to achieve the objective. Places the onus on the authority to justify its actions in the context of alternative courses of action.

Chapter Two

CCT for Professional Services

Contents

2.1 Background and Development of Professional Services CCT
2.2 The Defined Activities
2.3 New Accounting Provisions – the Statement of Support Service Costs
2.4 New Rules for Competitive Tendering
2.5 Summary

This Chapter continues the focus on the development and key features of compulsory competitive tendering. Chapter 1 considered the CCT regime relating to local authority blue-collar services, which encompassed detailed legal rules covering competitive tendering, accounting and financial requirements supported by strong enforcement powers wielded by the Secretary of State. This Chapter considers the extension of CCT in the 1990s into the field of local authority professional services: construction and property services, legal services, financial services, information technology services and personnel services. This area was also known as "white collar CCT". Determining the scope and terms of the white-collar regime proved to be very troublesome for the Conservative government and as a result its implementation was severely delayed, eventually being scheduled over the period 1996 to 2000. Surprisingly, that timetable survived the change of government in the 1997 general election largely intact.

2.1 Background and Development of Professional Services CCT

When the DOE published its proposals to widen CCT in 1985,[1] its eventual extension to cover local authority professional support services was mooted even then as a future policy development. The professional services were not only significant in their own terms regarding cost and numbers employed, but also contributed as overhead costs to the cost of work already carried out by DSOs under CCT. However this issue was not addressed until the 1990s, when it became part of the public sector reforms carried out by John Major's two administrations.

2.1.1 The consultation process

The consultations with local government and the relevant professional bodies were long and extensive, lasting from 1991 to 1994. An outline of the chief stages of the consultation process is set out below.

---

1 "Competition in the Provision of Local Services" (DOE).

Early stages

The extension of CCT into local authority professional services was only a part of a drive towards market testing in the public sector. This began with the Citizens Charter[2] of July 1991, which proposed a number of quality standards for public services including local government services. That was followed in November 1991 by the Treasury White Paper "Competing for Quality – Buying Better Public Services",[3] which emphasised the role of public sector managers as the purchasers of quality services, whether from the public or private sectors. Competition was to be the spur to greater efficiency and improvements in quality of service.

In parallel with this, at the departmental level (and following on from the findings of a preliminary study commissioned from the PA Consulting Group) the DOE released a consultation paper entitled "Competing for Quality" in November 1991. The paper contained a number of proposals to tighten the CCT regime in areas such as anti-competitive conduct (see Chapter 5) and also to extend CCT into a number of new services, including:

- construction-related services (architectural services, engineering services, property management services).
- corporate services (corporate and administrative services, legal services, financial services, personnel services, computing services).

It argued that the benefits competition had brought to blue-collar services should now be extended further:

> "2.1.2. Effective management should not be confined to manual services. The number of local authority employees engaged on the professional and technical activities considered in this paper is also in the region of 250,000–300,000, and the annual costs of their activities is estimated to be between £5 billion and £6 billion. The Government recognises that the differences between manual and professional activities may mean that the approach to the compulsory competitive tendering of the former followed under existing legislation is not appropriate to all of the latter, at least at this stage. It is quite clear, however, that the need for good management and value for money is common to both, and that these needs are most likely to be met if the existing organisation of services has to face the challenge of competition. This paper sets out the Government's proposals for applying this challenge as widely as possible to local authority professional and technical services."

While these proposals were being released for consultation, the government was already in the process of taking out the necessary enabling powers through a new Local Government Bill. These powers became section 8 (prescription of procedures for the separate evaluation of price and quality)

---

2 The Citizens Charter: Raising the Standard, Cm 1599 (1991).
3 Cm 1730 [1991].

and section 9 (prescription of anti-competitive conduct) of the Local Government Act 1992.

The actual proposals attracted a lot of criticism. In the consultation period that followed "Competing for Quality" the DOE received over 750 responses, many of them critical, including from bodies such as the Law Society and the Royal Institute of British Architects which represent professionals in both the public and the private sectors. The DOE released a second consultation paper in response in November 1992.[4] It contained revised proposals and conceded that further consultations would be necessary.

The eventual form of white-collar CCT was settled in consultations over 1993–94. These were led by a Competition Steering Group chaired by the DOE, and supported by a number of Service Working Groups. In particular, there were service working groups covering construction related services, corporate services, and housing management services (the DOE treating this as a part of the "white collar" group of CCT activities). The membership of these groups included officials from the DOE, the local authority associations, the Audit Commission and relevant professional bodies. A further working group considered the necessary accounting framework.

Following the completion of this exercise (which involved the commissioning of further consultancy studies), the DOE issued consultation papers containing formal proposals for implementation in the case of each activity. Plans to extend CCT to corporate and administrative services were shelved in December 1994. The final proposals for the remaining areas were released on the following dates, with draft statutory instruments and guidance notes attached:

- legal services – December 1993
- construction and property services – February 1994
- accounting framework – February 1994
- financial services – October 1994
- I.T services – October 1994
- personnel services – December 1994

After considering responses to these, the necessary secondary legislation was passed at the end of 1994 and into 1995.

2.1.2   Policy issues

The professional services that the government was proposing to subject to CCT shared certain characteristics, which differentiated them from the defined activities that had gone before:

(a) many elements of professional services work were not suitable for competition. Some were too closely connected to advising the council in its corporate capacity. There were also complex links with the local democratic process.

---

4   The Extension of Compulsory Competitive Tendering (DOE).

(b) there were wide variations between local authorities in the way that professional support services were organised. In some cases they were grouped together in central departments; in others there were varying degrees of decentralisation.
(c) the exercise of professional skill and judgment is more difficult to define and measure. In order to achieve service quality different approaches to the evaluation of tenders and the supervision of contracts would be needed.
(d) the cost of professional services was generally charged as overhead costs to other departments. However mechanisms for financial management were underdeveloped and incapable of revealing the true cost of the services. Since competitive tendering depended on accurate costing of the competing tenders, this was a significant problem.

These issues raised several policy questions throughout the course of the consultations. In particular, the government recognised that the different nature and organisation of local authority professional services would require some modifications to the CCT regime. The form of this modified regime evolved over the course of the consultation process.

Competition requirements

In blue-collar CCT the defined activities were framed so as to catch only the "contractor-side" of the activity (ie: its actual performance as opposed to its procurement and monitoring)) and so it was normal for 100% of the defined activity to be subjected to compulsory competition. The government originally intended to treat the construction-related services on the same basis (100% competition requirement). However it recognised that this would not be appropriate in the case of the corporate services, where it is more difficult to disentangle the contractor-side and client-side elements of work.

The preferred approach was to require that a percentage of the total annual value of work carried out by each professional service be exposed to competition. This meant including client-side elements in the defined activity and leaving local authorities the flexibility to choose exactly which work within a particular service they would put out to competition. On this basis the November 1991 consultation paper proposed the following competition requirements for the new defined activities:

- corporate and administrative services: 15%.
- legal services: 33%.
- financial services and personnel services: 25%.
- computing services: 80%.

Despite criticism in local authority circles that these figures were too high, the government made only one concession in the November 1992 consultation paper: that there should be a credit to take account of work already contracted out. There was though a change in the government's stance towards construction related work. Ministers accepted that a requirement for 100% competition would make it difficult for local authorities to retain the professional client side capacity that they needed to enable them to secure efficiency savings through market testing. Instead it was proposed to reduce the competition requirement from 100% to 90% to permit the retention of a small in-house capacity.

The competition requirement percentages went through further examination and consultations in the service working groups in 1993. In particular, there were a number of research studies conducted for the DOE by management consultants. For example, Coopers & Lybrand were appointed to consider the proposals for legal services, and construction and property services. They studied 24 local authorities, and concluded that while the legal services percentage could be comfortably implemented, that for construction and property services was too high to permit the retention of sufficient staff to form a viable client side. The government followed these findings and revised their proposals by raising the legal services percentage and reducing the construction and property services percentage. KPMG Peat Marwick carried out similar studies in relation to the other proposed services. Further consideration was also given to the matter of credits that authorities could deduct from the total value of work within each defined activity.

The outcome was a formulaic approach under which local authorities would be required to subject to CCT a percentage of the total defined activity (the competition requirement) less the value of any applicable credits. This final amount became known as the specified proportion. The specified proportion for each authority would be different because of inevitable differences in the value of applicable credits.

Measuring the cost of professional services

In the November 1991 Consultation Paper the government argued that CCT for the corporate services could be most effectively applied after the introduction of a consistent internal accounting regime. Existing accounting systems were seen as flawed because of a lack of financial management information and accountability. In a typical set-up, professional service departments would hold budgets funded by a crude apportionment of costs onto the budgets of other internal clients. These recharges would take the form of overhead costs. Under these systems there was rarely any agreement between the parties as to service levels or charges. Recharges would be imposed on the internal clients who consequently would have little say over the cost, efficiency or effectiveness of the service provided. It is not possible to establish the real cost of professional services under such a system and the lack of accountability hampered the development of any business ethos. A further problem was that the lack of transparency on costs gave local authorities scope to load support costs onto services which were not facing competition, so unfairly favouring services subject to CCT.

The government proposed that local authorities should be required to keep internal trading accounts for each corporate professional service, whether or not exposed to competition. To achieve this services would have to be clearly defined, forms and levels of service provision agreed with internal clients, charging mechanisms and standard unit costings similarly agreed, and time recording systems implemented. By this means the real cost of professional services could be measured and allocated to other departments on a consistent basis. The government believed that primary legislation would be required, but that once this had been enacted and a year had passed "bedding down" the new internal trading accounts, CCT in full could then be introduced.

The proposals were criticised as forcing local authorities to organise their professional services on the basis of accounting convenience rather than policy or need. Even the usually supportive Audit Commission warned that the accounting framework could become too bureaucratic, with costs exceeding likely savings.[5] Nevertheless the DOE had not changed its mind when it released its second consultation paper in November 1992. Indeed it now considered that internal trading accounts could be implemented by means of regulations under section 23 of the Local Government Finance Act 1982 (or section 105 of the Local Government (Scotland) Act 1973). This would have advanced the planned timetable for introducing internal trading accounts (and CCT after that). There were two other changes to the proposals, namely: that the requirement for internal trading accounts should be extended to the construction related services; and, that in addition local authorities be required to publish a statement of support service costs for each of the corporate and the construction related services.

Consultations continued within the framework of the Competition Steering Committee and the Accounts Working Group. Then in the new year the DOE suddenly dropped the idea of internal trading accounts altogether, proposing to leave in its place simply the requirement for the publication of a Statement of Support Service Costs (SSSC). It is probable that the strength of opposition to the imposition of internal trading accounts and the potential this opposition had to delay the introduction of CCT lay behind the change. In contrast, the SSSC would be an end-statement of what a particular support service cost the authority in any year. It left the underlying accounting methodology that reached that figure to the discretion of the particular authority.

The DOE described the purposes of SSSCs in the following terms:

- to demonstrate the costs to an authority of providing the respective support services, whether in-house or out-sourced;
- to stimulate the challenge of these costs by internal customers;
- to encourage the development of an internal market within local authorities;

---

5   See Cirell and Bennett in "Competitive Tendering for Professional Services" (1994) at Chapter K4 paragraph 14.

– to provide a basis on which the competition requirement for CCT could be calculated.[6]

The consultations that followed this paper lasted much longer than expected and it was not until November 1994 that the necessary regulations were made (followed up in December 1994 with DOE guidance and illustrative format for a SSSC).

The evaluation of quality

In relation to the original "blue collar" CCT activities, the government considered that quality considerations could be adequately dealt with in the detailed specification (see Chapter 5). However, it acknowledged that the situation with professional services was different. A DOE Minister told a Parliamentary Standing Committee during the passage of the Local Government Bill in February 1992 that "the assessment of quality in professional services is more complicated because the services are more difficult to specify and performance is harder to measure".[7] The government indicated its willingness in the November 1991 Consultation Paper to modify the statutory framework for tendering and permit the separate evaluation of the quality and price of individual tenders. This proposal was known as "double envelope" tendering (although it was only intended to apply in the construction related services – the corporate services having a different proposed regime). It was described as a system "under which unpriced tenders are initially evaluated against a pre-set quality threshold, and a second evaluation is then carried out so that the lowest priced tender is automatically accepted from those meeting or exceeding the quality threshold".[8] The proposal was introduced into Parliament as Clause 8 of the Local Government Bill 1991 while the consultation period was still open. It was eventually enacted (having been amended in its passage through the House of Lords) as section 8 of the LGA 1992. This provision empowered the Secretary of State to make orders prescribing separate procedures for the evaluation of the quality and the price of tenders. The power was limited to new defined activities created under section 2(3) of the LGA 1988 that involved professional services or the application of financial or technical expertise.

Meanwhile, in the consultations double envelope tendering was heavily criticised and in the second Consultation Paper of November 1992 it was dropped. Ministers conceded that the proposal was too rigid and could prevent local authorities from reaching appropriate judgments about the

---

6   "Competition in Professional White-Collar Support Services: Consultation Paper on Proposed Statutory Accounting Framework" (DOE) (February 1994).
7   Robert Key, Parliamentary Under-Secretary of State for the Environment, Standing Committee D, February 11 1992, col. 243.
8   This was similar to the much criticised system used for the allocation of ITV franchises by the Independent Television Commission under the Broadcasting Act 1990.

trade-off between price and quality. Instead the government proposed to allow local authorities to use their own procedures for tender evaluation provided these were fair and even-handed. That workhorse of the statutory regime, the prohibition of anti-competitive conduct, was therefore to fill the gap left by the rejection of double envelope tendering.[9] Section 8 of the LGA 1992 remained unused on the statute book.

2.2   The Defined Activities

The professional service activities were defined in a comprehensive manner to include both contractor and client functions. This allowed for the fact that the competition requirements applied to only a percentage of each defined activity. The defined activities were created by a number of orders made under section 2(3) of the LGA 1988. These orders added each activity to the list of defined activities in section 2(2) together with a new paragraph describing the extent of the activity in Schedule 1 of the Act. The descriptions of each defined activity that follow draw on the definitions provided by the Corporate Services Working Group.

2.2.1   Legal services[10]

This defined activity, which can be usefully divided into legal advice, legal representation and legal procurement, covered the provision of all legal services (whether by the Council's own staff or outsiders) to a local authority including the following:

(a) Legal advice to the Council itself, its committees, sub-committees, working groups, working panels and elected members.
(b) Legal advice to Council departments or officers, concerning the discharge of the Council's functions.
(c) Legal advice to Council departments, officers or other persons to ensure propriety in the discharge of the Council's functions. This included advice to statutory officers of the Council such as the Head of Paid Services, the Monitoring Officer and the Chief Financial Officer, independently of the Council itself. Also, to any other person including external bodies such as the Council's auditors or the local government ombudsman.
(d) Official legal representation of the Council (including the instruction of external solicitors and counsel) in connection with civil and criminal litigation in all courts (whether preparatory work, advocacy or

---

9   Guidance on the avoidance of anti-competitive conduct in white-collar CCT was issued through DOE Circulars in June and December 1994 (see Chapter 5).
10 Section 2(2)(j) and Schedule 1(11): created by S.I. 1994 No. 2884.

consequential action), contracts, conveyancing (and other property related legal work), statutory notices and orders, bye-laws, local Acts of Parliament, and insurance arrangements.
(e) The procurement, monitoring and supervision of any legal services described in (a) to (d) above. This was essentially what would be called the client function. It included the preparation of the service specification, the conduct of any competitive tendering, and the monitoring of in-house or external providers of legal services.

2.2.2   Construction and property services[11]

The defined activity covered services in the fields of architecture (including landscape architecture), engineering, valuation, property management, quantity surveying and building surveying.
It related to a number of functions, including:

− giving advice;
− establishing and managing capital and revenue programmes for the development and maintenance of relevant land;
− designing and planning development projects and maintenance work;
− managing such projects (financially and contractually);
− managing relevant land; and,
− procuring, monitoring, supervising or arranging payment for any of those things.

The scope of the defined activity was limited to work relating to "relevant land", that is land occupied by a council, or in which it had or was seeking to acquire an interest. This also included highways and land that the council managed or maintained by agreement. However for the purposes of managing land, local authority housing was excluded from the defined activity. This avoided an overlap with the defined activity of housing management. Work carried out under agency agreements with highway authorities and sewerage undertakers was also excluded from the defined activity.

2.2.3   Financial services[12]

The defined activity covered the following matters:

(a) the provision of financial advice to the council, committees or sub-committees, members, officers and to any other person concerning the discharge of the Council's functions.
(b) accounting services including the completion of statutory accounts, the maintenance of relevant records, administration of direct and

---

11 Section 2(2)(k) and Schedule 1(12): created by S.I. 1994 No. 2888.
12 Section 2(2)(l) and Schedule 1(13): created by S.I. 1995 No. 1915.

indirect taxation, and the development and maintenance of financial information and management systems.
(c) audit services, including liaison with external auditors and other bodies.
(d) administration, collection and recovery of local taxation.
(e) the provision of payroll facilities, collection of income, making of payments and recovery of debts.
(f) the administration of the authority's pension fund including management of investment and actuarial services.
(g) the arrangement and management of an authority's borrowing and investment, and the monitoring of its cash flow.
(h) administration of an authority's insurance arrangements.
(i) financial consultancy and research work.
(j) procuring, monitoring or supervising any of the above.

2.2.4   Information technology services[13]

This defined activity encompassed services that were designed to secure for an authority the availability and application of information technology. This included:

- giving advice to the council, committees, sub-committees, officers, members on IT matters that related to the discharge of the authority's functions.
- assessing and reviewing an authority's requirements for IT.
- the procurement, development, operation and maintenance of IT.
- user support and training.
- security of IT.
- contract management.

IT was defined widely to include any computer, telecommunications or other technology the principal use of which was the recording, processing and communication of information by electronic means.

2.2.5   Personnel services[14]

This defined covered the following areas:

(a) giving advice on personnel matters to the council, committees, sub-committees, officers, members or to any other person concerning the discharge of any of the authority's functions.
(b) the conduct of organisational and methods studies and works studies, including management service reviews and business planning.

---

13 Section 2(2)(m) and Schedule 1(14): created by S.I. 1995 No. 1915.
14 Section 2(2)(n) and Schedule 1(15): created by S.I. 1995 No. 1915.

(c) human resource management including recruitment, monitoring and appraisal of staff, maintenance of statistical records and management information systems, terms and conditions of employment, and redundancy arrangements.
(d) training and development of staff (but not ordinary supervision of trainees and other staff).
(e) personnel work connected with pay and non-pay benefits (eg – superannuation benefits).
(f) equal opportunities, health and safety, occupational health services, and other issues connected to staff welfare.

2.2.6 Exemptions

The main difference was in the treatment of incidental work performed by an employee (the cut-off exemption). Section 2(6) LGA 1988 was amended so that the exemption was construed against a specific percentage figure:

> "Work which is carried out by a defined authority through an employee and which would (apart from this subsection) fall within a defined activity shall not do so if the total amount of such work performed by such an employee occupies less than 50 per cent of his working time."

2.3 New Accounting Provisions – the Statement of Support Service Costs

To facilitate CCT, local authorities were required to publish details of the costs of their professional support services in a Statement of Support Service Costs (SSSC). This applied from 1995/96 for London and metropolitan authorities, and from 1996/97 for the remaining authorities.

SSSCs became the basis of the government's new internal accounting framework for local authority professional services when its original conception of internal trading accounts was dropped in early 1994. The requirement was originally contained in the Accounts and Audit (Amendment) Regulations 1994[15] (which amended previous regulations dating from 1983). This was in turn replaced by consolidating regulations entitled the Accounts and Audit Regulations 1996.[16]

Regulation 10 required local authorities to publish certain matters relating to the cost of certain "specified activities" in the form of a statement. This had to be done as soon as reasonably possible or within nine months (whichever was sooner) of the conclusion of an audit. The contents of the statement were prescribed by the Schedule to the Regulations, and the statement itself had to be open to public inspection and copying. Under the Regulations, the specified activities were the defined activities of legal services, construction and property services, financial services, IT services and personnel services.

---

15 S.I. 1994 No. 3018.
16 S.I. 1996 No. 590.

CHAPTER TWO

The Regulations did not prescribe the format for a SSSC but both the DOE and CIPFA used the following illustrative format.

The SSSC: Illustrative Format (DOE, CIPFA)

1. Specified Support Service Activity	Legal	C & P	Finance	Etc....

2. Cost of activity, excluding charges from other specified activities
3. Add charges from other specified activities
4. Cost of activity
5. Deduct charges to other specified activities
6. Net Cost of activity
7 – 13. [Miscellaneous adjustments]
14. TOTAL

The crucial figure above for the purposes of CCT was line 4 (which had also to be shown in the local authority's annual accounts). The DOE recommended that local authorities used this figure to represent the cost of the defined activity and as the basis for calculating the specified proportion of the activity that had be put out to competition. However ascertaining the cost of an activity (line 4 above) was not a straightforward operation. In particular, it included the following operations:

(i) identifying all of the work falling within a specified activity, not just the proportion that would be subject to competition. This included work that was already contracted out as well as work undertaken in-house. The value of defined activity work carried out under a works contract had to be included in the SSSC of the local authority commissioning the work and not that of the authority that bid for and actually carried out the work.[17] Also both direct costs and overhead costs were counted.

(ii) allocating work between defined activities in cases where work was capable of falling within more than one activity.[18]

(iii) excluding defined activity work performed by an employee that was incidental to other work (ie – the "cut-off" exemption under section 2(6)). Work that was incidental to a defined activity because it fell below the cut-off, could not be counted towards the value of a

---

17　DOE Letter: CCT: White Collar Services: Joint Arrangements (18 May 1995).
18　See the consolidating regulations S.I. 1996 No. 590: Schedule 1 paragraph 1(3). This provision mirrors section 2(5) LGA 1988 (allocation of work capable of falling in more than one defined activity).

specified activity for the purposes of that activity's SSSC. Furthermore, guidance produced by CIPFA (and commended to local authorities by the DOE) stated that the 50 per cent cut-off related to individual defined activities and not to the total time spent on two or more defined activities. Therefore if a hypothetical member of staff spent 45 per cent of her time on financial services and another 25 per cent on IT services, her work would not fall under the CCT regime or appear on a SSSC. While this interpretation might be questioned, in practical terms it was probably the easiest approach to adopt. Otherwise it would have been necessary to apportion the work between the two specified activities which would then be shown under separate columns on the SSSC.

2.4 New Rules for Competitive Tendering

The competitive tendering regime for professional services was substantially the same as that for the blue-collar services but there were a number of differences in detail that are outlined in the following sections.

2.4.1 The works contracts provisions

Local authorities had to comply with the requirements contained in sections 4 and 5 LGA 1988 in relation to works contracts. The implementation dates for CCT were specified in the relevant orders "defining" each activity under section 2(3). These dates were not uniform because they had to take account of the local government reorganisations of the 1990s. There was also a de minimis exemption for any individual contract valued at or below £25,000.[19]

2.4.2 Functional work: calculating the specified proportion

The Secretary of State made regulations under section 6(3) of the LGA 1988 requiring local authorities to expose a "specified proportion" of the work within each defined activity to competition every year.[20] It followed that the value of work an authority was required to expose to competition might vary from year to year. Therefore an authority might satisfy the specified proportion in one year, yet find that it needed to expose further work to competition the next.

The various regulations defined the specified proportion by means of a formula:

$$T - (A + B + C + D + E + F + G).$$

---

19 S.I. 1996 No. 770
20 S.I. 1994 No. 3164 (Legal services); S.I. 1994 No. 3166 (Construction and Property services); S.I. 1995 No. 2916 (Financial services); S.I. 1995 No. 2813 (Information technology services); S.I. 1995 No. 2101 (Personnel services).

"T" was the total value of work, while and "A" to "G" represented credits that were deductible from it (although there were slight variations in the way that the credits applied to different activities, as will become clear). The deduction of further allowances for work that had already been contracted out or externalised naturally followed on from the formulation of the primary CCT legislation, which only bit on work that was undertaken in-house.

(1)   Calculating "T": the total value of work

T represented the cost to a defined authority of "specified work"; that is to say all the work falling within the definition of the relevant defined activity except work carried out by a bidding authority pursuant to a works contract. The cost was the total annual estimated cost including overheads. The correct method of calculating T was the subject of much argument. DOE guidance defined T in the following terms:

> "The starting point for deciding what proportion of ..[work].. must be exposed to competition ... is determining the total value of work falling within the defined activity. Subject to the cut-off (ie the exemption provided under s.2(6) of the 1988 Act as modified), this is the full or gross cost of performing that work (whether directly or through provision under contract) including overheads and the cost of bought-in goods and services."[21]

The guidance went on to say that the Statement of Support Service Costs (SSSC) offered a basis for calculating the value of T, the relevant part of the SSSC being the amount represented by line 4 (see back).

(2)   Credits under the formula

The formula allowed authorities to deduct from the cost of T, a number of credits. The most significant of these was Credit A, which ensured that all authorities could retain in-house and free from competition a certain amount of work (either in the form of a competition-free percentage or as a de minimis allowance – see below). The remaining credits were all intended to recognise parts of work that had already been subject to competitive pressures.

Credit A

This was the most significant of the credits. A local authority was permitted to deduct from the value of T either a stated competition free allowance (expressed in terms of a percentage) or a de minimis allowance, whichever of the two was the greater. The purpose of the competition free allowance was to give local authorities the maximum flexibility in selecting and organising work for competition.

---

21   See for example, "Implementation of CCT for Legal Services" at paragraph 16 (DOE Guidance Note) (December 1994).

The de minimis allowances served two purposes. As was the case with the blue-collar activities, they excluded from the CCT regime, those authorities where the value of the work performed was too low for competition to produce net savings. However, they also provided an irreducible minimum core of service provision, which remained competition free on a permanent basis. Only the excess value of services was ever liable to face competition.

The various regulations set the following values for Credit A in relation to the professional services:

(i) legal services: "an amount equal to 55 per cent of T or £300,000, whichever is greater".
(ii) construction and property services: "an amount equal to 35 per cent of T or £450,000, whichever is greater".
(iii) financial services: "an amount equal to 65 per cent of T or £300,000, whichever is greater".
(iv) I.T services: "an amount equal to 30 per cent of T or £300,000, whichever is greater".
(v) personnel services: "an amount equal to 70 per cent of T or £400,000, whichever is greater".

Credit B

The following amount could deducted from the value of T:

> "for the period ending on 31st March 1999 or five years after work was awarded, whichever is the shorter, an amount equal to the cost of specified work which is being carried out by a defined authority following voluntary competitive tendering"

This credit was available to local authorities that had already market tested parts of their professional services, and had awarded the work in-house. The DOE first announced it in a press release on 13 September 1993. It was originally intended that local authorities should have to demonstrate to their auditors "their voluntary competitive tendering exercise was of equivalent rigor to that which would be expected under the CCT legislation". However this was a role that the auditors were unwilling to assume and it also raised the prospect of an inconsistent application of the exemption across the country. Therefore the government settled on a requirement that at least three external contractors as well as the in-house team were invited to tender for the work. In the regulations this is expressed in the definition of voluntary competitive tendering. The award of work had to have taken place before 1 April 1994 in order to qualify.

Where voluntary competitive tendering led to the award of work to an outside contractor, this could be counted against the specified proportion at the end of the formulaic calculation (see below).

Credit C

The following amount could be deducted from the value of T as credit C:

> "an amount equal to the cost of specified work carried out by a defined authority on behalf of a school with a delegated budget provided under scheme prepared in accordance with section 33 of the Education Reform Act 1988"

The reason for this credit or exemption was again the presumption of prior market testing. Under the Education Reform Act 1988, local education authorities were required to prepare schemes to delegate elements of the education budget to the local management of the governors of schools. This was known as LMS (Local Management of Schools) and left schools with considerable discretion over how to spend the designated elements of their budgets, hence the presumption of prior market testing.

Credit D

The following amount could be deducted from the value of T as credit D:

> "until 1st April 1999, an amount equal to the cost of specified work which is being carried out by a defined authority in connection with functional work falling within the defined activity mentioned in section 2(2)(h) of the Act (housing management) where that functional work is not subject to section 6 of the Act"

This credit was intended to recognise the close links between housing management and the professional support services. It allowed local authorities to establish comprehensive housing management arrangements (such as "one stop shops" for tenants providing housing, benefits and other related services) by postponing the requirement to tender relevant support services until the main body of housing management work was brought into CCT.

Credits E and F

The aim of these two credits was essentially the same: to take account of the value of professional support services work that had already been tested under CCT conditions. Credit E operated in relation to work under the LGA 1988 and was defined as follows:

> "an amount equal to the cost of specified work carried out by a defined authority in connection with functional work falling within any other defined activity where that functional work is being carried out by a defined authority in accordance with the provisions of the Act"

An example might be a personnel department's advice to a DSO on the subject of redundancies, structuring or changes to employees' terms and conditions in preparation of a bid to be submitted by the DSO under CCT for work falling under another defined activity. The cost of this advice would normally be recharged as an overhead to the DSO concerned, and so would be counted towards the price of the DSO bid. As such, the cost would be tested in competition as part of the DSO bid to carry out the other defined activity. In the event that the DSO bid was successful, credit E would permit the value of the personnel department's advice to be deducted from the T value of the Personnel Services defined activity and thereby prevent it from being subjected to competition twice over.

Credit F was defined in similar terms but related to professional services support costs for construction and maintenance work carried out under the LGPLA 1980. The purpose and effect was the same.

However there was a loophole in the wording used for Credit E, in that it related to work carried out "in connection with functional work falling within any other defined activity". This was significant in relation to the professional services where only a specified proportion of the defined activity was required to face competition. Take as an example the cost of I.T support towards a successful in-house bid to carry out financial services. For the purpose of calculating the specified proportion of I.T work, the cost of I.T support towards the whole of the financial services defined activity could be counted towards Credit E. This would be so, despite the fact that only a proportion of financial services work would actually have been tested in competition. Therefore, a part of the I.T work claimed under Credit E could not have been previously tested in competition (the original justification for the credit).[22]

Credit G

This was available only in the case of construction and property services, information technology services, and personnel services. The form taken by this credit differed between the three defined activities.

(i) In relation to construction and property services, a credit was available for certain work in progress. This enabled the local authority to continue performing certain types of work until a natural break had been reached, avoiding the potential problems involved in handing over unfinished work to an external contractor. These would include problems such as the division of liabilities regarding the on-going work, and the practical difficulties for the contractor of picking up a number of files on a set date at different stages of completion. There were other implications regarding the applicability of TUPE, in that the transfer of on-going work would have indicated the transfer of an undertaking and so the application of TUPE (see Chapter 6).

---

22 This is discussed in Cirell and Bennett "Competitive Tendering for Professional Services" at Chapter C2.29.

The credit allowed for the deduction from the value of T of the following:

> "for the allowable period, an amount equal to the cost (including overheads) of the work falling within paragraphs 12(3)(d) and (e) of Schedule 1 to the Act, where that work has been started by a defined authority before the commencement of the allowable period"

The "allowable period" began on the date that CCT first applied to that particular defined authority, and ended at two natural break-points in the performance of the work concerned. For the work in paragraph 12(3)(d) (design and planning of development projects and maintenance work, including feasibility studies, investigatory work, and the preparation of plans, costings and reports) the end point would be the date on which that work was completed. For the work in paragraph 12(3)(e) (establishment and management of capital and revenue programmes for the development and maintenance of relevant land) the end point would be the certification of satisfactory completion.

(ii) In relation to I.T services: the credit arose from situations where local authorities had voluntarily contracted out other services that required I.T support, and the contractor had chosen to use the authority's I.T facilities for the purpose of carrying out that work. In such a situation the I.T work performed by the authority would have been indirectly market tested, and the credit was allowed by the DOE to reflect this situation.

Interestingly the DOE accepted in a press release of 18 May 1995 that it would not consider a contractual requirement for the contractor to use the authority's I.T facilities, to be anti-competitive if it were operationally necessary. This meant that the credit could be claimed even where the contractor was given no choice over using the facilities. This position was subsequently confirmed by departmental guidance issued in DOE Circular 5/96.

(iii) In relation to personnel services: the credit applied to:

> "an amount equal to the cost of specified work falling within paragraph 15(1)(g) of Schedule 1 to the Act where that work is wholly or partly funded by a grant made pursuant to section 1 of the Education (Grants and Awards) Act 1984"

The type of work referred to was "training a defined authority's employees including, in particular, arranging, monitoring and evaluating training and development programmes" where this was wholly or partly grant aided.

(3)   Deductible allowances outside of the formula

The DOE accepted in various guidance notes that the formula provided for the calculation of the specified proportion was not comprehensive and that local authorities could make allowances for other matters as well as those mentioned in the formula.

Work already contracted out

A basic premise of CCT was that it only applied where a defined authority used its own staff to carry out defined activity work. Therefore, work within any particular defined activity that had already been contracted out could be counted towards the specified proportion for that activity (so reducing the amount of work that the authority was required to put to compulsory competitive tendering). This principle was stated in DOE Guidance Notes on CCT for Legal Services (December 1994):

> "24. Any element of legal work which is already contracted out serves to reduce the amount of work within the specified proportion which is undertaken in-house and thus the amount of in-house work which must be awarded through competitive tendering. This does not need to be provided for by a specific deduction from the competition percentage. Instead it flows from the formulation of the legislation, which only bites on work undertaken in-house.
> 25. In deciding what their obligations under CCT may be, authorities should, therefore, deduct from the specified proportion the value of any contracted out legal work, regardless of whether the contract was awarded through competitive tendering or by any other means. In the case of legal services, work undertaken by barristers is treated as contracted out, although no formal contract exists. The remainder of the work within the specified proportion which is undertaken in-house must, after the implementation date, be awarded through CCT..."

This principle also applied where an authority commissioned work to be carried out on its behalf under a works contract. The work, which would be included within the commissioning authority's "T" value for the defined activity, would count towards the satisfaction of its specified proportion, just as it would were it being performed by a private contractor.

Work indirectly contracted out (the "pre-shrunk allowance")

This allowance reflected the fact that where work in any defined activity was contracted out, in addition to losing the main body of work, the local authority also lost the element of professional support services work associated with it. This support work would then be performed externally and the costs charged, albeit indirectly, to the local authority. The DOE permitted local authorities to claim an allowance for this indirectly contracted out work (also known as the "pre-shrunk" allowance) within the parameters set out in the DOE Guidance Notes on CCT, taking for an example again those for Legal Services:

"26. Some legal work may be undertaken by the private sector as part of a contract or contracts for other services. Where this falls within the defined activity, authorities will wish to consider whether it represents a material proportion of the cost of legal services. If so they will wish to seek their external auditor's agreement to this being recognised as contracted out work."

The cost of bought-in goods and services

The DOE accepted that in certain circumstances the cost of bought-in goods and services could be counted towards the satisfaction of the specified proportion. This was because such purchases were deemed to introduce competitive pressures. For this purpose a distinction was drawn between goods and services that did defined activity work and counted towards the specified proportion, and those that merely supported it and did not. In relation to financial services, the DOE guidance cited the external printing of invoices, the delivery of council tax demands and fees for external legal advice, as examples of goods and services that "did" defined activity work. In contrast the buying of stationary, electricity and telephone charges merely supported defined activity work and did not introduce competitive pressures to the local authority's service provision. While both would form part of the total cost of the defined activity work (the "T" value) only the former could be deducted from the specified proportion. This was admittedly a complicated distinction to draw.

"Double-counting" allowance.

Because of the comprehensive definitions given to the professional defined activities, which included support costs, a professional service could at the same time be an activity in its own right and a support service to another service. That of course included other professional services. For example, I.T work would count towards the T value of the I.T defined activity, and also as an overhead cost towards the financial services defined activity etc.[23] Local authorities were given an allowance where there was this element of double-counting so that work did not have to be exposed to competition twice over.

2.4.3 Other provisions for functional work

Once the specified proportion of work within a defined activity had been ascertained for the year ahead, the CCT rules for functional work were substantially the same as those considered earlier in Chapter 1 regarding blue-collar services. There were however a few modifications to the regime, which are considered below.

---

23 See the cost of an activity represented by line 4 of the illustrative format of the SSSC in 2.3. This was suggested by the DOE as the basis for the value of "T" and was reached by the inclusion of charges from other specified work.

(1) Treatment of sub-contracted work

The definition of functional work in section 3(4) of the LGA 1988 included work that was carried out otherwise than by a defined authority but that was dependant upon, or incidental or preparatory to other functional work. This provision was omitted in the case of professional services. Work of this sort was treated as a contracted out service and taken into account accordingly in calculating the specified proportion (see above).

(2) Treatment of time periods in the tendering process

The requirement that an authority issued invitations to tender between 3 and 6 months after advertising the work was dropped.[24] This provided local authorities with a degree more flexibility over the timetabling of CCT. However all of the other time periods under the 1993 Competition Regulations[25] and EC public procurement law did apply.

(3) Minimum and maximum contract periods

The Secretary of State did not issued regulations under section 8 LGA 1988 to specify minimum or maximum contract periods in relation to the professional services and housing management. However this omission did not release authorities from the general requirement to ensure a reasonable exposure of services to competition. In particular, where a contract concerned the continuous provision of a service, the examples given being architectural advice and housing management, the DOE indicated through guidance in a departmental circular that contracts should normally be no longer than 5 years in length.[26]

2.4.4 Changes resulting from the Beresford review

The government rapidly became disillusioned with the way in which professional services CCT was working. The early indications suggested that an early review of the regime was needed. Local authorities were complaining about implementation costs, contractors were complaining that competition was being frustrated by the authorities, the Audit Commission considered that the credits and allowances were open to abuse, and DOE research suggested that very little work was actually being exposed to competition.[27]

Acting on these concerns, the Local Government Minister, Sir Paul

---

24 Requirement contained in section 7(3)(a) – dropped by the relevant section 2(3) orders for each defined activity.
25 S.I. 1993 No. 848.
26 DOE Circular 5/96 paragraph 16.
27 "The Exposure of Professional and White Collar Services to CCT" Report by Newchurch & Co. for the DOE [November 1996].

Beresford initiated a review of the regime for professional services and housing management between December 1995 and March 1996. The outcome of the review and the government's proposals for change were then released in a consultation paper in June 1996.[28] This was in turn followed that November by a draft circular. New regulations, consolidating the previous regulations, were issued by the Secretary of State in February 1997.[29]

The new regulations significantly changed the existing rules for calculating the specified proportion. The value of T was redefined to prevent the double counting of overheads. Only overhead costs that did not form part of another defined activity would henceforth count towards the T value of any single defined activity. Defined activity overheads would be counted towards their own T value and no others. In terms of the SSSC, this change meant that line 2 rather than line 4 would be the best indicator in future of the value of T. This change also meant that the double counting allowance, which was considered open to abuse, was abolished. All the other allowances that had been outside the original formula were brought together within a new and comprehensive formula for calculating the specified proportion:

$$T - (A + B) - (C + D + E + F + G + H)$$

The new credits were framed on the following basis:

(i) Credit A represented indirectly contracted out work.
(ii) Credit B represented all bought-in goods and services (ending the previous distinction between bought-in goods etc that "did" a defined activity and those that merely supported it).

Under the new formula, the combined value of Credits A and B would be deducted from T before going onto the next part of the formula. Previously both these items were deducted at the end from the specified proportion itself. Deducting them at an earlier stage from the value of T, meant that more work would be brought into competition. The remaining credits were:

(iii) Credit C was the competition-free allowance/de minimis allowance formerly represented as Credit A.[30]
(iv) Credit D was the old Credit B relating to voluntary competitive tendering.
(v) Credit E was a new allowance for any work that had been awarded

---

28 "Changes to CCT Framework for Professional Services and Housing Management" (DOE).
29 S.I. 1997 No. 175.
30 The competition-free percentages have changed in some cases. For financial services it is now 60% for county councils and 50% for the rest. 60% is also the new figure for IT and personnel services.

(vi) Credit F was the former Credit C relating to work carried out for schools with delegated budgets under LMS.
(vii) Credit G was the former Credit D relating to the support of housing management work.
(viii) Credit H was the same as the previous Credit G but only in relation to personnel and IT work.

under the ordinary CCT principles whether awarded in-house or externally.

The new regulations have been given only a brief consideration here for two reasons. The first is that they were issued too late in the day to have any bearing on the white-collar CCT tenders undertaken by the two local authorities that are the subject of case studies in Chapters 7 and 8 of this book. The second is that the new government plans to make further significant changes to the formula (pending the establishment in a few years time of a new best value regime for local government in place of or alongside CCT). Fuller consideration will become more profitable only when the dust has settled.

2.5 Summary

The different character of professional services dictated the need for a modified form of CCT in this area. It took shape as widely drawn defined activities from within which authorities were required to subject only a proportion of each activity to competition. The resulting accounting provisions and competition requirements certainly added a new dimension of complexity. The white collar regime took a long time to establish and it would appear that the last government was still dissatisfied with its creation almost to the end, fearing that it was insufficiently rigorous for competition to bear fruit. It should be noted nevertheless that much of the government's concern focussed on the lack of private sector success in general in winning contracts. This concern ignored the potential benefits that could accrue through competitive pressure on costs even where contracts have been awarded in-house. Unlike the situation with blue-collar services, the professional services regime was not in place long enough for its financial effects to be fully assessed.

Chapter three

CCT for Construction and Maintenance work under the Local Government, Planning and Land Act 1980

Contents

3.1 Activities covered by the Act
3.2 The CCT Requirements
3.3 Requirements for Accounts, Financial Returns and Disclosure of Information
3.4 The Enforcement Provisions

This Chapter completes the focus on the development and key features of compulsory competitive tendering by examining its application to local authority construction and maintenance work. This was the first area to which the principle of CCT was introduced, dating back to Part III of the Local Government, Planning and Land Act 1980. At that time CCT was not a "flagship" policy but just a part of a mammoth piece of local government legislation. The purpose of Part III was to promote greater efficiency and to regulate the activities of local authority direct labour organisations (DLOs). This was to be achieved by putting DLOs on a commercial footing: requiring them to compete for the right to perform construction and maintenance work, to maintain trading accounts for the work they carried out and to achieve specified rates of return on capital employed. Most of its provisions came into force on 1 April 1981.[1] They were to form the sole plank of CCT law for the next seven years. The legislation was then significantly amended through the LGA 1988[2] and again by the LGA 1992.[3] These amendments brought its CCT provisions substantially, although not totally, into line with those of the later Acts.

3.1 Activities covered by the Act

The LGPLA 1980 applied to construction and maintenance work carried out by a local authority or development body.[4] The Act was self-contained, in that its CCT rules could not be extended to new local authority services, other than by changes to the definition of construction and maintenance work itself. This was defined in section 20(1) as:

"(a) building or engineering work involved in the construction, improvement,

---

1 LGPLA 1980 (Commencement No.5) Order 1981; S.I. 1981 No.341 (except for s.16).
2 Section 32 and Schedule 6 LGA 1988.
3 Section 11 and Schedule 1 LGA 1992.
4 As defined by section 20.

maintenance or repair of buildings and other structures or in the laying out, construction, improvement, maintenance or repair of highways and other land, and (b) the gritting or clearing of snow from highways, and (c) the maintenance of street lighting".

The maintenance of street lighting was added to the terms of the definition by the LGA 1988. Unlike the latter Act, there was no comprehensive description of the activities intended to fall within the definition. Instead reference had to be made to other sections of the Act and to the regulations made under it. In this respect, section 10 was of interest because it required local authorities to keep separate accounts for certain descriptions of construction and maintenance work. These descriptions referred to "general highway works and works in connection with the construction and maintenance of a sewer", "works of new construction", and "works of maintenance". These terms helped to clarify the overall scope of construction and maintenance work, although difficulties did arise distinguishing between the particular descriptions of work for the purposes of the section 10 accounting provisions. Broadly speaking therefore, the Act applied to work involved in construction, the maintenance and repair of highways and buildings, and those activities specifically mentioned in section 20 namely the gritting or clearing of snow from highways, and the maintenance of street lighting.

There was little in the way of departmental guidance on the extent of these provisions, although the DOE advised authorities that the term "construction and maintenance work" included painting and decorating.[5] This was disputed by some local authorities, on the grounds that painting jobs while they were always a form of "maintenance" would not always be "building work" in the sense conveyed by section 20. Only where painting was linked to other construction and maintenance work (eg – painting a new building, or following replastering work or filling in cracks) should it be considered to fall within the Act; by itself, painting work should not count. This argument was pursued by the council in *Wilkinson v Doncaster MBC*[6] but was rejected in the Court of Appeal. The council's auditor had sought rectification of the DLO revenue accounts on the basis that painting work had been wrongly excluded. Sir John Donaldson MR said that painting could not be isolated in this fashion:

"'Building work' in the context of this definition, bearing in mind that it refers to 'construction, improvement, maintenance or repair', in my judgment means work of the type done by builders, and 'painting work' is clearly within that category".

The Department of Transport also indicated in guidance that all maintenance work on trunk roads except for grass cutting, sweeping and cleaning of

---

5   Joint Circular DOE 19/83 and Welsh Office 26/83.
6   unreported judgment delivered in the High Court on 21 December 1983; confirmed by the Court of Appeal (1985) 84 L.G.R. 257.

gullies, and cleaning of road signs should be regarded as falling under the LGPLA 1980 provisions.[7]

An element of discretion was conferred on local authorities by section 20(5). Work ancillary to construction and maintenance work was permitted to be included alongside it where it could not be undertaken efficiently on a separate basis.

Exemptions

A number of activities were exempted from the requirement of competition, either by the provisions of the Act itself or by regulations made under it.

Firstly, section 20 excluded the following types of work from its definition of construction and maintenance work:

(1) work in parks, gardens, playing fields, open spaces or allotments, except in so far as it related to a building or structure.
(2) the routine maintenance of buildings by employees (with duties relating to the relevant buildings) who spent the greater part of their time on non-LGPLA 1980 work.
(3) work undertaken for the purposes of a dock or harbour undertaking.
(4) work carried out under certain approved training schemes.

Secondly, work carried out by small DLOs was exempted under section 21 of the Act – the de minimis provision. This applied where an authority did not in the previous year at any one time employ more than a set number of people in carrying out construction and maintenance work. Employees engaged wholly or mainly in the design, development or control of construction and maintenance work were not counted towards that number. The Act originally set the qualifying threshold number at 30 but gave the Secretary of State a reserve power to specify a lower number if he desired. Following the passage of the LGA 1988, the government consulted with local authorities and their associations on a proposal to reduce the limit on the exemption to 5 employees. The reasoning behind this proposal was to bring work covered by the LGPLA 1980 into line with the de minimis provisions of the LGA 1988. To this end, the DOE calculated that the existing exemption of 30 persons equated to approximately £600,000 worth of work per annum, so it followed that an exemption of five employees would equate to £100,000 and so harmonise the two sets of provisions. After lobbying, the Secretary of State compromised and specified a new limit at 15 employees.[8]

Where an authority employed more than 15 people to carry out work at any time, it lost the benefit of this exemption in the next financial year. If the only reason for employing more than this number was necessity to carry out

---

7 Department of Transport Trunk Road Management and Maintenance Notice 4/83.
8 Local Government (Direct Labour Organisations) (Specified Number of Employed Persons) Order 1989 (S.I. 1989 No. 1589).

urgent and unforeseen work, then the Secretary of State could decide to direct that the Act need not apply (section 21(6)).

A third category of exemptions arose from powers reserved to the Secretary of State under sections 7 and 9 of the Act to specify descriptions of work that were to be subject to competition and to specify the conditions of competition. These powers were exercised in the 1989 DLO Competition Regulations[9] (as amended). Until the 1 April 1995, these made provision for four types of exempted work: (a) emergency work; (b) extension work; (c) gritting/snow clearance on highways; and (d) competition free allowances. After that date only the first two remained.

(a)   Emergency work

This was exempted from a requirement to seek competitive tenders for reasons of urgency and practicality. However the government considered the original exemption to be drawn too widely and so potentially subject to abuse. It used the 1989 Regulations to introduce a more restrictive definition of eligible work from 1 April 1990. This covered:

> "work of any description the necessity for which could not reasonably have been foreseen by the local authority or development body concerned and which is:
> (a) required to avert, alleviate or eradicate in their area, or any part of it, the effects or potential effects of any emergency or disaster which involves or is likely to involve risk of serious damage to or destruction of property or risk of injury or danger to health or life;
> (b) required to be put in hand as a matter of urgency within 48 hours of the emergency or disaster occurring; and
> (c) not work on a scale or of a nature normally undertaken by that authority or development body."

The sub-paragraphs b) and c) were additions to the previous definition and their effect was to remove most routine emergencies from the scope of this exemption. An example of this would be the repair of burst water pipes in local authority housing. In many cases this would previously have been done by the authority's employees as emergency work, but because of c) above (it is work of a scale and nature normally undertaken by that authority) the right to continue to do this work had to be tested in competition.

(b)   Extension contracts or jobs

Circumstances could arise where a local authority might agree to carry out activities going beyond an existing works contract or job. This might occur

---

9   S.I. 1989 No. 1588.

where unforeseen additional works became necessary or there had been a cost overrun. It is a common commercial practice. The government had always allowed such extension contracts to take place, subject to constraints to prevent their being misused as a means of awarding extra work to DLOs without competition. The position was tightened under the 1989 Regulations (Regulations 7 and 9):

- the exemption was restricted solely to construction work; it no longer applied to maintenance work;
- the value of the extension contract/job could not exceed that of the original by more than 10% (previously up to 25% had been allowed);
- the original contract/job must have involved work of a similar description carried out on the same or an adjacent site;
- the original contract/job must have been awarded to the DLO within the last 12 months (previously it was 2 years) following a tendering exercise which involved at least three private contractors;
- the DLO must have won the original contract/job as the lowest priced tender;
- there must have been no previous extension.

Since this exemption was framed so as to cover a "further contract" or "further job", it is doubtful that it applied in the case of a contractual option to extend the original contract/job. Therefore by building an option to extend into a contract/job from the beginning, it should have been possible to avoid the restrictive conditions of this exemption.

(c) "Winter maintenance"

There used to be an exemption for work involved in the gritting of highways in icy or snowy weather and clearing snow from highways. It was abolished with effect from 1 April 1995.

(d) Competition free allowances

These existed in relation to the different financial thresholds for types of works contracts and functional work set by the Regulations (see below). A specified percentage of the value of work carried out in the previous financial year as "small" contracts/jobs (those whose value fell below the relevant financial threshold) would be allocated to the local authority to award as it saw fit, either with or without competition. The number and size of competition free allowances (CFAs) steadily reduced over the course of time. The last, relating to general highway works, was abolished with effect from 1 April 1995.

3.2   The CCT Requirements

The LGPLA 1980 was similar to the LGA 1988 in that it divided construction and maintenance work carried out by local authorities into works contracts and functional work, and required local authorities to go through different prescribed tendering procedures in each case. The CCT requirements were contained partly in the Act itself, and partly in regulations issued by the Secretary of State. The inter-action between these two sources made the competition provisions of the 1980 Act unnecessarily cumbersome and complex, particularly when compared to those of the 1988 Act.

3.2.1   The introduction of CCT

The government did not attempt to introduce competition along the lines later used for defined activities under the LGA 1988; that is different activities at different times in different areas.[10] This was perhaps a sign of confidence on the part of the government that there was already a well developed private sector in this field that would be able to respond effectively to the opening up of this public sector market.

Instead, a number of DLO Competition Regulations were issued to control the amount of construction and maintenance work that was subject to competition at any particular time. Control was exercised through the definition (and progressive tightening) of exempted work, combined with the use of financial threshold values. This was the path taken by Secretaries of State in a number of regulations issued between 1981 and the passing of the LGA 1988.[11] Those currently in force are the 1989 DLO Competition Regulations[12] as amended in 1994 and 1995.[13]

These regulations were not subject to detailed scrutiny in Parliament. The statutory instruments that carried them were issued under the negative resolution procedure; that is, they did not have to be approved by a vote before taking effect but were subject to annulment in pursuance of a resolution of either House.

3.2.2   The statutory requirements for works contracts

The 1980 Act defined works contracts in section 5. Wherever a local authority carried out work for another legal person, by agreement, and that work was not in the nature of agency work discharging the functions of another public body or a Minister of the Crown, it was undertaken as a works contract. Any work that was not undertaken pursuant to a works contract was classed as functional work (see 3.2.3).

It should be noted in passing that in the case of all works contracts there had to be a separate statutory authority to carry out the work in question. Often cited in this respect is section 1(1)(d) of the Local Government (Goods and Services) Act 1970, which provides for the carrying out of works of

---

10   Regarding which, see Chapter 1 at 1.3.3.
11   S.I.s 1981 No. 340, 1982 Nos. 325 and 1036, 1983 No. 685, 1987 No. 181, and 1988 No. 160.
12   S.I. 1989 No. 1588.
13   S.I.1994 Nos. 338, 567 and 1439, and 1995 No. 677.

maintenance by a local authority of land or buildings for which another public body is responsible.

Before a local authority was permitted to enter into a works contract under which it was to carry out work, certain requirements had to be satisfied. These were rather complicated to unravel, being found partly in section 7 of the Act itself and partly in the regulations issued by the Secretary of State. They related to the need for a specified tendering procedure to be followed, including (after 1988) the avoidance of anti-competitive conduct (called here the "competition condition").

The tendering procedures prescribed under section 7 were based upon certain "prescribed amounts" or financial threshold values for works contracts that were specified by the Secretary of State in regulations. Those set by Regulation 3 of the 1989 DLO Competition Regulations were for the following amounts:

- general highway works, £25,000;
- the construction or maintenance of a sewer, £50,000;
- works of new construction, £50,000;
- works of maintenance, £10,000.

In determining the value of a works contract for the purpose of these prescribed amounts, the value of any other contract made within the preceding six months for work of the same or similar description on the same or an adjacent site had to be brought into account. This requirement was intended to prevent work being artificially split up into smaller contracts in order to stay below the financial thresholds.

According to section 7(1)(a) of the Act, a local authority could only enter into a works contract whose value exceeded the prescribed amount as the result of the "acceptance of a tender". The conditions for this were defined in section 7(3) as follows:

- the contract was made by the acceptance of an offer to carry out the work in question;
- the offer was made in response to an invitation to submit such offers;
- at least three other persons (not being other local authorities or development bodies) were also invited to submit such offers.

On the other hand, under section 7(1)(b), a works contract whose value was equal to or less than the prescribed amount could only be entered into after complying with conditions set down in regulations issued by the Secretary of State. Regulations 5 and 6 of the 1989 Regulations set a single competition condition, applicable to works contracts for general highways work not exceeding £25,000 (a 40% CFA was abolished from 1995), new construction works not exceeding £50,000 and maintenance work not exceeding £10,000. Somewhat perversely, the condition (for entering into applicable works contracts at or below those values) was the same as that set in section 7(3) of the Act itself for contracts entered into above those values: that it must be done as the result of the acceptance of a tender. Essentially, this rendered the prescribed amounts for works contracts redundant, as the same conditions for competition now applied whether the contract value was above, equal to, or below the prescribed amount. Incidentally, no condition was set in relation to sewering work so it must be presumed that there was no requirement to go out to competition where a sewer contract did not exceed £50,000.

The "competition condition" was added to the Act by amendment through the LGA 1988. It was set out in section 7(1A) and (1B) as follows:

> "(1A) A local authority may not enter into a works contract under which they are to carry out work unless the competition provision is fulfilled, that is, the other party to the contract, in entering into it and doing anything else in connection with it before entering into it, did not act in a manner having the effect or intended or likely to have the effect of restricting, distorting or preventing competition.
> (1B) Subsection (1A) above shall not prevent the local authority from entering into the contract unless the local authority have become aware, before entering into the contract, of the failure to fulfill the competition condition".

The drafting of these provisions left the local authority seeking to win the works contract in an exposed position, dependant on the body awarding the contract to comply with the statutory requirements, whilst itself facing the liability of sanctions by the Secretary of State where they were not met. The only DOE guidance on this matter, regarding the tendering procedures (the competition condition not having yet been enacted) dates from 1981, in Circular 10/81:

> "Under Section 7(3) the primary responsibility is laid on the contractor authority, not the client authority, for satisfying itself that at least three other persons were invited to tender and that the requirements have been complied with. If necessary, therefore, an authority invited to tender for a works contract of or above the various amounts prescribed under Section 7(1) of the Act should seek confirmation from its prospective client that three other tenders have been invited. It is suggested, however, that this cumbersome procedure could be avoided if client authorities, in inviting DLOs to tender for a works contract of or above the prescribed amounts, state in their letters of invitation that at least three other tenders have been sought."

This guidance was never updated.[14] The drafting of section 7(1B) was more helpful in that it allowed the contractor authority to enter into a works contract unless it was "aware" of a transgression, although this only operated in relation to section 7(1A). There being no stated requirement for an authority to make reasonable inquiries of the person letting the work, a state of ignorance might have been enough to trigger the exclusion, although

---

14   Although DOE Circular 19/88 restated this guidance in relation to works contracts covered by the LGA 1988.

"wilful blindness" would probably have been unreasonable in the Wednesbury sense.[15] This was an inherently difficult area to regulate, and perhaps all that these provisions could reasonably have hoped to catch was wilful collusion by a bidding authority in anti-competitive practices.

3.2.3 The statutory requirements for functional work

Turning next to functional work, this was defined by section 8 to cover all construction and maintenance work carried out by a local authority, otherwise than under a works contract, in performance of or connected with:

- its functions;[16] or
- its obligations under any arrangements, agreements or requirements of statute, to discharge the functions of a Minister of the Crown or other public body ("agency agreements").

Before carrying out functional work, section 9(2) required the local authority to prepare a written statement showing the cost of the work (or at least the method by which this would be calculated). It was required to credit this amount to a DLO revenue account prepared in accordance with section 10 (see later).

Section 9 then followed a two-track approach similar to that employed by section 7 for works contracts. In particular, section 9(3)(a) empowered the Secretary of State to specify in regulations descriptions of functional work, which a local authority was not permitted to carry out without first complying with conditions set out in section 9(4) of the Act. The following descriptions of functional work were specified for this purpose by Regulation 8 of the 1989 Regulations:

- general highway works;
- works for the construction and maintenance of a sewer, over £50,000;[17]
- works of new construction;
- works of maintenance.

Under section 9(3)(b), regulations could also specify different descriptions of functional work, which an authority was not permitted to carry out without first complying with conditions set out in the regulations themselves. This provision was last used in relation to general highway works not exceeding £25,000 in value, to provide for a 40% competition free allowance. This was abolished in relation to England, from 1 April 1995. From that date there-

---

15 S. Cirell and J. Bennett in the Encyclopedia of Local Government Law and "CCT: Law and Practice" (1990) (Longman).
16 Definition of an authority's "functions" considered by Lord Templeman in *Hazell v Hammersmith LBC* [1992] 2 AC 1.
17 For this the financial thresholds are based on the estimated cost of a "job" which is defined as "all the functional work which can reasonably be carried out most economically and efficiently under one arrangement".

fore, all functional work had to comply with the section 9(4) conditions, with the sole exception (as was the case in the regulation of works contracts) of sewering work valued at or under £50,000. Since the regulations did not set any conditions in relation to this, it may be presumed that sewering work to this value could be carried out without competition.

In its original form, section 9(4) required two things: that tenders were invited from at least three persons, and that afterwards the authority provided written details on request showing who was to undertake the work, its estimated cost and the price of every tender submitted. Amendments introduced by the LGA 1988 added requirements that:

- at least three persons who were not local authorities or development bodies and who were included on a list maintained by the authority for these purposes, be among those invited to tender;
- the local authority complied with any requirements made in regulations issued by the Secretary of State relating to the inclusion of prescribed matters in invitations to tender (such as the time and method for responding) and prescribed requirements as to responses; and,
- the local authority complied with the "competition condition" (the ban on anti-competitive behaviour).

The "competition condition" was contained in section 9(4)(aaaa), and like section 7(1A), the parallel provision for works contracts, it was introduced to bring the rules governing construction and maintenance work under the LGPLA 1980 into line with those governing defined activities under the LGA 1988. A further step was made in this direction in the LGA 1992, which introduced the requirement that invitations to tender be issued on the basis of a detailed specification of the work that was the subject of the tender.

3.3 Requirements for Accounts, Financial Returns and Disclosure of Information

These provisions were an integral part of the government's aim of improving the efficiency of local authority DLOs. At least initially they were probably seen as being more significant by the government than the competition provisions. Their foundation lay in the accounting provisions of sections 10–14. These were very detailed and closely linked in with the competitive tendering requirements. On the basis of these accounts, section 16 imposed duties to meet financial objectives specified by the Secretary of State. Finally there were requirements to prepare and make available for inspection annual reports on construction and maintenance work under section 18.

3.3.1 The accounting provisions

A local authority which carried out construction and maintenance work under works contracts or by way of functional work, was required to keep a separate

DLO revenue account in respect of each description of work specified in section 10(2). These descriptions were, in broad terms:

- general highway works and works in connection with the construction or maintenance of a sewer;
- other works of new construction over £50,000;
- other works of new construction not exceeding £50,000;
- other works of maintenance.

Local authorities that had small DLOs are exempted from this requirement by section 11. They did not need to account separately for any description of work if they did not at any one time in the previous financial year employ more than 15 persons in carrying out work of that description. Therefore, while they still had to keep accounts for construction and maintenance work as a whole, those accounts do not need to specifically identify such de minimis descriptions of work. The qualifying number of persons was reduced to 15 from 30 in 1989.[18] It did not include anybody involved wholly or partly in the design, development or control of work. In this way, section 11 was framed in similar terms to section 21 (the general de minimis provision), with the difference that the latter provision referred to numbers employed in construction and maintenance work as a whole.

In the case of a works contract, the price was credited to the revenue account. If it was functional work, section 12(1) – (4) required the local authority to credit to the account the amount in the written statement made under section 9(2) before the commencement of the work in question. A wide power to give directions as to the contents of accounts was reserved to the Secretary of State by section 12(5).

Local authorities were required to prepare a set of financial documents relating to a financial year, no later than the following 30 September. By virtue of section 13, these had to include all of the DLO revenue accounts relevant to the authority and a statement showing whether the authority had met any financial objective set under section 16. A requirement to prepare a balance sheet was removed by an amendment introduced through the LGA 1988.

3.3.2 The financial provisions

To reflect the true economic costs of operating a DLO, local authorities were required by section 16 to meet financial objectives specified by the Secretary of State. This requirement was closely linked to the accounting provisions discussed above. The original terms of section 16 required that the revenue from work of each description under section 10(2) showed "such positive rate of return on the capital employed for the purpose of carrying out the work as the Secretary of State may direct". It was not intended that the

---

18   S.I. 1989 No. 1589.

precise rate should represent the current cost of capital at any given moment but rather the opportunity cost of tying up capital over a period of time. The rate that the government decided on was 5% (influenced by the then required rates of return for nationalised industries). It was published in an Annex to DOE Circular 10/81 as the Local Government (Rate of Return on Capital) Directions 1981. This 5% required rate of return was subsequently to be adopted for the financial performance of DSOs under the LGA 1988.[19]

The Secretary of State later gained more flexible powers as a result of changes introduced in the LGA 1992. These widened the references to rate of return on capital employed to "such financial objective as the Secretary of State may specify". Following this the Financial Objectives Specifications 1994 were issued as Annex A to DOE Circular 12/94. The new rules required DLOs to ensure that revenue equalled expenditure in respect of each description of work, taking into account, as a part of expenditure properly charged to a DLO revenue account, a capital financing charge of 6%.

3.3.3 Disclosure of information

A local authority carrying out construction and maintenance work was required under section 18 to prepare an annual report no later than 30 September following the financial year to which it related. The report had to include such information as the Secretary of State might direct. The Secretary of State exercised this power in the Local Government (DLO) Annual Report Directions 1982 which were published as an Annex to DOE Circular 6/82. In the main body of the circular at paragraph 6, it was explained that

> "these annual reports will be important not only in providing, as already required by the Act, an assessment of the financial performance of individual DLOs, but also in making public information not hitherto available about other features of local authorities' DLO operations...".

To this end, local authorities were directed to publish information that included:

- documents prepared under section 13 (copies of the revenue accounts and statement showing whether the authority had met the section 16 financial objective);
- the total value of construction and maintenance work performed under both works contracts and as functional work;
- the value of work exempted from competition;

---

[19] The accounting rules behind the rate of return calculation were revised in 1991 to overcome examples of creative accounting in the treatment of fixed assets. One particular loophole had the result that assets not acquired outright (for example, leased or otherwise obtained on credit) did not need to be counted as capital employed in the calculation.

- the value of work won by the DLO in competition;
- details of functional work awarded to DLO where it had not submitted the lowest priced tender.

In the following year, in Circular 26/83, the Secretary of State expressed broad satisfaction with the response to the directions. Section 18 was subsequently amended through the LGA 1988, which brought about two main changes. Firstly, the inclusion of the section 13 documents was made a statutory requirement, by virtue of section 18(1A). Secondly, the report had to be sent to the Secretary of State and to the local authority's auditor no later than 31 October of the following financial year. The auditor's role was to consider the statement relating to the achievement of the financial objective under section 16 and give the authority and the Secretary of State his written opinion.

In October 1992, the Secretary of State wrote to the Local Authority Associations for the purpose of consulting on changes to the DLO annual reports (and the equivalent reports for DSOs under the LGA 1988). Local authorities were to be requested to supply certain information (some of it new) on pro forma sheets. The Secretary of State had a clear power to direct further disclosure but was expecting and got co-operation from the local authorities. The 1982 Directions remained in force.

3.4 The Enforcement Provisions

Section 17 (now defunct) contained the only sanctions available under the original version of the Act. Where a local authority failed to meet the section 16 financial objectives in respect of any description of work, it had to notify the Secretary of State within six months of the end of the financial year. If this happened in three consecutive years, it was required to prepare a report for transmission to the Secretary of State. The Secretary of State could more generally direct a local authority to prepare, within a specified time, a special report on any aspect of construction and maintenance work. On the expiry of the time specified (and whether or not a report had been received) the Secretary of State could issue a direction under section 17(5) to prevent the local authority from carrying out construction and maintenance work in the future.

The Act gave no indication of the grounds on which a special report would be required. However, an Environment Minister told the House of Lords during the passage of the original Bill, that a persistent failure by a local authority to accept the lowest tender in favour of its own DLO's bid might be one such ground. This was restated in DOE Circular 6/82. In Circular 19/83 the grounds were widened to cover evidence of abuse of proper contractual and tendering procedures such as the use of contract compliance clauses to distort competition. Section 17 orders were only used on two occasions, and the section was replaced through the LGA 1988 by two new provisions, sections 19A and 19B. These new sections closely followed the lines of sections 13 and 14 of the LGA 1988.

Section 19A allowed the Secretary of State to serve on a local authority a notice for the purpose of getting information. The notice could be served where it appeared to the Secretary of State that any of seven grounds listed in section 19A(1) had been met. These grounds arose in relation to decisions by a local authority to undertake construction and maintenance work, or in relation to the actual performance of such work, in breach of:

- section 7 (rules on entry into works contracts);
- section 9(2) – (7) (rules on performance of functional work);
- section 10 (duty to keep DLO revenue accounts etc.);
- section 12(1) and (5) (accounting rules);
- section 13 (duty to prepare financial documents);
- section 16(1) – (3) (duty to meet financial objectives);
- section 18(1) – (2A) (duty to prepare an annual report).

This was a marked change from the old power under section 17. It gave a very specific indication of what the government saw as the important parts of the legislation. Considerable flexibility was preserved because of the prohibitions of anti-competitive conduct contained in section 7(1A) and section 9(4)(aaaa).

Where it appeared to the Secretary of State that any of the above grounds was applicable, a written notice could be served on the local authority stating that fact and requiring a response to it within a stated time. The response could be in the form of a denial that the ground applied or an admission coupled with reasons why the Secretary of State should not go on to serve a direction on the authority under section 19B. A direction under section 19B could order the absolute or conditional cessation of all or any part of construction and maintenance work. This directly accorded with section 14 LGA 1988 and its sanctions are more fully considered in the discussion of that provision.

Finally, nothing in sections 19A or 19B prejudiced any other remedy available to a person in respect of a failure to observe Part III of the Act.[20]

Summary

The LGPLA 1980 established the earliest version of CCT. It was amended by the LGA 1988 to bring its provisions substantially into line with those for defined activities under the later Act. In most respects this involved a considerable strengthening of the original provisions. However despite these amendments there remained points of detail where the two CCT regimes differed. The LGPLA 1980 was also a very complicated and inelegantly drafted piece of legislation. It can only be wondered whether it might have been simpler to allow the LGA 1988 to subsume construction and maintenance work as one or more additional defined activities.

---

20 Section 20(7).

PART TWO

LEGAL AND PRACTICAL ISSUES RAISED BY COMPULSORY
COMPETITIVE TENDERING

Chapter 4
EC Public Procurement Law and its Implications for CCT

Chapter 5
The Limitation of Local Authority Discretion in the Contract Tendering Process

Chapter 6
TUPE and its Implications for CCT

CHAPTER FOUR

EC PUBLIC PROCUREMENT LAW AND ITS IMPLICATIONS FOR CCT

CONTENTS

4.1 Background
4.2 The Overlapping Scope of the EC and CCT Regimes
4.3 The EC rules and their Interaction with CCT
4.4 Summary

One of the principal legal issues arising from CCT was its interaction with the public procurement law of the European Community, which predates CCT and has now, indeed, outlived it. The EC public procurement regime is concerned with the purchasing decisions and procedures of public authorities across the Community. It seeks to ensure that these do not discriminate against contractors from other member states. Although sharing certain features with CCT, the purpose of the EC rules is different: the opening up of existing markets whereas CCT aimed, at least in part, at the creation of new markets. Local authorities affected by compulsory competitive tendering and also those that chose to voluntarily contract out parts of local service provision were directly affected by the EC rules. Voluntary competitive tendering still is. The consequent inter-action of the two legal regimes raises a number of issues, some problems and some opportunities.

4.1 Background

The purpose of EC public procurement law is to break down the barriers hindering contractors based in one member state of the Community from being awarded contracts by public bodies in another member state ("intra – EC trade"). It is a part of the goal of establishing a common market.

There is potentially a very large public procurement market in the EC. In the mid-1980s the Cecchini survey[1] carried out on behalf of the EC Commission, estimated that ECU 530 billion (£358 billion or 15% of the Community's GDP) was spent in 1986 by public bodies across the EC on the procurement of supplies and works. Of this, ECU 240–340 billion was contractual procurement (made after tendering or negotiating a written contract of a limited duration) and was theoretically subject to EC – wide competition under the public procurement rules that then existed. Those rules dated from 1971 and 1977 but despite this, the historical division of

---

1   P. Cecchinni/M. Catinat/A. Jacquemin, The European Challenge 1992: The Benefits of a Single Market [Gower, 1988].

the market on national lines was still very much in evidence. Only ECU 5 billion out of the contractual procurement total above had been awarded to EC contractors from outside the awarding states.

The EC law of public procurement is derived from the Treaty of Rome 1956[2] itself and the directives enacted under it. The directives were framed with the aim of creating a common core of EC rules to exist inside each member state legal system alongside any relevant national rules. EC directives provide a blueprint for national implementation measures to follow within a specified period. The first to be enacted was the Public Works Contracts Directive of 1971. This provided that contracts for specified types of works and of a certain financial value had to be advertised across the EC by way of a notice in the Official Journal of the European Communities (OJEC). Technical specifications used in contract documents were to be described by reference to European standards wherever possible rather than national standards. Common procedures and time limits were to be followed in the course of tendering. The aim was to put contractors from other EC states on an equal basis in bidding for work to domestic contractors of the state of the public authority awarding the work. A second directive dealing in a similar manner with the procurement of supplies followed in 1977.

These directives were ineffective in breaking down national hindrances to intra-EC trade as the results of the Cecchini survey showed (see above). There were a number of explanations for this. In many instances the existing rules had either been ignored or abused. This included the non-advertisement of work and authorities taking undue advantage of exemptions or derogations intended for exceptional use. Another common form of avoidance was the artificial splitting of single work requirements into a number of smaller contracts. This enabled authorities to let a number of small value contracts that would be de minimis under the EC rules rather than a single large contract that would be covered by the rules. There were other factors as well. Many types of contracts such as those made by public utilities had been excluded from the scope of the directives. Little progress had been made on identifying common European standards in the area of technical specifications. This meant that most contractual documents continued to use national technical standards, which disadvantaged other non-national EC contractors. Finally there were no common remedies for breaches of the directives. Each state had its own remedies and procedures, which again disadvantaged non-national EC contractors.

These deficiencies were acted upon in the "1992 programme" for the completion of the internal market, which was the next stage of development in this field.[3] Five new public procurement directives were enacted. Two amended the existing regimes for works and supplies. One brought contracts for services under EC public procurement rules for the first time. Another extended a minimal legal regime to contracts made by public utilities. A final

---

2   As amended: in particular Articles 12, 28, 43 and 49.
3   COM(85)310 final.

directive provided for the harmonisation of remedies in this field across the EC.

The following directives now make up the whole of EC public procurement law. Every procurement contract entered into by a public authority will be covered by one of them (or else will fall within a recognised exemption):

- Public Works Contract Directive 71/305/EEC as amended by Directive 89/440/EEC.
- Public Supplies Contract Directive 77/62/EEC as amended by Directive 88/295/EEC.
- Compliance Directive 89/665/EEC;
- Utilities Public Supplies and Works Contracts Directive 90/531/EEC;
- Public Services Contract Directive 92/50/EEC.

It has been seen that European directives have to be implemented through national measures.[4] For a long time in the UK this was done through administrative guidance. DOE Circulars would remind local authorities of their obligations as contracting authorities in procuring supplies and works. For example, DOE Circular 15/83 that introduced a revised edition of model standing orders for local authorities advised:

> "7. Attention is drawn in the Model to the requirements of the EEC Directives. In this connection it should be noted that these requirements must be complied with in all cases where they are relevant. Contracts which may be required to be advertised in the Official Journal of the European Communities can be exempted from such requirements only in accordance with the provisions contained in the Directives themselves."

This continued up to 1990, when DOE Circular 16/90 was released to explain the amended public works contracts regime. This means of implementing the directives was never challenged but was nevertheless of dubious legality under European law because mere administrative measures do not provide legal certainty.[5] Since 1991 the provisions of the directives have been more formally implemented through a series of regulations made under section 2(2) of the European Communities Act 1972. The current regulations are listed below:

- Public Works Contracts Regulations 1991, as amended 1995.[6]
- Utilities Supply and Works Contract Regulations 1992.[7]

---

4 Article 249 EC Treaty.
5 *Commission v Belgium* Case 102/79 [1980] ECR 1473.
6 S.I 1991 No. 2680.
7 S.I 1992 No. 3279.

- Public Services Contracts Regulations 1993.[8]
- Public Supplies Contracts Regulations 1995.[9]

The Compliance Directive was implemented as a part of the above regulations. The Public Works Contract Regulations 1991 and the Public Services Contract Regulations 1993 ("Works Regulations" and "Services Regulations") are of most relevance to the subject of compulsory and voluntary competitive tendering.

4.2 The Overlapping Scope of the EC and CCT Regimes

The EC regime covers contracts for the procurement of supplies, works and services. It therefore overlapped with many of the activities covered by CCT. Both regimes also rely (or relied) on financial threshold values to exclude small or de minimis contracts from their scope. This Part considers the extent of the overlap between the two regimes in relation to activities and financial thresholds.

4.2.1 The overlap of activities

(i) Procurement of works

The Works Regulations define "works" through a Schedule, which reproduces the EC general industrial classification used in the Directive. Under the general heading of "building and civil engineering" the activities listed include most forms of construction and civil engineering work, demolition work, the installation of building fittings and fixtures, and building completion work such as plastering, painting and glazing. As outlined in Chapter 3, CCT applied to local authorities carrying out construction and maintenance work under Part III of the LGPLA 1980. From this, it can be safely said that the overlap between the two regimes encompassed all "pure" construction activities carried out by local authorities (except those exempted from CCT under the LGPLA 1980 or its regulations). However, the position was less clear-cut in relation to the CCT activities of maintenance work, the gritting and clearing of snow from highways, and the maintenance of street lighting. These activities are not mentioned in the Schedule to the Works Regulations, in what is an otherwise comprehensive list. They are probably outside the scope of the EC regime.

(ii) Procurement of services

The scope of the Services Regulations is defined by reference to a Schedule, reproduced from the original directive, based upon the Common Product

---

8   S.I 1993 No. 3228.
9   S.I 1995 No. 201.

Classification (CPC) of the United Nations. Service activities are divided into two parts for regulatory purposes. Schedule 1A services are subject to the full regulatory regime. In contrast, Schedule 1B services are subject to a minimal regulation pending a future review by the EC Commission.

Therefore the critical overlap in the EC and CCT regimes involved the services listed in Schedule 1A of the Services Regulations. These appeared to overlap with services subject to CCT in the following areas:

(1) Schedule 1A(1) the "Maintenance and repair of vehicles and equipment" which corresponded to the defined activity of repair and maintenance of vehicles.
(2) Schedule 1A(6) "Financial services" and (9) "Accounting, auditing and book-keeping services", which corresponded to the defined activity of financial services.
(3) Schedule 1A(7) "Computer and related services", which corresponded to the defined activity of IT services.
(4) Schedules 1A(11) "Management consultancy etc" and 1B(22) "Personnel placement and supply" which corresponded to the defined activity of personnel services.
(5) Schedule 1A(12) "Architectural services: engineering services..." which corresponded to the defined activity of construction and property services.
(6) Schedule 1A(14) "Building-cleaning services and property management services" which corresponded to the defined activities of building cleaning and construction and property services.
(7) Schedule 1A(16) "Sewerage and refuse disposal service: sanitation and similar services" which corresponded with the defined activity of refuse collection and probably also street cleansing.

The remaining defined activities would have fallen under Schedule 1B either in a specific category like "legal services" or as part of the catch-all "other services" category.

Unfortunately, many overlaps were less than clear-cut. Some CCT services, or parts of CCT services, could be placed in one or more of the CPC categories and therefore potentially into either of Schedule 1A or 1B. In other cases, such as building maintenance, it was even open to question whether the Works Regulations or the Services Regulations applied (see below). This situation came about because the public procurement directives and their implementing regulations were intended to form the whole of EC public procurement law. Every contract let by a public authority had to fall within the scope of one of the regulations or into a recognised exemption. This meant that an authority planning to let, for example, a building maintenance contract under CCT might face a dilemma as to which part of the EC rules was applicable. It might come under the Works Regulations if it could be fairly regarded as incidental or ancillary to other activities listed in the Works Regulations Schedule (perhaps the installation of plumbing, central heating and insulation, plastering, tiling, painting, glazing and paper hanging). If not, then it had to either fall under the Services Regulations Schedule 1A (14) ["Building cleaning services and property management services"], or Schedule 1B (27) ["Other services"]. The resolution of this ambiguity had important legal consequences because the EC regulatory regime was different in each case.

However in most cases the question would be whether a defined activity fell under the Services Regulations Schedule 1A or 1B. And it would be most complicated under white-collar CCT where local authorities could choose which areas of work within each defined activity should count towards satisfying the competition requirement. For example, local authorities were required to subject at least 30% of the value of personnel services work to competition.[10] The competition requirement might be satisfied by tendering "the conducting of organisational and method studies and work studies", which would fall into "management consultancy services" in Schedule 1A. If so, this overlap would result in the full application of the EC rules. On the other hand, if an authority decided to tender "human resource management including ... recruitment" that would overlap with "personnel placement and supply services" in Schedule 1B. In that case only parts of the EC regime would have to be followed (the requirement to use non-discriminatory technical specifications and the duty to file reports).

Another example of the difficulties that might arise concerned the classification of computer services as a Schedule 1A service. IT support can be an important component of many white-collar services. Services Regulation 2 provides that where a contract contains a mix of work, whether it falls under Schedule 1A or 1B depends on the value of consideration attributable to each service category. Therefore it is possible that a contract ostensibly for the delivery of a Schedule 1B service (the financial service of non-domestic rates and council tax collection) could be brought by its reliance on IT support into Schedule 1A.[11]

However while these ambiguities were problematic they could also be seen as affording contracting authorities a degree of flexibility in packaging contracts. This was become particularly significant when considered alongside the issue of financial thresholds (see below). For example, an authority might deem it to be more advantageous for a sizeable maintenance contract to be considered under the Works Regulations rather than the Services Regulations so as to take advantage of the higher financial threshold applicable in that case (see below). Cirell and Bennett have described this as a "tactical consideration".[12] However if a contracting authority is too blatant in attempting to avoid competition it may be challenged under the compliance provisions of the Regulations themselves (see later). Under the CCT regime,

---

10   S.I 1995 No. 2101.
11   Lee Digings and John Bennett "EC Public Procurement Law and Practice" at Chapter C2.
12   Cirell and Bennett, Compulsory Competitive Tendering – Law and Practice, at p. H154.

it would also have been open to challenge by the Secretary of State on the ground of anti-competitive conduct.

4.2.2   Financial thresholds

The EC public procurement rules are triggered once contracts exceed a specified financial threshold. Contracts valued below this threshold are treated as de minimis. In this respect it bears some similarities to the way CCT operated although the thresholds work in slightly different ways.

The EC rules have been implemented in Works Regulation 7 and Services Regulation 7. The thresholds are recalculated every two years. At the time of the case study research presented in this book the figures were £3,950,456 [ECU 5 million) for works, and £158,018 [ECU 200,000] for services, both net of VAT.[13] The EC thresholds are calculated on the basis of a contract's estimated cost over its lifetime.

There are "aggregation rules" to frustrate attempts to avoid the thresholds by artificial subdivision of work. Where a work or a single requirement for services has been subdivided into different lots, each of which is the subject of a contract, the values of these lots are aggregated for the purpose of calculating whether the threshold has been reached. An exception is allowed for small contracts of less than ECU 1,000,000 for works or ECU 80,000 for services, provided that the sum of such contracts does not exceed 20% of the total estimated value of all the contracts. The circumstances in which the aggregation rules applied were considered by Keene J in *R v Portsmouth CC ex parte Bonaco Builders*.[14] He said, obiter, that where the activities embraced by each contract had a particular outcome, and an end result that made functional sense, they should be aggregated.

In circumstances where the contracting authority has been divided into "discrete operational units" the effect of the aggregation rules has been modified by Services Regulation 7(8). A discrete operational unit is defined as one to which decision-making about contracts has been devolved and whose decisions are taken independently of the rest of the authority. An example would be a locally managed school with a delegated budget (but not a DSO, which would probably lack the necessary degree of autonomy). In these circumstances and provided that the contracts are for the sole purposes of the discrete unit, the aggregation rules will only bite in relation to the unit itself.

By 1995 there were no remaining financial threshold values for CCT in relation to construction and maintenance work under the LGPLA 1980.[15] This meant that there was little chance of the two regimes overlapping

---

13   Valued at 1996 prices.
14   The Times 6 June 1996.
15   The de minimis provisions related to the number of workers employed not the financial value of the work in question (ss.11 and 21). For the use of financial thresholds in the competition provisions of the 1980 Act (ss.7 and 9) see Chapter 3.

because few local authorities were likely to carry out works of new construction [or maintenance] to a level over the EC works threshold. Only the largest authorities or those in receipt of EC structural funds [to whom the EC rules automatically applied] could have expected to be covered by both regimes.

That was not the case for defined activity work under the LGA 1988, where the blue-collar activities had a de minimis threshold of £100,000 [ECU 133,576].[16] There were somewhat higher thresholds for housing management and the professional services defined activities. On its face, this was a lower threshold than that under the EC rules. However, the CCT threshold was based upon gross estimated expenditure in the coming financial year (a figure calculated on the basis of expenditure incurred in the preceding financial year), whereas the EC threshold is based on estimated value over the life of the contract. Therefore, a 4-year building cleaning contract valued at £45,000 per annum would be de minimis for CCT purposes (assuming it represented all the defined activity) but would be caught under the EC rules (because 4 × £45,000 = £180,000). In practice this meant that any services contract that was not within the de minimis exemption for CCT, would almost certainly be covered under the EC rules.

The EC aggregation rules could affect the way that contracts were packaged for CCT purposes, in that they might compel authorities to package work into larger contracts than the DOE considered necessary to attract private sector bids. This was greater potential for this in the case of public works contracts because of the higher threshold that applied to them.

4.3 The EC Rules and their Interaction with CCT

CCT required a local authority to carry out a tendering exercise wherever it wished to retain the option of performing relevant work in-house. This automatically triggered the operation of the EC rules, forcing the authority to operate the two legal regimes in tandem. The following sections will outline the requirements of the EC rules and the effect they had on the operation of CCT. For this purpose, the EC rules are represented by the Services Regulations, unless otherwise indicated. The Works Regulations are similar in all essential respects.

4.3.1   General principles

Two ground rules governed the inter-action of the two regimes. Firstly, the EC rules are complementary to national public procurement rules. They do not replace them. This point was made by the ECJ in relation to the Works Directive in *C.E.I v Association Inter-communale des Ardennes*:[17]

---

16   S.I 1988 No. 1372.
17   Case 27-29/86 [1987-7] ECR 3347; [1989] 2 CMLR 224.

"[15] The directive therefore does not lay down a uniform and exhaustive body of Community rules. Within the framework of the common rules which it contains, the member states remain free to maintain or adopt substantive and procedural rules in regard to public works contracts on the condition that they comply with all the relevant provisions of Community law and in particular, the prohibitions flowing from the principles laid down in the Treaty in regard to the right of establishment and the freedom to provide services."

Secondly, the EC rules must prevail over any inconsistent national rule, under the doctrine of the supremacy of EC law. The application of this calls for careful consideration, because both the EC and the CCT rules contain a mix of obligatory and discretionary elements. The obligatory elements of each must be followed until they conflict, when the EC rules will prevail. Where they do not conflict, the discretionary elements of each can be followed within the limits of the discretion conferred. However, the exercise of discretion under one regime must be guided where relevant by any obligatory provision of the other.

4.3.2   Choice of procedures

Regulation 10 requires, for the purpose of seeking offers for a public services contract, that a contracting authority shall use the open procedure, the restricted procedure or the negotiated procedure. The open procedure is one where all interested persons may tender for a contract. The restricted procedure is one where the authority selects those contractors that it invites to tender. The negotiated procedure is one in which the authority selects contractors with whom it wishes to negotiate contractual terms. The steps involved in each procedure are governed by Regulations 11, 12 and 13 respectively.

The choice of procedure is a matter for the contracting authority and any relevant national rules, subject to the provisions of Regulation 10. Those provisions limit the circumstances in which the negotiated procedure may be used. The negotiated procedure was in any case incompatible with CCT and so was not an option for local authorities in the UK at the time of this study.

It is foreseeable that the limitations on the use of the negotiated procedure by Regulation 10 will assume greater importance following the abolition of CCT, although it is too early as yet to be sure. This is because the circumstances in which it is permitted, of which there are eight, are all exceptional in nature. Routine public service contracts will never be eligible for the negotiated procedure. CCT is being replaced from 2 January 2000 by the duty of best value regime, which is likely to bring about an increasing number and variety of partnerships between local authorities and the private and/or voluntary sectors.[18] These partnerships will be mostly contractual, and it will not be possible simply to negotiate them into existence because Regulation 10

---

18   Part I Local Government Act 1999; see also the commentary in Appendix 2 of this book.

will prevent this. Therefore any "best value" regime based on partnerships with the private or voluntary sectors is likely to follow either the restricted or the open procedures of the EC public procurement regime. In other words, competition is likely to remain the foundation of local service provision in the UK.

To return again to the question of the compatibility of the EC public procurement procedures with CCT, the negotiated procedure clearly was not compatible. The open procedure might have been, but only if an authority decided in advance that it would invite tenders from every person expressing an interest after the contract has been advertised. That ran the risk of the whole procedure becoming oversubscribed and unwieldy. Therefore an authority would probably prefer to select from those expressing an interest, the contractors that it considered most suitable to invite to tender. This is closest in form to the restricted procedure. The restricted procedure consists of the following stages.

(1) The contracting authority must advertise its intention to place the contract by dispatching a contract notice to the OJEC.
(2) The authority must allow at least 37 days from the dispatch of the notice to receive any expressions of interest in bidding for a contract.
(3) The authority must select from persons expressing an interest, those that it wishes to invite to tender. Interested persons may be excluded on prescribed grounds of ineligibility or because they fail to satisfy minimum standards of economic and financial standing or ability and technical capacity that are required by the authority. The manner in which these matters can be evaluated is governed by Regulations 14–17.
(4) The authority must dispatch invitations to tender to those persons selected and allow at least 40 days for the submission of tenders. This will be followed by the evaluation of the submitted tenders and the decision to award the contract. There are certain post-award requirements, which are considered later.

The time limits are measured from the day after the dispatch of the contract notice or the invitations to tender. There is scope to shorten these time limits where they have been rendered impracticable for reasons of urgency, or where a prior indicative notice (see below) has been published. Further time limits govern the response to requests for additional information about the contract documents.

This two-stage format is closest to that required under CCT with some differences relating to the time limits for different stages of the procedure. In fact there had been no time limits under the LGPLA 1980 for construction and maintenance work, and originally only one under the LGA 1988 in relation to defined activities. That was the requirement contained in section 7(4)(a) for invitations to tender to be issued between 3 and 6 months after advertisement of the work. In neither of these instances was there any inconsistency with the EC rules, so local authorities could easily comply with both regimes.

Through the 1993 Competition Regulations, the CCT time limits were brought fully into line with the EC rules.[19] The 37 day and the 40 day limits above were imposed in CCT situations that were outside the Works or the Services Regulations (perhaps because of contracts falling below the financial thresholds). The phrasing of the 1993 Regulations would appear to have left authorities free to use the shortened time limits permitted by the EC rules, in the appropriate situations when the Works Regulations and the Services Regulations did apply. However such behaviour would have run the risk of challenge by the Secretary of State as being anti-competitive. The same fate would probably have faced an authority that was tardy in responding to requests from contractors for additional information, despite the absence of a specific CCT time limit for this.

The other time limits introduced by the 1993 Competition Regulations related solely to defined activity work under the 1988 Act. They were additional to the EC requirements and had to be complied with in full. These were the requirements to announce the award of the contract within 90 days of the closing date for the receipt of tenders (Regulation 5b), and for the commencement of work within 30 to 120 days of the announcement of the award (Regulation 3).

In circumstances where an open or restricted procedure had been discontinued because of irregular tenders or otherwise unsuitable responses, Regulation 10 does permit the use of the negotiated procedure. The selection of persons to negotiate must be from all those who tendered in the discontinued procedure. Local authorities prepared to do this had to be aware that such post-tender negotiations ran the risk of being deemed anti competitive behaviour by the Secretary of State. Guidance on this point was contained in DOE Circular 5/96. In particular, where the DSO was given the opportunity to revise its tender, or to tender to a revised specification of the contract, the same opportunity had to be extended to every other tenderer or candidate who met the original specification.[20]

4.3.3   Advertising requirements

The EC rules introduce two new advertising requirements to a competitive tendering process: the prior information notice and the contract notice. Both must be sent for publication in the Official Journal of the European Communities (OJEC).

(i)   Prior information notice

A contracting authority must sometimes give advance warning of its intention to contract through a prior information notice published in the OJEC (Regulation 9). In the case of Schedule 1A public service contracts, this must be done at the beginning of each financial year. The notice must

---

19   S.I. 1993 No. 848.
20   DOE Circular 5/96 Annex B paragraph 17.

follow the format set out in Schedule 2A of the Services Regulations. In particular it should state the value of services required under each category in Schedule 1A (but only if it is in excess of ECU 750,000) and the envisaged commencement date of the tendering procedure. There is no requirement for a prior information notice in relation to services listed in Schedule 1B.

The prior information notice is also a requirement in the case of public works contracts. In this case, the notice must be sent to the OJEC as soon as possible after the contracting authority has decided to approve the planning of the works in question (Works Regulation 9).

There was no equivalent to the prior information notice in CCT.

(ii)   Contract notice

A contract notice must be sent to the OJEC at the beginning of the tendering procedure, and must follow a format prescribed in Schedule 2 of the Regulations. There is a different form of notice for each type of procedure (open, restricted or negotiated) but most elements are common to all. In particular, a contract notice will cover matters such as:

- the information and formalities necessary for the authority to appraise the minimum standards of economic or financial standing and ability or technical capacity required of the contractor;
- the award criteria chosen by the authority.

Under the restricted procedure an authority may choose to leave these matters to the invitation to tender stage (Regulation 12(10)). Also under the restricted procedure, the authority may use the contract notice to predetermine the range within which the number of persons it invites to tender will be fixed, provided that this is between 5 and 20.

The equivalent provision under CCT was the requirement to advertise work in a local newspaper and a relevant trade journal under section 7(1) LGA 1988. There was no such requirement in the LGPLA 1980 relating to construction and maintenance work. To comply with EC law the advertisement could not contain any information additional to that contained in the contract notice, nor could it be published before the contract notice had been sent to the OJEC (Regulation 29). To do either would have given an unfair advantage to contractors based in the UK, and so breached EC law. Additional information required for CCT purposes (the references to the availability for inspection and copying of a detailed specification of the work) could be included in the contract notice under the heading of "Other information". The CCT advertisement could then either duplicate the contract notice in full or with the details purely concerned with EC law deleted.

Contracting authorities are permitted to include in their contract documentation information concerning where a contractor may obtain information about employment protection and working conditions obligations that will apply to the services to be provided. If so, then under Regulation 26 the authority should ask contractors to indicate that they have taken these matters into account in preparing tenders.

4.3.4 Service specifications

CCT required local authorities to prepare a detailed specification of the services to be provided under a contract, which was to be available for inspection and copying. The EC rules have no similar requirement, beyond the publication of certain sparse details in the contract notice. However, they do contain a number of rules about the use of technical specifications in contract documents, including for this purpose the service specification.

Technical specifications are all the technical requirements defining the characteristics of the supplies, works or services in question so that they are fit for their intended purpose under the contract. Regulation 8 requires that all such technical specifications are specified in the contract documents and are defined wherever relevant to "common European specifications". These are agreed EC-wide standards. Their use is intended to eliminate the disadvantage faced by persons from other EC states when tendering for contracts in the UK.

4.3.5 Selection of contractors

The Regulations allow contracting authorities to exclude contractors from the tendering process on one or more of the grounds of ineligibility set down in Regulation 14. They may also determine their own minimum standards in relation to contractor's economic and financial standing and ability and technical capacity. To be satisfied that contractors can meet these minimum standards, authorities may request information and references in accordance with Regulations 15, 16 and 17.

Grounds of ineligibility

Regulation 14 lists a number of grounds on which an authority may treat a contractor as ineligible to tender. An authority will therefore be entitled to require information relevant to any of those grounds. These include insolvency, professional misconduct, failure to meet obligations to pay taxes or social security contributions and serious misrepresentation in supplying information required by the authority in accordance with the Regulations. Contractors may also be treated as ineligible if they are not licensed by the relevant state authorities or are not registered on the appropriate professional or trade register for their country of origin.

The Regulation allows contractors to produce, as conclusive evidence that a ground does not apply, an extract from a judicial record, a certificate issued by the competent authority or a suitable declaration on oath. This is a permissive requirement, intended to allow for the fact that the different member states issue different types of document for these purposes. The extract from a judicial record is a form of proof that a contractor is not bankrupt or has not been convicted of a criminal offence that is used in a number of member states including Italy. In other states, relevant authorities issue certificates to confirm that a contractor has fulfilled its tax or social security obligations. In the UK there is neither and so a statutory declaration would have to serve instead.

The problem for UK local authorities operating under CCT was how far they would be allowed to make full use of Regulation 14. If full use were to be made of it, the detail requested of contractors (presumably in a pre-tender questionnaire) would have been considerable, running the risk of challenge from the Secretary of State as anti-competitive conduct. In this respect, DOE Circular 10/93 warned authorities to avoid "unnecessarily detailed pre-tender questionnaires". This was afterwards replaced by a more ambiguously worded stipulation in Circular 5/96: that questionnaires should seek only "information which is essential to the proper carrying out of the service". There may have been some mileage in an argument that because something is permitted by Regulation 14 it is "essential"; but probably not very much.

Minimum standards

The EC regime leaves contracting authorities with a wide discretion to determine the minimum standards of economic/financial standing and technical ability/capacity that they will require of contractors. This was recognised by the ECJ in *Gebroeders Beentjes BV v The Netherlands*[21] where it said in relation to the relevant provisions of the original Public Works Contracts Directive (Articles 25–28):

> "[17] ...The purpose of these Articles is not to delimit the power of the member states to fix the level of financial and economic standing and technical knowledge required in order to take part in procedures for the award of public works contracts but to determine the references or evidence which may be furnished in order to establish the contractor's financial and economic standing and technical knowledge or ability...."

The EC rules are explicit about the evidence that authorities can request and consider in assessing contractors against minimum standards. A side effect of this was to give local authorities a greater degree of flexibility in the context of CCT. It is something to which they can point to show they are acting reasonably and not anti-competitively. The Local Government Management Board has used the EC rules as its framework in the 1994/95 guidance papers on the assessment of quality.[22]

Evidence of economic and financial standing

Regulation 15 permits authorities to request of contractors and to consider:

---

21 Case 31/87 [1988] ECR 4635; [1990] 2 CMLR 287.
22 See Chapter 5 at 5.4.2.

- appropriate bankers' statements or evidence of professional risk indemnity insurance.
- statement of accounts
- statement of overall turnover and turnover in respect of the services that are the subject of the contract in the previous 3 financial years.

Other appropriate information may also be requested. This was confirmed by the ECJ in *C.E.I v Association Intercommunale des Ardenne*.[23] The case concerned Article 25 of the original Works Directive, which was the equivalent provision to Regulation 15 above. The applicant was excluded from consideration despite having submitted a lower tender because the total value of its work in hand exceeded the maximum limit allowed under Belgian rules. The question arose whether a reference establishing the value of an interested person's work in hand was valid. The ECJ held that it was, because the enumeration of references under Article 25 was not exhaustive and the Directive did not prohibit a non-discriminatory national rule that limited the amount of current work in hand.

Evidence of ability and technical capacity

Regulation 16 permits an authority to have regard to a contractor's ability in terms of its skills, efficiency, experience and reliability. With regard to its technical capacity a number of other matters can be inquired about and considered. These include:

- educational and professional qualifications of managerial staff and those actually responsible for providing services under the contract.
- record over the previous 3 years of providing services of the type in question.
- the technicians or technical bodies responsible for service provision (especially quality control) and whether they are of independent status.
- average annual manpower and number of managers over previous 3 years.
- tools, plant and equipment available to contractor.
- quality assurance measures and research facilities.
- where relevant, the result of any check on the contractor's capacity carried out by a competent official body in the state in which the contractor is established.
- whether contractor holds quality assurance certification based on the EN 29000 European standards series or equivalent.
- proportion of work contractor intends to subcontract.

Supplementary information

A contracting authority may request further information, within the limits of

---

23 Case 27-29/86 [1987-7] ECR 3347; [1989] 2 CMLR 224.

Regulations 15 and 16, to supplement or clarify any matters relating to minimum standards.

Alternative proof of economic standing, ability etc

Many member states (not the UK) operate official lists of recognised service providers. The lists are held by government departments, have a statutory basis and registration is obligatory for contractors wanting to carry out public contracts of any significant value in certain fields. On being registered, contractors are issued with a certificate that classifies them according to the type of work they are competent to do and the value of contracts that they are financially capable of performing. Regulation 18 stipulates that where a contractor can produce a certificate of registration issued by the relevant official body in the state in which the contractor is established, this may serve as an alternative means of proof regarding many of the matters covered by Regulations 15 and 16. The certificate must specify the information submitted to the official body on which basis the contractor was registered and the classification given.

Use of approved lists of contractors

Many local authorities hold pre-existing lists of contractors approved by them on economic and technical grounds. DOE Circular 16/90, which gave guidance on the implementation of the Works Directive, said that "there is no reason why they should not be used as an aid to the selection of participants, provided that the selection is not discriminatory or based solely on those listed." One problem is that the criteria used to draw up the lists are unlikely to be those required for the prospective contract under consideration. Therefore, the use of lists is potentially discriminatory unless firms on the list reapply for each new contract.

Number of participants

Regulation 12 permits contracting authorities to predetermine through the contract notice a range of anything from 5 to 20 persons to whom it will extend invitations to tender. In any event the number invited to tender should be sufficient to ensure genuine competition. The Council and the Commission have agreed that this number must be at least three.[24] This tied in with the equivalent CCT provisions.

4.3.6   Use of non-discriminatory contract conditions

The ECJ has indicated that it will allow other non-discriminatory requirements to be made of contractors. This was the effect of its ruling in

---

24   Confirmed in DOE Circular 16/90.

Gebroeders Beentjes BV v The Netherlands.[25] A Dutch land consolidation committee rejected the lowest bid from the complainant on the grounds that it was less well qualified than other tenderers by reason of its inability to employ long term unemployed workers. The particular requirement contained in the invitation to tender was that tenderers be in a position to employ long term unemployed people registered at a local labour exchange. The Court noted that such a condition bore no relation to any checks on a contractor's suitability in terms of financial standing or technical ability. It also did not relate to the possible award criteria. However the Court accepted that it could be compatible with the Directive, should it comply with all the relevant provisions of Community law, in particular the freedom to provide services, freedom of establishment and prohibition of discrimination on grounds of nationality.

The Court said that discrimination would be apparent if only domestic tenderers could satisfy the condition, or that tenderers from other member states would have difficulty complying with it. It was a question of fact for determination by the national court whether the condition was in all the circumstances directly or indirectly discriminatory. The matter was accordingly remitted back to the Dutch court.

The Commission has said of this judgement:[26]

"Although the Beentjes case concerned long-term unemployment, there is no reason to suppose that objectives other than the reduction of long-term unemployment would fall outside the area of liberty left to the member states by the Directive 71/305. Other categories of unemployment, for example, of the young, would appear to be an equally legitimate concern. The same probably applies to a broad range of social matters including, for example, professional training, health and safety, labour relations and the suppression of racial, religious discrimination or discrimination on the grounds of sex. In these areas too, the procurement Directives neither forbid nor expressly authorise Member States to regulate the matter. Accordingly, they and procuring entities are free under Community law to pursue such objectives, provided they respect the Directives' provisions and the constraints of the Treaty. It also follows that Member States are free under Community law to restrict the capacity of procuring entities to pursue objectives of this kind."

The Commission went on to consider the character of non-discriminatory contract conditions. It clarified that they were conditions in the sense that any firm awarded the contract would be obliged to accept them. They stood independently of the selection and award criteria. So, for example, an authority could not list willingness to employ long-term unemployed people as a criterion for identifying the most economically advantageous tender. This

---

25 Case 31/87 [1988] ECR 4635; [1990] 2 CMLR 287.
26 Public Procurement: Regional and Social Aspects, COM(89) 400 final (Commission communication of 22 September 1989) (89/C 311/07) at paragraph 46.

was because the employment of such persons would not offer any economic advantage to the contracting authority (whatever social good it might do for the long term unemployed and the local area) and therefore it could not count as a factor in evaluating a tender for most economic advantage.

On the question of whether a condition infringed the principle of non-discrimination on grounds of nationality, this was something that would depend on the precise condition and its effects on non-national EC contractors and would need to be assessed on a case-by-case basis. A condition that the winning contractor employ a particular number or percentage of unemployed persons (whether young, long-term, or in general) would probably not be discriminatory because all contractors would face the same opportunities or problems in meeting this. However a requirement to employ a percentage of local labour probably would. In that situation, local firms would have the advantage of already employing locals and of familiarity with the local labour market. The condition that was in question in the *Beentjes* case fell between these two examples. The successful contractor was to employ a percentage of long-term unemployed persons (non-discriminatory) registered at a local employment office (potentially discriminatory). Whether this was actually discriminatory was unclear to the ECJ, which remitted the issue back to the Dutch court for determination. Had there been a commitment by the contracting authority to make available to any contractor a pool of appropriate labour (perhaps through an employment agency) then the condition would probably be non-discriminatory and so would stand.

To digress for a moment to an example from the UK, in the 1980s several local authorities requested contractors to indicate whether they proposed to use their own labour force or rely on local recruitment. Following complaints from the Commission that the wording was discriminatory, because it could imply that contractors intending to recruit local labour would be more favourably treated, the DOE instructed authorities in Circular 16/90 not to use this requirement. Cirell and Bennett have suggested that a clause requiring contractors to make their "best endeavours" to recruit a reasonable proportion of their labour locally, would be suitably non-discriminatory.

The Commission gave other examples of what it considered to be potentially non-discriminatory conditions:

- requirements to employ a percentage of trainees (but not if limited to trainees on registered national schemes)
- requirements to employ a percentage of women or people in some other category not based on nationality
- requirement that contractor respects local terms and conditions of employment, at least regarding its contract operations within the territory of the contracting authority (as opposed to employees providing support services based in a different state).

For contracting authorities in the UK, the Commission's expansiveness is of less practical use because of its earlier concession that member states are free under Community law to restrict authorities from pursuing such objectives. This is the sting in the tail because Part II of the LGA 1988 will severely restrict their freedom to entertain non-commercial considerations in the course of procurement procedures. That legislation goes to the heart of tendering procedures because even asking questions or dispatching draft terms of contract referring to non-commercial considerations is prohibited. The non-commercial considerations themselves are listed in section 17(5) of the Act, the most significant of them being "workforce matters". This is defined in section 17(5)(a) as "the terms and conditions of employment by contractors of their workers or the composition of, the arrangements for the promotion, transfer or training of or the other opportunities afforded to, their workforces".

The full extent of the restriction imposed by Part II LGA 1988 is considered in greater detail in Chapter 5. However the ban on workforce matters would appear to rule out most of the conditions discussed above by the Commission (quotas for women, trainees or local labour, imposition of terms and conditions of employment typical to the local area and type of work, and so on). What is left might include some health and safety matters, and probably would include environmental matters.

There is also the express exception for race relations issues contained in section 18 of the Act. Under this provision, local authorities are permitted to ask certain approved questions of contractors. These questions have been set out in DOE Circular 12/88 but their use is potentially discriminatory in EC law. This is because the wording of the questions is specific to the UK (referring to UK legislation, institutions and codes of practice) so making them easier for a British contractor to answer than a continental counterpart. The Secretary of State has declined to revise the approved questions, advising local authorities instead to apply them while bearing their EC obligations in mind.[27] The Commission for Racial Equality (CRE) has written to local authorities, and advised them to ask contractors from outside the UK to "frame their response in the context of the anti (race) discrimination law and codification of good practice (if any) in force in the member state from which the application is being made".[28] This could be done in one of two ways. The first would be to ask non-UK contractors to disregard the first six questions and instead answer a seventh, framed in the terms of the CRE letter above. However, such a broadly worded question could lead to generalised and unhelpful responses. The second approach is to amend the preamble to the approved questions, asking for answers to the six questions in terms of the equivalent legislation in the contractor's state of origin. This adapts the questions in full to the situation of those contractors.[29]

---

27 Letter of Secretary of State to the Association of Metropolitan Authorities on 17 March 1994.
28 Letter from Chairman of Commission for Racial Equality to Local Authority Chief Executives 25 April 1994.
29 Cirell and Bennett "Compulsory Competitive Tendering: Law and Practice" at page H171.

4.3.7 Tender evaluation

According to Regulation 21, a contracting authority shall award a contract on the basis either that it is the most economically advantageous to the authority, or that it offers the lowest price. The contract notice or the invitation to tender should state on which basis the authority intends to proceed. The contracting authority therefore needs to have formed a view on its award criteria at an early stage, something that was not explicitly required under CCT rules (although the need for this was mentioned in guidance on the avoidance of anti-competitive conduct).

"Most economically advantageous"

Local authorities have been advised by HM Treasury to use the "most economically advantageous" option. This offers the greatest flexibility to authorities. Regulation 21 allows the use of criteria including period for completion or delivery, quality, aesthetic and functional characteristics, technical merit, after-sales service, technical assistance and price. The criteria should be stated, where possible in descending order of importance, in the contract notice or the contract documents. Again this demands a degree of forward planning that was not explicitly required under CCT. However since an individual criterion such as "quality" or "technical merit" can encompass a variety of factors, this is not excessively onerous.

In any case, the contracting authority must base its assessment of the most economically advantageous tender on objective criteria. The decision cannot be arbitrary. In the *Gebroeders Beentjes*[30] case, the contracting authority awarded the contract on the basis of the Dutch "Uniform Rules on Invitation to tender". These provided that "the contract shall be awarded to the tenderer whose tender seems the most acceptable to the awarding authority". The ECJ found this phrasing to be dubious, its compatibility with the Directive dependant on how it was interpreted by the Dutch courts. If it were to be interpreted as conferring unrestricted freedom of choice, it would be incompatible with the Directive. However this would not be so if it were to be interpreted as giving the contracting authority discretion to compare different tenders and to award the contract to the most advantageous on the basis of objective criteria (such as the criteria listed in the Directive).

Treatment of variations – post tender negotiations

Under Regulation 21(4), contracting authorities intending to award contracts to the most economically advantageous tender, may consider offers that offer variations on the requirements specified in the contract documents provided that they meet pre-stated minimum criteria. The intention to consider variations and the minimum criteria must first be included in the contract

---

30 Case 31/87 [1988] ECR 4635; [1990] 2 CMLR 287.

documents. Such consideration, in other words post-tender negotiations, must be undertaken with care. A joint statement published by the Council of Ministers and the Commission[31] provides some guidance on this subject. Negotiations concerning the fundamental aspects of a tender, in particular its price, are ruled out because they distort competition. However discussions to clarify or supplement matters raised by a particular tender would be permissible, provided they are not discriminatory.

Guidance on the avoidance of anti-competitive conduct contained in DOE Circular 5/96 was more restrictive. It advised that contracts should be retendered where post-tender negotiations had led to changes to the service specification, with all persons originally invited to tender, being offered the chance to tender again.

Treatment of "abnormally low tenders"

Tenders submitted to a contracting authority that appear to be abnormally low in relation to the transaction must be examined according to Regulation 21(7) before a decision is taken to reject them. The authority must request in writing details of the relevant parts of the tender and verify them in the light of any explanations received. Explanations should be justifiable on objective grounds, and listed by way of example are reasons such as economy of method, originality, the choice of technical solutions and exceptionally favourable conditions available to the tenderer. Where the award criterion is the lowest price, the rejection of the lowest priced tender must be notified to the Commission.

The nature of the equivalent provision in the original Works Directive was considered by the ECJ in *SA Transporoute et Travaux v Minister of Public Works*.[32] The contracting authority rejected a tender on the grounds that it was "obviously abnormally low". It argued that the prices in the tender bore no relation to reality and so it was pointless to ask the contractor for an explanation. The ECJ took little time in rejecting this argument:

> "[17] ... The aim of the provision, which is to protect tenderers against arbitrariness on the part of the authority awarding the contract, could not be achieved if it were left to that authority to judge whether or not it was appropriate to seek explanation..."

These provisions were considered again in *Fratelli Costanzo SpA v Commune di Milano*.[33] A tender for works to renovate a football stadium for the 1990 Football World Cup, had been rejected as abnormally low on the basis of a mathematical formula, under the provisions of an Italian law implementing the Directive. The contracting authority argued, with the decision in *Transporoute* in mind, that the use of such a formula was an absolute safeguard

---

31 attached to Directive 89/440/EEC.
32 Case 76/81 [1982] ECR 417.
33 Case 103/88 [1989] ECR 1839.

against arbitrariness and was also faster than seeking explanations. However the ECJ refused to accept this:

> "[18] That argument cannot be upheld. A mathematical criterion for exclusion deprives tenderers who have submitted exceptionally low tenders of the opportunity of demonstrating that those tenders are genuine ones. The application of such a criterion is contrary to the aim of Directive 71/305, namely to promote the development of effective competition in the field of public contracts."

The ECJ went on to say that the aim of the Directive would be jeopardised if authorities were to depart to any material extent from its provisions. Such a departure was therefore not permissible.

The approaches of CCT and the EC rules to the rejection of an abnormally low tender coincided where a lower priced bid from an outside contractor was rejected in favour of an in-house bid. In a CCT situation, this had always to be carefully justified to minimise the possibility of the Secretary of State making a finding of anti-competitive conduct. However, the CCT rules were silent in the situation where a lower bid is rejected in favour of another outside bid. Such a rejection could never be anti-competitive in CCT terms. This is not the case with the EC rules, which level the playing field, treating outside contractors on the same basis as in-house teams.

4.3.8 Post-award requirements and other matters

Three requirements are placed upon contracting authorities after the award of a public services contract. These are the publication of a contract award notice in the OJEC, a duty to give reasons to unsuccessful contractors, and a duty to prepare various statistical returns for transmission via HM Treasury to the Commission.

Contract award notice

Regulation 22 requires a contracting authority to send a contract award notice to the OJEC within 48 days of the award of a Schedule 1A or 1B services contract. The format of the notice is governed by Schedule 2E of the Regulations and includes the name of the successful tenderer, the number of offers received, and the range of prices submitted.

The Regulations have made specific provision to cover the CCT situation where an authority decided to award the work in-house (which is necessary because the in house unit is a part of the local authority and the authority cannot contract with itself). Therefore, Regulation 21(9) defines an offer so that it "includes a bid by one part of a contracting authority to carry out work or works for another part of the contracting authority when the former part is invited by the latter part to compete with offers from other persons". However, a question mark remains because Regulation 2 defines "to award" as "to accept an offer made in relation to a proposed contract" and there can after all be no legal contract between different parts of the same local authority.

An alternative view of this situation is that there is no award but rather a withdrawal of the work from competition. If that is the case then Regulation 23(4) requires that the OJEC be informed, and reasons given for the decision to any participant in the tendering who so requests. Another view is that the regulations, being ones to implement EC legislation, should be interpreted purposively in line with the decision in *Litster v Forth Dry Dock and Engineering Co.*[34] Therefore, an appropriately modified contract award notice should be sent to the OJEC.

Duty to give reasons

Regulation 23 requires that the contracting authority give to any eliminated contractor who requests it, the reasons for the rejection of its application to be considered or for the rejection of its tender. This must be done within 15 days of the request. This duty is more limited than its CCT equivalents (section 9(8) LGPLA 1980 and section 12 LGA 1988) which were duties owed to any person.

Statistical returns

Regulation 23 also requires contracting authorities to draw up a written record in relation to each contract awarded, which must be forwarded to the Commission (via HM Treasury) on request. The report should deal with a number of specified matters including the price of the contract, the reasons why contractors were selected or rejected for invitation to tender, and likewise for choosing the successful contractor and not the others. In the event of an in-house win, similar considerations to those discussed in relation to contract award notices would apply (see above).

4.3.9   Enforcement

The Compliance Directive required member states to provide a direct remedy for breach of the public procurement directives and implementing laws. This has been implemented in the UK in the case of services through Regulation 32.

The obligation on a contracting authority to comply with the regulations is made a duty owed to services providers (any person who sought, seeks, or would have wished to become so – Regulation 4). The breach of this duty is not a criminal offence but is actionable by any service provider who, in consequence, suffers or risks suffering loss or damage. Proceedings must be brought in England, Wales and Northern Ireland before the High Court and before the Court of Session in Scotland. An aggrieved services provider must first inform the contracting authority of the apprehended breach before beginning

---

34   [1989] IRLR 161, H.L.

an action. This is equivalent to a letter before action in civil proceedings and allows a little time for matters to be resolved out of court. However, a services provider must be prepared to act swiftly, because the limitation period for bringing an action is the same as in an application for judicial review: that is promptly and in any event within 3 months of the grounds for the action first arising.

Once an action has been brought, the court has a number of options. It can issue interim orders that suspend procurement procedures or decisions reached under them. Then, where a breach is established and providing that no contract has been entered into, the court can set aside the decision, order the amendment of contract documents, and/or award damages. Once a contract has been entered into the court may only award damages. This distinction may provide certainty in contractual relations with the private sector but not where the work has been won in house, because there is no contract. A decision to award work to a DSO is therefore always vulnerable to the full range of remedies including setting aside.

Another source of uncertainty is that the regulations do not make clear the basis on which any damages are to be awarded. Before the conclusion of a contract it would be expected that only tort-based damages would be available. However the decision in *Blackpool and Fylde Aeroclub v Blackpool B.C*[35] opens the possibility of contractual damages being awarded (in that case, contractual damages were awarded where a local authority failed to follow its stated tendering procedures).

The advantage for a contractor in using the EC remedies over those of CCT was that they could be sought directly rather than by persuading the Secretary of State of the correctness of its view, and the prospect of damages. A further advantage was that the provisions against anti competitive behaviour in CCT would protect a litigious contractor from the authority's disfavour in the future.

There are two leading cases under the EC rules to date. One is *General Building and Maintenance plc v Greenwich LBC*.[36] The plaintiff sought an injunction to restrain the council from awarding a housing maintenance contract, until it had been allowed to submit a tender. GBM argued that the council had been wrong to consider matters of health and safety in deciding not to invite it to tender. As would be expected in the light of earlier discussions, the application was dismissed.

The other is *R v Portsmouth CC ex parte Coles and George Austin (Builders) Ltd*.[37] in which the Court of Appeal decided that a challenge to a local authority that had awarded a contract in-house could only be brought under the UK Regulations and not the Directives themselves. That was because the Directives contained a "lacuna" in that their provisions were predicated on the award of a contract, a situation that did not arise in the case of an in-house award. The UK Regulations had addressed this particular problem by

---

35 [1990] 3 All ER 25.
36 The Times 9 March 1993.
37 The Times 15 November 1996.

the manner in which an "offer" was defined through Works Regulation 20(8) and Services Regulation 21(9).

4.4 Summary

The EC rules provide a parallel set of tendering procedures and requirements for local authorities to meet when carrying out compulsory (and voluntary) competitive tendering. This can increase procedural difficulties but also provided authorities with a ready to hand and legitimate framework for adapting CCT to their own policy priorities. In particular, the EC rules provide a basis for building qualitative criteria into the selection of contractors and the evaluation of tenders. The scope that the EC rules provide would be considerably greater were it not for the constraints imposed by Part II of the LGA 1988 (see Chapter 5).

Chapter Five

The Limitation of Local Discretion in the Contract Tendering Process

Contents

5.1 Background
5.2 Restricting Contract Compliance Policies: the Prohibition of Non-Commercial Considerations under Part II of the LGA 1988
5.3 An Overview of Anti-Competitive Conduct
5.4 Examples of Anti-Competitive Conduct in the Tendering Process
5.5 Summary

The exercise of local authority contractual powers is governed by the general principles of contract law, supplemented in some cases by special rules. Most of these are better considered by reference to other general works on local government law.[1] Before the advent of CCT these rules did not impinge to any great extent on the conduct of local authority contract tendering procedures. In particular, the Secretary of State was not a significant player. All this has changed because of CCT and its associated provisions.

5.1 Background

Before the days of CCT (and the EC public procurement regime), local authorities were relatively free to exercise their powers to contract as they saw fit. Basically, a local authority could choose how to conduct its own tendering procedures. That is not to say that local authority discretion was unfettered: procedures and decisions were subject to judicial review, the scrutiny of the district auditor, and perhaps the attention of the Local Government Commissioner or Ombudsman. However there was no detailed prescription, no rule book that had to be followed; and central government, in the form of the Secretary of State was not major player. In particular, there was no detailed legal prescription of procedures to be followed or what factors could or could not be taken into account by local authorities in their decision-making. The legal background under which local authorities exercise their contractual powers, outside of the CCT (and EC) regimes, is considered next.

Local authorities are required to make standing orders covering contracts for the supply of goods and materials or the execution of works under section 135 of the Local Government Act 1972. These must make provision for competition and regulate the manner in which tenders are invited. However they may also exempt contracts valued below a given price or where the authority considers that special circumstances demand it. The content of the

---

1   See Cross on Local Government Law and other works in this area.

standing orders is also left up to individual local authorities. Whilst the DOE has issued Model Standing Orders, following consultations with local authority associations, these are not binding.[2] Therefore there was (and still is) considerable scope under section 135 LGA 1972 for an individual authority to determine its own rules and practices.

Persons contracting with a local authority are not bound to inquire whether standing orders have been followed, and non-compliance with standing orders will not invalidate a contract. The most an aggrieved contractor might achieve against an authority is an order of mandamus compelling an authority to follow its standing orders. This is unlikely to be of much use because standing orders generally make provision for their own suspension, and the courts would probably delay issue of mandamus to allow the authority the opportunity to do so.[3] More recently the courts have held that an invitation to tender may give rise to an implied contractual obligation to consider any particular conforming tender on the same basis as all other conforming tenders.[4]

It was against this background that CCT was first introduced through Part III of the LGPLA 1980. As described in Chapter 3, this required local authorities to go through competitive tendering by seeking tenders from at least 3 private contractors, but did not go beyond that to prescribe the conduct of tendering or the basis on which contracts would be awarded. However, after experiencing the operation of the Act in its early years, the government became concerned that many local authorities were conducting the tendering process in a way that favoured in-house bids over those from outside contractors. Its frustration was expressed in DOE Circular 19/83:

> "23. The Secretaries of State restate their fundamental opposition to the imposition of irrelevant and extraneous requirements and conditions of contract which are anti-competitive in effect and, very probably, in intention too. Such conditions are considered to militate against the principle that an authority should seek the best value for money for its ratepayers through fair, unbiased competition between DLOs and private contractors. Action has already been taken in the 1982 Employment Act to make unlawful conditions which attempt to impose obligations to employ only trade union labour...
> 24. . . . .
> 25. The Secretaries of State also emphasise that it is essential for authorities to observe the accepted principles of good tendering practice and to treat all tenderers equally...

---

[2] Model Standing Orders: Contracts (3rd Edition, 1983): see also DOE Circular 15/83.

[3] See *R v Hereford Corporation ex p Harrower* [1970] 1 WLR 1424.

[4] See *Blackpool and Fylde Aero Club Ltd. v Blackpool BC* [1990] 1 WLR 1195. However, in *Fairclough Buildings Ltd. v Port Talbot BC* (1992) 62 BLR 82, the council was held to have acted reasonably in withdrawing a company originally invited to tender from its tender list, on the ground that the council's chief architect was married to one of the company directors.

26. The Secretaries of State consider wholly unacceptable any arrangements under which DLO "tenders" are revised with knowledge of contractors' prices, or which give the DLO any other advantage in competing for work. Such practices are totally contrary to responsible tendering procedures. Revised tenders should be obtained only where there is a justifiable reason for doing so, such as a change in circumstances which will substantially alter or add to the scope of the work; and, when such action is necessary, equal opportunity for retendering should always be given to contractors and DLO alike.

27. The Secretaries of State also restate their views ... that failure to accept the lowest tender, except in circumstances where there are legitimate grounds for passing it over, undermines the fundamental principle of competitive tendering, and calls in question the fundamental basis in which tenders were sought. As such it is to be deplored, irrespective of whether the DLO is involved."

In its 1985 Consultation Paper, the government proposed new powers to combat this "anti-competitiveness" by local authorities in contract tendering processes. These were enacted through the LGA 1988.

5.2 Restricting Contract Compliance Policies: the Prohibition of Non-Commercial Considerations under Part II of the LGA 1988

Contract compliance is the practice of furthering social or political ends through the contractual process. It is the utilisation of a public authority's buying power in the market as a bargaining device to compel contractors to accept or to work towards its desired social or political goals; goals that might not bear any direct relationship to the subject matter of any particular contract. Widely practiced in the USA, contract compliance has also been a feature of local government in the UK. It has been used for a variety of purposes including the promotion of health and safety standards and the combating of racial and sexual discrimination. The use of contract compliance in these areas was justified on the grounds that public money should not be used to profit businesses that discriminated or that owed their competitiveness to unsafe working conditions. However it was also used, particularly in the 1980s, for more controversial ends such as to protect trade union closed shop arrangements, and blacklist firms involved in trade disputes or linked to nuclear or defence installations or unpopular foreign governments. The government found the use of contract compliance for these ends increasingly intolerable. The 1985 consultation paper proposed to ban the use of non-commercial considerations in the contractual process. This was enacted as Part II of the LGA 1988.

5.2.1 The exclusion of non-commercial considerations

Under section 17(1) LGA 1988 local authorities are required to carry out a number of functions relating to public supply or works contracts without reference to non-commercial considerations. The contracts covered by the section include contracts for the supply of goods, materials and services and for the execution of works – the same sorts of contract that are covered by the EC public procurement rules and, in its day, by CCT.

The regulated functions are listed in section 17(4) and cover the entire contractual tendering process, including matters such as:

- the inclusion or exclusion of a person from an approved list of contractors.
- the selection of persons for invitation to tender.
- the acceptance of a tender.
- the selection, nomination or approval of persons to be subcontractors for the purposes of a contract.
- the termination of a contract.

Furthermore, by virtue of section 19(10) an authority will also be caught where it asks a question relating to a non-commercial matter of any potential contractor, or submits to him a draft contract or draft tender that includes provisions relating to non-commercial matters. This provision meant that references to non-commercial matters in contract documents relating to a CCT tender (or indeed any tender), including a pre-tender questionnaire, had to be removed in order to comply with section 17.

Section 17(5) lists the non-commercial matters or considerations that are to be excluded. They include the following:

(a) the terms and conditions of employment of workers (see below).
(b) whether contractors employ subcontractors on the basis that subcontractor employees are self-employed.
(c) involvement of contractors in irrelevant fields of Government policy such as defence or foreign policy.
(d) involvement of contractors in individual trade disputes (so for example a contractor cannot be required to cross or not to cross official picket lines).
(e) location of a contractor's business activities or origin of contractor's supplies.
(f) Political, industrial or sectarian affiliations of contractors or their directors, partners or employees.
(g) Financial support or lack of it by contractor to any organisation to or from which the authority gives or witholds support
(h) Use or non-use of technical or professional services provided by the authority in relation to building regulation approvals.

The most significant of the non-commercial considerations listed above is that relating to "workforce matters" found in section 17(5)(a):

"the terms and conditions of employment by contractors of their workers or the composition of, the arrangements for the promotion, transfer or training of or the other opportunities afforded to, their workforces;"

This provision covers matters such as rates of pay, and the proportion of trainees, women and members of ethnic minorities in the workforce.[5] The effect of section 17 is to render unlawful most forms of contract compliance. The following sections will examine areas where non-commercial matters may still taken into account during the contractual process.

Race relations

Local authorities have a duty to carry out their functions with regard to the need to eliminate unlawful racial discrimination and to promote equality of opportunity and good relations between people of different racial groups (section 71 Race Relations Act 1976). It was argued during the passage of the Local Government Bill that this might be prejudiced by the exclusion of non-commercial considerations from the contract tendering process. Therefore the government introduced a limited exception to the general exclusion, through an amendment that became section 18 of the LGA 1988.

The exception is strictly limited to two areas:

- asking approved questions and/or making approved requests for evidence relating to workforce matters;
- including terms or provisions relating to workforce matters in draft contracts or tenders; and considering the responses to these.

Questions and requests for evidence must be approved by the Secretary of State. Following consultation with industry, local authority associations and the Commission for Racial Equality, six questions have been approved for this purpose. They were released as Annex B of DOE Circular 8/88:

1. Is it your policy as an employer to comply with your statutory obligations under the Race Relations Act 1976 and, accordingly, your practice not to treat one group of people less favourably than others because of their colour, race nationality or ethnic origin in relation to decisions to recruit, train or promote employees?
2. In the last three years, has any finding of unlawful racial discrimination been made against your organisation by any court or industrial tribunal?
3. In the last three years, has your organisation been the subject of formal investigation by the Commission for Racial Equality on grounds of alleged unlawful discrimination?
    If the answer to question 2 is in the affirmative or, in relation to question 3, the Commission made a finding adverse to your organisation.
4. What steps did you take in consequence of that finding?
5. Is your policy on race relations set out:
    (a) in instructions to those concerned with recruitment, training and promotion;

---

5   DOE Circular 8/88.

(b) in documents available to employees, recognised trade unions or other representative groups of employees;
(c) in recruitment advertisements or other literature?
6. Do you observe as far as possible the Commission for Racial Equality's Code of Practice for Employment, as approved by Parliament in 1983, which gives practical guidance to employers and others on the elimination of racial discrimination and the promotion of equality of opportunity in employment, including the steps that can be taken to encourage members of the ethnic minorities to apply for jobs or take up training opportunities?

Description of evidence
In relation to question 5: examples of the instructions, documents, recruitment advertisements or other literature.

While the scope of these questions is pretty extensive there are important limitations. The asking of approved questions etc must be reasonably necessary to secure compliance with the Race Relations Act 1976. The section 18 exception is also only available pre-contract; contracts may not be terminated by reference to race relations matters. Finally, in asking these questions local authorities must take care to adapt them so that contractors from other EC countries can meaningfully answer them. This issue is considered in Chapter 4.

Sex and disability discrimination

Neither the Sex Discrimination Act 1975 nor the Disabled Persons (Employment) Act 1944 place duties on local authorities analogous to section 71 of the Race Relations Act 1976. Without a statutory role for promoting equal opportunities there is no clear basis on which local authorities can take these matters into consideration during the contractual process.

The issue in relation to sex discrimination was considered by the Divisional Court in *R v Islington LBC ex parte Building Employers' Confederation* ("BEC").[6] After the LGA 1988 came into force, the council revised its standard contract clauses for potential contractors. The revised clauses provided for the council's continuing interest in contract compliance policies, covering areas such as racial discrimination, sexual discrimination and health and safety policies. The BEC challenged the legality of these clauses by way of judicial review. One of the clauses at issue was Clause 3, which ran as follows:

"3(1) The Contractor shall at all times comply with the requirements of:
(a) the Race Relations Act 1976;
(b) s.6(1)(a) and (c) and 2(b) of the Sex Discrimination Act 1975;

---

6   [1989] IRLR 382.

(c) any Act, rule, statement, code of practice, manual or other instrument or document amending or replacing either of the foregoing enactments."

The following sub-clauses required contractors to give the council reasonable access to documents and to supply the council on request with a breakdown of its workforce by race and grade as required, so that the council could satisfy itself as to the contractor's compliance with clause 3(1). The Divisional Court considered that clause 3(1) related to non-commercial considerations, namely workforce matters. Sub-clause 1(a) because it related to race relations matters was covered by the exception to the general exclusion of non-commercial considerations provided by section 18 (so long as it was reasonably necessary to ensure compliance with section 71 Race Relations Act 1976).

In relation to sub-clause 1(b) the council argued that it had been carefully framed so as to exclude reference to non-commercial considerations. For example, section 6(1) of the Sex Discrimination Act 1975, which is reproduced below, states:

"It is unlawful for a person, in relation to employment by him at an establishment in Great Britain, to discriminate against a woman:
(a) in the arrangements he makes for the purpose of determining who should be offered that employment, or
(b) in the terms on which he offers her that employment, or
(c) by refusing or deliberately omitting to offer her that employment."

The council pointed out that clause 3(1) did not require contractors to comply with section 6(1)(b) of the Act, which refers to terms of employment. It argued that the "composition" of the workforce referred to by section 17(5)(a) was limited to matters such as requirements for the employment of a certain proportion of women or people from ethnic minorities. The Court rejected this approach as too narrow. The "composition" of the workforce was a term broad enough to cover any decision or practice that would have a bearing on the future composition of the workforce (such as hiring and firing staff). Therefore, sub-clause 1(b) did relate to non-commercial matters and, there being no saving provision akin to section 18 for sex discrimination matters, was unlawful.

Later on in the course of the judgement, Parker J considered the general question of whether local authorities could lawfully ask questions of contractors and impose on them contractual terms relating to their compliance with the general law. The council had argued that so long as they did not specifically require a particular term or condition to be included in the contract of employment, they could impose on the contractor all the terms and conditions they desired by simply saying "the contractor shall" and then setting out a list of obligations covering matters such as pay and remuneration to be given to the workforce. This was firmly rejected. The purpose of the Act was to prevent local authorities from interfering with the provisions of employment contracts. The use of such a device would clearly defeat that purpose.

However Parker J did not totally exclude the lawfulness of imposing terms requiring compliance with the general law:

> "...it is necessary that I should stress that I do not, by what I have said, intend to hold that a local authority is not to include in its contracts provisions requiring the contractor to comply with the general law. It is only to the extent that there are specific obligations so included which cover such matters as pay, hours of work, what a particular employee is or is not permitted to do and so on that there would be an infringement."

Health and safety

DOE Circular 8/88 offers the following guidance to local authorities about health and safety considerations:

> "8. It has never been the Government's intention to prevent authorities taking account of contractors' health and safety records during the contractual process. Whilst the Government would want questions kept to the minimum necessary, there is no reason why authorities should not make reasonable inquiries about contractors' health and safety records and their arrangements for making their employees aware of their health and safety obligations."

This would appear to cover authorities wanting to ask questions before awarding a contract. It is less clear whether conditions can be imposed on a contractor for the duration of a contract. This question was also considered by the Divisional Court in the *BEC* case. The council's standard contract terms and conditions included in Clause 4 a requirement for a contractor to comply with a long list of provisions relating to the safety, health and welfare of employees and others. These provisions ranged from statutes such as the Factories Act 1961 and the Health and Safety at Work Act 1974, to "such safety policy statements and safety codes of practice as the Council may from time to time adopt or require and notify to the contractor". It was, as Parker J described it, "a formidable list".

The Court rejected BEC's contention that the conditions of employment referred to in section 17(5)(a) covered all the physical conditions in which employees worked. It referred only to the actual contractual terms and conditions as between the contractor and the workers. However for a clause to offend it only had to relate to a non-commercial matter. The Court did not review the entire list of obligations for compatibility with section 17(5)(a) but was of the view that clause 4 would have to be "very considerably amended" if it was to be so compatible. Therefore it would appear that conditions relating to health and safety can be imposed but only if they do not relate to the actual terms and conditions of employment contracts.

The council did win on one particular point, namely a requirement for a contractor to maintain one safety officer on-site for every 300 manual operatives. This was specifically upheld because section 17(5)(a) only applied to workers and a safety officer was not a worker for this purpose. This distinction may be extendible by analogy to other supervisory or managerial staff.

Comparability of pensions

The TUPE Regulations provide that where there is a relevant transfer of an undertaking, the new employer takes over responsibility for the employment contracts of persons employed in the undertaking on their existing terms and conditions. The DOE has taken the view that, in order to protect themselves from claims for unfair dismissal, local authorities should insist that the new employer offer comparable pensions arrangements or compensation to transferred employees. It has indicated that such a stipulation would not contravene section 17, which does not (notwithstanding section 17(5)) prevent authorities from referring to matters that are in substance commercial matters affecting their financial position.[7]

Management systems

Reasonable inquiries about management systems are not likely to infringe section 17. They can be reasonably construed as being "commercial" in character and if the safety officer point above is correct, inquiries about managers will not be considered to be about the composition of the workforce. The same points will probably apply to quality management systems. In particular DOE guidance in Circular 8/88 says that authorities are not prevented from asking questions about the qualifications of a contractor's workforce, or from requiring that certain types of work are performed by persons holding appropriate qualifications.

The DOE has also indicated in Circular 5/96, where it is essential for service delivery, that local authorities may require contractors to follow any relevant professional code of practice (or European equivalent).

Environmental issues

The environment is clearly a non-commercial consideration, but because it has not been specified as such in section 17(5) there is no reason why an authority should not take it fully into account.

5.2.2   Other legal implications

Local authorities are also required to notify the persons affected, of certain decisions taken by the authority under Part II of the 1988 Act. The duty is outlined in section 20 and covers decisions such as excluding a person from

---

[7] "Handling Pensions Matters in Relation to CCT" DOE Letter to Local Authorities on TUPE – 15 March 1995.

an approved list, not inviting a person to tender, rejecting a tender and terminating a contract. If requested in writing within 15 days of such notification, an authority must supply written reasons for its decision to the person concerned.

The duty imposed by section 17 does not give rise to any criminal offence. However a breach of the duty is actionable by any person who suffers loss or damage as a result. It is specifically provided that any potential contractor, former potential contractor or body representing contractors shall have sufficient interest to bring an application for judicial review. Where a tender has actually been submitted, the extent of damages is limited to damages in respect of expenditure reasonably incurred for the purpose of submitting the tender.

5.2.3 Summary

The ban on non-commercial considerations places severe constraints on the exercise of local authority discretion, in particular in the field of social policy. It shared this characteristic with the prohibition of anti-competitive conduct in Part I of the 1988 Act, which is considered next. There are however two important differences:

- the exclusion of non-commercial considerations has been fully debated and approved in Parliament (through the affirmative resolution procedure).
- there is no enforcement role for the Secretary of State.

This makes it, in constitutional terms, a less arbitrary and more accountable form of legislation than the ban on anti-competitive conduct.

5.3 An Overview of Anti-Competitive Conduct

From the standpoint of the Secretary of State, the prohibition of anti-competitive conduct was the workhorse of the CCT regime. It extended his remit into the far-flung reaches of what had been local decision making. It is of particular interest because it was largely developed outside the primary legislation, through departmental circulars and regulations. Despite this lack of Parliamentary scrutiny it had a farther reaching effect on local authority practice than almost any other part of CCT law.

5.3.1 The legal background

The statutory basis of the ban on anti-competitive conduct lay in the various competition conditions found within the LGA 1988. These were also imported into the LGPLA 1980. The issue of anti-competitive conduct was so significant because it was directly linked in both Acts to their respective enforcement provisions (sections 19A–19B LGPLA 1980 and sections 13–14

LGA 1988). The Secretary of State issued guidance to local authorities on the sorts of conduct that might be considered anti-competitive when deciding whether to exercise his enforcement powers. The Secretary of State also took out powers through section 9 of the LGA 1992 to define anti-competitive conduct by regulation. The same provision empowered the Secretary of State to issue mandatory guidance under the regulations about anti-competitive conduct.

The competition conditions

Local authorities could not engage in conduct having the effect or intended or likely to have the effect of restricting, distorting or preventing competition. This applied to work carried out pursuant to a works contract[8] as well as to functional work (see below) within any defined activity under the LGA 1988, and was imported on the same basis into the LGPLA 1980.[9] It was most likely to be relevant to functional work under the LGA 1988, and here the relevant provision could be found in section 7(7) (the fifth condition for the performance of functional work):

> "The fifth condition is that the authority, in reaching the decision that they should carry out the work and in doing anything else [whether or not required by this Part] in connection with the work before reaching the decision, did not act in a manner having the effect or intended or likely to have the effect of restricting, distorting or preventing competition."

Four points can be drawn from the wording of this provision:

(1) It applied where a local authority awarded work to its DSO, but never where work was awarded to an outside contractor (even if the authority had acted with bias, although in that case other remedies might be available). CCT was not a part of general competition law, but rather a specific type of public law, designed to break down the inefficiencies perceived to flow from the monopoly status of local authorities as providers of local public services. It was not concerned with "fair competition" in general, but with fair competition between DSOs and outside contractors.
(2) It only concerned the authority's conduct before it decided to award the work to the DSO. The contract implementation period and matters arising over the operation of the contract were not covered.
(3) It was framed in negative terms. The Secretary of State had the power to take enforcement action under sections 13 and 14 of the Act where he considered that an authority had engaged in anti-competitive conduct. Because the condition was framed in negative terms, the

---

8 Section 4[5] LGA 1988.
9 Sections 7[1A] and 9[4][aaaa].

burden of proof was on the local authority to give reasons that it had not acted anti-competitively. The reluctance of the courts to interfere with the exercise of the Secretary of State's discretion (as demonstrated by the *Knowsley* decision) left the Secretary of State in a very powerful position indeed.[10]

(4) It did not indicate the nature of the conduct that might "restrict, distort or prevent competition". It is on this last point that the remainder of the Chapter will concentrate.

In the normal course of events, government departments issue administrative guidance on the meaning and practical application of all types legislation through circulars and letters. The limitation of "legislating" through these circulars is that they are not legislative instruments. Of course, there is good reason to suppose that a local authority will, in normal circumstances, follow advice given in a circular. Professor Keith Davies has given two explanations for this. Firstly, it is easier for an authority to be told what to do than to work things out for itself. Secondly the government departments are more likely to be expert in the subject matter of a circular than the authority, especially where novel legislation is concerned. Davies sums up quite colourfully by saying:

> "To depart without good cause from what a circular generally prescribes is to be the odd man out. It would be rather like navigating a reef strewn sea and throwing the charts or the radar overboard."[11]

The exact status of the provisions in a circular will sometimes depend on the original legislation in question. Some statutes have given ministers the power to issue directions, and this is frequently done by way of a circular. However the competition provisions of the LGA 1988 did not give any such status to circulars. This left them occupying a legal grey area. The attitude of the courts to such circulars is one of suspicion, the reasoning behind which was famously outlined by Streatfield J in the 1940s case of *Patchett v Leathem*:[12]

> "Whereas ordinary legislation, by passing through both Houses of Parliament or at least lying on the table of both Houses is thus twice blessed, this type of so called legislation is at least four times cursed. First, it has seen neither House of Parliament; secondly it is unpublished and inaccessible even to those whose valuable rights of property may be affected; thirdly it is a jumble of provisions, legislative, administrative or directive in character and sometimes difficult to disentangle one from the other; and fourthly it is expressed not in the precise language of an Act of Parliament or an Order in Council but in

---

10 This is discussed in Chapter 1.
11 Keith Davies – "Local Government Law" 1st edition 1983 at p. 242 [Longmans].
12 (1949) 65 TLR 69.

the more colloquial language of correspondence which is not always susceptible to the ordinary canons of construction."

The DOE circulars that were released on CCT (19/88, 1/91, 10/93 and 5/96), indicated the sorts of behaviour that the Secretary of State might have deemed to be anti-competitive, and put local authorities on notice that enforcement action might follow. The legal significance of this sort of departmental guidance lies in a local authority's duty to properly exercise its discretion according to ordinary public law principles. Therefore if an authority were to pay no regard to a circular it could very well find its decisions challenged on judicial review for irrationality or "Wednesbury unreasonableness", because it had ignored a factor that was relevant to its exercise of discretion. The guidance contained in a circular must therefore be carefully considered, alongside all other relevant considerations, before a decision is reached. Where this has been done, a departure from the terms of a circular should be safe from challenge by way of judicial review.

Nevertheless, if the Secretary of State felt that the authority had conducted itself in an anti-competitive manner, then the enforcement mechanisms of sections 13–14 LGA 1988 could be put into motion regardless. This was of course part of the Secretary of State's discretion under the CCT legislation, also reviewable on public law principles. The *Knowsley* decision showed that once the section 13–14 enforcement mechanisms were rolling it was very difficult to successfully challenge the Secretary of State.

However because the introduction of CCT attracted wide opposition among local authorities (not least because of the threat to their own workforces), some authorities were prepared to follow their own course and declined to follow the guidance given in the circulars. Because of the non-binding nature of the circulars they were perfectly entitled to do this, provided they had considered the guidance before reaching that decision and were prepared to take the chance of being challenged by the Secretary of State.

The difficulty for the DOE, was that whatever draconian powers it possessed, there was only a finite workload it could manage at any one time. The guidance given through departmental circulars could not in law be framed in a manner that fettered the Secretary of State's discretion. This is because the Secretary of State cannot pre-judge a situation that may call for the exercise of a statutory discretion, so closing his mind to the specific circumstances of each individual case.[13] The consequence of this was that every complaint

---

13 *R v Secretary of State ex p Sherif* (1986) The Times 18 December (unlawful fettering of discretion in situation where Secretary of State refused to make a discretionary grant on the basis of the over rigid wording of the Department's explanatory memo). See also *R v Home Secretary ex p Bennett* (1986) The Times 18 August (circular for the approval of rent allowances, contained criteria that were held to be too rigid, and leaving no scope for reasoned arguments on the complainant's behalf, so unlawfully fettering the Home Secretary's discretion).

about an authority's anti-competitive conduct would have to be considered on its merits, something that often involved a lengthy correspondence with the authority concerned.

These limitations led to the government legislating for a power to specify forms of conduct as anti-competitive by regulation. This was done through section 9 of the LGA 1992. This gave the Secretary of State the power to prescribe by regulations, conduct that was to be regarded as anti-competitive, or alternatively conduct that was not to be so regarded. In a sense therefore the power was a two edged sword. It could be used to either promote private sector competition or to assist in-house service providers depending on the political stance of the sitting Secretary of State.

Section 9(3)(e) enabled the Secretary of State to issue guidance as to anti-competitive conduct under the authority of any section 9 regulations. Significantly, at section 9(3)(f) there was also a power to:

> "require the extent (if any) to which there has been a contravention of guidance issued by the Secretary of State under the regulations to be taken into account in any determination of whether or not [there has been anti-competitive behaviour]."

Presumably this meant that the Secretary of State could issue guidance to the effect that X was anti-competitive, and require that the extent of contravention of that guidance be "taken into account" by the Secretary of State in making a determination as to whether there had been anti-competitive conduct. This has been described as guidance with a mandatory nature.[14] However it seems debatable how far the new type of guidance will be different to the previous sort. The Secretary of State must still make a "determination" that the conduct in question is anti-competitive and as an exercise of discretion this would still be subject to judicial review. In a similar way, the Secretary of State will still be subject to the rule that he must not fetter his discretion in advance, but must remain open to persuasion in every case.

Therefore the true significance of section 9(3)(f) would appear to be that it highlighted to local authorities the importance that the Secretary of State would attach to any such guidance issued. This would, in effect, have raised the hurdle over which the authority would have to jump, in order to satisfy the Secretary of State that it had not acted anti-competitively.

5.3.2 The development of "anti-competitiveness" as a control over local authorities

The substantive development of anti-competitive conduct can be traced through the line of DOE Circulars 19/88, 1/91, 10/93, the white-collar circulars of June and December 1994, and finally 5/96. The overall trend was

---

[14] Cirell and Bennett "Compulsory Competitive Tendering: Law and Practice" at 16.28.

one of increasingly detailed guidance covering every aspect of the competitive tendering process.

An overview of this development would have to begin with DOE Circular 19/88, in which the Department adopted a distinctly minimalist stance on the definition of anti-competitive conduct, stating in paragraphs 32–33:

> "(32) ...Anti-competitive behaviour is by its nature difficult to define exhaustively. Section 7 (7) therefore makes it a condition of compliance that authorities should not do anything which actually has the effect, or is intended or likely to have the effect of restricting, distorting or preventing competition. The Act does not define anti-competitive behaviour in more detail and it is therefore for individual authorities to decide, according to the circumstances of particular cases, whether the way they propose to package work, invite tenders, appraise competing bids etc is or is not likely to infringe this provision.
> (33) Authorities acting in good faith should have nothing to fear. The Department is aware, however, of cases where ground maintenance work is being packaged into such large amounts as to cast doubts on the likely ability of contractors – which tend to be smallish firms – to compete for it. Since they might well compete for more manageable blocks of work such behaviour on the part of authorities could well be regarded as anti-competitive by the Secretary of State. Other sorts of behaviour likely to be regarded as anti-competitive will include giving contractors too little time to respond to tender invitations; seeking detailed and sensitive information about companies which go beyond that needed to assess their ability to carry out work properly; requiring contractors to provide excessive performance bonds; taking into account any of the non-commercial considerations which are separately proscribed in Part II of the Act; and rejecting lower tenders from contractors in favour of the DSO's bid without good reason."

The reference to authorities acting in "good faith" proved to have little worth in practice. Many contractors complained, even at an early stage in the implementation of CCT, to the DOE alleging anti-competitive practices by local authorities in their handling of the competition process.[15] Particular matters of concern were the refusal to make available local authority assets, the demanding of "excessive" performance bonds, and the addition of various extraneous cost items onto the price of outside tenders during the tender evaluation process. The DOE took up these complaints, using the enforcement powers available under the CCT legislation. As the litigation in the *Knowsley* case showed, where the Secretary of State considered conduct to be anti-competitive it was very difficult for local authorities to challenge his discretion with any real chance of success.

---

15 According to a Parliamentary written answer, in the period up to 13.4.89 approximately 80 complaints had been received by the DOE, about half of which related to local authorities refusing to make depots available to contractors: Hansard (17.4.89) HC Vol. 151 Col. 36.

Following its early experience of the operation of the Act, the DOE put somewhat sterner guidance out for consultation in a draft circular in 1990. The result was DOE Circular 1/91 of March 1991, which replaced the relevant guidance in Circular 19/88, including the assurance that authorities "acting in good faith" had nothing to fear. It replaced it with 44 paragraphs of detailed guidance largely concerned with the financial evaluation of tenders, the availability and treatment of assets in the tendering process, forms of contract packaging and the use of performance bonds.

It was following this, that the Secretary of State acquired the powers to issue regulations specifying anti-competitive conduct through section 9 LGA 1992. This power was exercised in the 1993 Competition Regulations.[16] They set time limits for various stages of CCT, specified the persons responsible for various operations under CCT, and dictated the method of calculation to be used to identify the lowest cost tender. In addition, Regulation 15 gave the Secretary of State the power to issue guidance on anti-competitive conduct, and stated that in any determination as to whether there had been anti-competitive conduct "there shall be taken into account the extent of any contravention of the guidance issued".

New guidance along these lines was issued that year through Circular 10/93. This guidance covered local authority functional work only, and replaced in its entirety DOE Circular 1/91. The non-imperative terms of the new circular lend support to the interpretation of its originating power, section 9(3)(f) discussed above. For example, the guidance alerted readers that it did not reiterate all the matters covered in the 1993 Competition Regulations, and that neither the Circular nor the Regulations were to be taken to be exhaustive.[17] Clearly where guidance is not exhaustive then there is room for an authority to argue that it has a special case. The language used by the Circular strengthens this impression. For example, the word "should" is widely used instead of the clearly imperative "must". Clearly the Secretary of State was still mindful of the rules against fettered discretion.

In other respects, Circular 10/93 simply built on its predecessor. It was no longer necessary to cover the financial aspects of tender evaluation in detail (that was done by the 1993 Regulations) but nevertheless there were still 64 paragraphs of detailed guidance. Certain matters were covered by guidance for the first time including responsibility for the competition process, the use of quality assurance certification and the transfer of undertakings.

In June and December 1994, the DOE issued separate draft guidance about anti-competitive conduct in relation to the new white-collar defined activities.

Then in 1996, DOE Circular 5/96 consolidated and replaced all previous guidance. It appeared to mark a new approach from the DOE. It attempted to draw back from trying to guide authorities through every nook and cranny of the tendering process. Instead local authorities were encouraged to show

---

16 S.I. 1993 No. 848.
17 DOE Circular 10/93 at para.4.

proper regard for the way in which markets for the individual services operated in practice. The guidance suggested that this could be demonstrated where authorities followed five key principles:

(1) ensuring that the competition process was conducted, and was seen to be conducted, in a fair and transparent manner;
(2) identifying the way in which the market operated for the service in question, and ensuring that tendering practices were consistent with securing a good competitive response;
(3) generally specifying the output to be achieved rather than the way in which the service was to be performed in detail, so that the evaluation of bids and the monitoring of performance could concentrate on the ability of contractors to achieve the full requirements of the specification including real service quality;
(4) adopting clear procedures for evaluating tenders to ensure that the required quality can be achieved;
(5) acting fairly between potential contractors to ensure that the conduct of tendering does not put any one of them at a disadvantage.

The most significant practical change came in relation to the second principle. The guidance recommended that authorities carry out what was effectively a preliminary market testing exercise. It stated that they should be able to demonstrate they have considered the market and consulted with a reasonable range of prospective tenderers about the way work was selected and packaged for competition. This resulted in many authorities advertising their intention to carry out CCT in advance and inviting responses along the lines indicated from prospective tenderers.

Having started by offering general principles, the rest of Circular 5/96 reverted to type. The 5 principles were subsequently developed over 39 paragraphs in the main body of the Circular and in 2 appendices (one of which contained a further 23 paragraphs of suggested good practice).

5.4 Examples of Anti-Competitive Conduct in the Tendering Process

This section considers a few of the areas where the government's position on anti-competitive conduct impinged on the exercise of local discretion in contract tendering and associated matters.

5.4.1 Separation of the client and contractor roles

One of the biggest practical problems posed by CCT was the extent to which a local authority was required to separate, in organisational terms, its role as a service client from its role as a service contractor. Traditionally, local authorities have been organised around departments or directorates which undertook both the planning and monitoring of services (client role) and the provision and supervision of those services (contractor role). At the top and bottom of the hierarchy in such departments the roles tended to be distinct but in between the distinction could become blurred with individuals spending their time in both roles (referred to as twin-hattedness). This was especially true of professional staff.

The LGPLA 1980 and LGA 1988 did not directly tackle this problem, but the wording of the legislation appeared to imply that some separation was necessary. For example, section 7 LGA 1988 referred to the "local authority" publishing notice of the work, but to the local authority "through their direct labour organisation" preparing a bid for the work. There were other reasons to suppose that the two roles should have been separated under CCT:

- a duality of roles in one person, could give rise to actual or perceived conflicts of interest: for example, if officers who advised on the evaluation of tenders, also advised the DSO on the preparation of its bid. That would be a conflict of interest, which would call into question the integrity of the whole tendering process. It could also be deemed to be anti-competitive conduct by the Secretary of State.
- CCT required the maintenance of trading accounts for each defined activity. To fulfil this requirement the costs of the contractor role had to be separated from the costs of the client role. This would be easier to do where the roles were clearly separated and there were no or fewer twin-hatted employees with chargeable time that needed to be apportioned.
- in management terms, twin-hattedness could lead to a loss of employee focus with a possibly adverse effect on DSO competitiveness

This subject is suffused with jargon, which can obscure as well as illuminate. A "hard split" is where the client role is located in a separate part of the organisation to the contractor role (two separate departments, two separate committees). A "soft split" is where existing organisational arrangements are retained but the employees within them are allocated to client or contractor roles for the duration of the CCT process. The prohibition on anti-competitive behaviour was only applicable prior to a decision to award a contract, so organisational arrangements thereafter for the period of the contract were not affected. In between these extremes innumerable variations are feasible.

There are arguments on both sides as to how far the separation of roles should go.[18] The lack of detailed guidance from the DOE contributed to the uncertainty. Local authorities certainly feared the prospect of their organisational arrangements being deemed to be "anti-competitive". The Audit Commission took the toughest line on separating the client and contractor roles. It

---

18 Some of these arguments are reviewed in a CIPFA Competition Joint Committee Occasional Paper "Compulsory Competition and the Separation of Duties" (1995).

issued its own guidance to local authorities in January 1989, which on balance favoured hard splits.[19] The Audit Commission's stance was summarised in a chart, which is reproduced below.

The DOE's silence eventually came to an end. In the "Competing for Quality" Consultation Paper of November 1991, the government proposed to issue regulations to underpin the organisational response to CCT. Further details came in the June 1992 Paper. The proposed regulations would follow the principle that "those with responsibility for the competition process should have no direct interest in the result and ensure that no individual has day to day responsibility for both client and contractor side tasks during the competition process". This indicated that the government would pursue a minimalist approach to the client–contractor split. It did not intend to use the proposed regulations to prescribe how local authorities should be structured. The regulations would merely set out the minimal framework needed to ensure the desired separation of responsibilities.

The proposals were implemented by the 1993 Competition Regulations.[20] Regulation 4 listed a number of "relevant operations", that none but a few specified individuals could carry out concurrently with advising the DSO. Conduct contravening the Regulation was deemed to be anti-competitive. The "relevant operations" were:

Options for the Client-Contractor Split

	Unacceptable arrangement	Undesirable arrangement	Possible arrangement	Ideal arrangement
MEMBERS	Same committee	Same committee	Same committee plus DSO and client sub-committees	Client Committee & DSO Committee
OFFICERS	Same officers	Different officers in same department	Client Department & DSO	Stand-alone or umbrella DSO Client Department plus contract supervision unit

---

19 Audit Commission Occasional Paper No. 7 "Preparing for Compulsory Competition" (1989).
20 S.I 1993 No. 848 Reg.4.

1. the selection of the newspaper or journal in which the CCT notice was to be published;
2. the selection of the persons to be invited to tender and sending to them the necessary documents;
3. the calculation any "prospective costs";
4. receiving, opening or evaluating the DSO bid or any tender submitted;
5. taking the decision as to who should win the work.

The only individuals permitted to work or take responsibility in both areas were the following:

1. the head of paid service (or in the event of his absence, his deputy).
2. the chief officer directly accountable to the head of paid service for the discharge of the relevant operation (or in his absence, his deputy).
3. any persons employed by the authority to give legal, financial or other professional advice in relation to the authority's business, other than advice within the same description of work for which tenders were invited.

The Regulations did not deal with councillors who were involved on both sides of the client/contractor division. This was a concession after the June 1992 paper had proposed regulating this area as well. Instead DOE Circular 10/93 recommended that councillors should when dealing with any of the relevant operations above, follow the principles set out in the National Code of Local Government Conduct. Under the Code a councillor's "private or personal interests" in a matter under discussion should be disclosed, and if appropriate a councillor with such an interest should withdraw from the discussion. Involvement in DSO business is not a private or personal interest under the Code, something that the guidance acknowledged, but it stated that it should be treated as such nonetheless.[21] This guidance was repeated in the Circular 5/96.

5.4.2   Service quality issues

In the early days of CCT, the government took the view that desired standards of service quality could and should be written into the service specification. For example, DOE Circular 1/91 said:

> "30. Authorities will clearly want to ensure a high level of quality in the provision of services and this will naturally be reflected in the specifications drawn up as a basis for contracts ..."

However local authorities were faced with a tricky balancing act with regard to the content of specifications. They had on the one hand to be clear,

---

21   DOE Circular 10/93 at para.13.

accurate and precise so as to give contractors an equal chance in preparing bids as a DSO, which would have been undertaking the work for years. On the other hand specifications were not to be too detailed because this would deny contractors the opportunity to put forward innovative ideas for improving services. Local authorities were also warned that asking too many detailed questions could be anti-competitive.

Assuming that those difficulties were overcome, then issues of quality could be disposed of at the front end of the tendering process. A local authority would satisfy itself before inviting tenders, that its selected contractors were technically and financially viable to carry out the kind of work that was the subject of the contract. Then at the final evaluation of tenders (assuming the tender submitted met the terms of the specification) it would not usually be necessary for it to look beyond the offered price in deciding where to award a contract. A decision to reject a lower tender in favour of the DSO would therefore be anti-competitive unless sound reasons could be shown to justify that course.

This approach to quality issues continued in Circular 10/93. By that time quality assurance certification had become a feature in local authority services. Some local authorities had taken to insisting that contractors hold quality assurance certification such as the BS 5750 series. The DOE disapproved of this practice. Its view was that the presence or absence of such certification could not on its own, be considered sufficient to indicate the competence of a contractor to carry out work. Certification was still not common and so such a requirement might be considered to restrict competition. Where authorities did refer to quality assurance certification in their contracts, the guidance said that it should be open to contractors to demonstrate that they were in the process of undergoing certification or already operated equivalent management systems.

Change came about because of the influence of white-collar CCT. It has been seen in Chapter 2 that the government recognised that quality in white-collar services work was harder to specify and measure than in blue-collar work. It accepted that local authorities, in addition to stating quality standards in service specifications, should be able to devise their own methods for evaluating quality, provided that these were fair and even-handed. This new approach was broached in the white-collar CCT guidance of June and December 1994, in which the DOE said:

> "The Secretary of State accepts that it is for local authorities to decide on the appropriate balance between price and quality and to select the appropriate tender accordingly. Selection should be made on the basis of an evaluation procedure which is rigorous and even-handed as between in-house and external bids. Decision making should be fully documented, enabling an authority to demonstrate the basis for decisions taken, if called upon to do so."

The Secretary of State specifically commended to local authorities the advice contained in a Local Government Management Board (LGMB) guidance paper released in 1994. That was the product of consultations between the local authority associations and the LGMB concerning the assessment of quality in white-collar CCT. It advised local authorities to devise their own measures for quality and to fully integrate them into their contract documentation and tendering processes. It used the Public Service Contract Regulations 1993 as a framework for the assessment of quality within the CCT regime. A guidance paper in much the same terms relating to blue-collar CCT was released by the LGMB in 1995 and was similarly commended by the Secretary of State.

The integrated CCT guidance, offered in Circular 5/96, largely restated this new approach to quality. The relevant guidance is quoted below.

> "19. The Secretary of State takes the view that most quality and environmental standards, together with equal opportunities issues, can be explicitly stated in the specification for the service or work in question. ... The Secretary of State accepts, however, there may be elements of performance which are difficult to quantify and therefore price realistically, and these need to be included in the evaluation. An authority should notify any such elements of performance which it wishes to include in the specification to all tenderers and give details of how the evaluation for these items will be carried out, at the time of invitation. The outcome of any such non-financial evaluation should be reported as part of the evaluation process. Authorities will be expected to be able to give a clear and soundly reasoned account of both why the elements considered are important and how they have been handled in relation to each tenderer."

5.4.3   The financial evaluation of tenders

The primary CCT legislation made no mention of the principles that should govern tender evaluation. The government tried to overcome this deficiency by classifying the use of certain conventions of tender evaluation as anti-competitive conduct.

Early conflicting approaches to the financial evaluation of tenders

(A)   Local authorities

The majority of local authorities took the view that the proper way to evaluate outside tenders was to assess the true cost to an authority of contracting out the work. The true cost was not just the price of the tender but also a number of other costs that the authority would bear as a result of contracting out – often known as extraneous costs. Some of these costs are outlined below:

> (1)   the potential redundancy costs of council staff, no longer needed for the contracted work and who could not be redeployed within the authority. Furthermore, some councils had voluntary severance

schemes that offered payments to redundant staff above the statutory minimum redundancy payments.[22]

(2) the cost of added years of service. Under the Local Government (Compensation for Premature Retirement) Regulations 1982 local authorities have the discretion to notionally enhance the number of years of reckonable service to be taken into account for ascertaining the pension entitlement of employees aged 50 and over who already have at least 5 years of service. Where this discretion is exercised, the authority pays a lump sum into the superannuation fund.

(3) the need to pay frozen holiday pay to employees on termination of employment with the authority. In the early 1980s the employment conditions of local authority manual workers were changed so that they were relieved of the need to work for 12 months before earning a leave entitlement. At that time, a years leave entitlement was frozen for each worker, to be paid out on termination of employment.[23] Where this eventuality was brought forward by CCT, local authorities argued that either the whole sum or the financial cost of the early pay-out should be included in the evaluation.

(4) the cost of loyalty or retention payments made to DSO staff after the decision to contract out work to the private sector in order to retain their services up to the hand-over date. Some authorities had experienced a loss of disillusioned staff in these circumstances.

(5) payments made to staff in lieu of notice, where the contract commencement date fell within a redundant employee's notice period.

(6) the continuing cost of overheads. Certain costs that were included in a DSO bid (accommodation, storage and corporate functions and support services) would not necessarily be saved if the work were to be won by an outside contractor. It was argued by some local authorities that these costs should therefore be added on to outside tenders.

(7) client supervision costs. Local authorities argued that the cost of supervising a new private contractor would exceed that of supervising the existing DSO, because of its unfamiliarity with the work.

(8) losses made on disposal of assets no longer required where work was to be awarded to an external contractor.

(9) the cost of requiring an external contractor to hold a performance bond, to cover the cost to the authority of arranging alternative service provision in the event that the contractor should become bankrupt or otherwise default.

(10) DSO/DLO required rate of return on capital employed. Local authorities argued that they were entitled to assume that they would

---

22 This was ruled ultra vires by the High Court in Allsop v North Tyneside D.C (1992) The Times 12 March. The unlawfulness centred around the interpretation of s.111[1] LGA 1972.
23 The 1982 Compensation for Premature Retirement Regulations: see (2).

receive this as an income benefit from the operations of DSOs. This would be lost if the DSO were closed.

(11) long term effect on prices of an authority having no DSO. One reason for the original establishment of in-house workforces, was to protect the authority from private sector monopolies and cartels. The continued presence of a DSO would, it was argued, have a beneficial downward effect on private sector prices. This item is inherently difficult to quantify.

(12) costs to be incurred in the cancellation of contracts, for assets that would no longer be required if the work was awarded to an outside contractor.

(13) the costs of progressive employer practices, such as the employment of disabled people and trainees in above average numbers. Such costs, it was argued, should be deducted from the DSO bid.

The extent to which extraneous costs have been used in the evaluation of tenders has varied between authorities. However where they were taken into account, the effect could often be to push the price of outside tenders above the price of the DSO bid, even when they might have had a cheaper "price for the job" at the start of the tender evaluation. This has never been popular with the contractors or the government.

(B)   The government

The government's view of tender evaluation in relation to CCT under the LGPLA 1980 was that the lowest price should be accepted, whether that came from the DLO or a contractor, unless good reason could be shown to the contrary. Statements by government ministers during the passage of the Local Government Bill in 1987 (to become the LGA 1988), were more emollient but still consistent with this approach. For example, the then Secretary of State, Mr Nicholas Ridley, said on 6 July 1987 in the House of Commons, that:

> "...despite much scaremongering to the contrary, proper tender appraisal is not a simple matter of whose tender is the lowest..."

DOE Circular 19/88 said little directly on the subject of tender evaluation, except that local authorities could legitimately take potential redundancy costs into account "as part of their assessment of the overall cost to ratepayers of accepting a contractor's bid".[24] This showed an acceptance of the principle that the wider costs of awarding a contract to an external tender could be evaluated. In the Circular's own words "authorities acting in good faith should have nothing to fear".[25]

---

24   Circular 19/88 para.34.
25   ibid para.33.

(C) The Audit Commission and CIPFA

The Audit Commission took a similar but stricter line to that outlined in Circular 19/88. In an article in the Law Society Gazette,[26] the Controller of the Audit Commission said that a local authority was allowed "for the purposes of comparison, to add to contractors bids those costs which it would not be incurring if the contract were awarded to the in-house operation". But, he added that only costs "which arise as an inevitable consequence of the in-house operation losing the tender competition may be taken into account in this way".

In a letter to local authorities, dated 9 August 1989, the Audit Commission indicated, on this basis, that authorities taking account of costs such as frozen holiday pay and central overheads would be acting anti-competitively. The views of the Audit Commission were of strong persuasive value, especially if a local authority was resolved to "play by the rules". However, they were not binding.

The Audit Commission's views were often contradicted by the views of CIPFA expressed in its Code of Competition. CIPFA tended to adopt a more relaxed view on the treatment of extraneous costs.

(D) DOE Circular 1/91

Following its own experience of the working of the Act and complaints from contractors, the DOE brought out a draft circular for consultation in 1990, which was followed in March 1991 by Circular 1/91. This was far more specific than Circular 19/88, withdrawing six of its predecessor's paragraphs relating to anti-competitive conduct including the principle that "authorities acting in good faith should have nothing to fear".[27] Its approach closely matched that of the Audit Commission in that the chief consideration was whether or not a cost item inevitably flowed from the award of work to an outside contractor. If it did not, and yet an authority had taken account of it in a tender evaluation, a suspicion of anti-competitive conduct would arise and, authorities were warned, sanction under sections 13 and 14 of the Act might follow.

The following cost items could according to the new Circular be legitimately taken into account:

- potential redundancy costs;
- the additional cost of disabled employees and trainees;
- the net costs of cancelling contracts for which an incoming contractor did not wish to take responsibility;
- losses incurred on the disposal of depots and vehicles made available to an incoming contractor but unwanted.

---

26 The Law Society's Gazette 27 November 1989.
27 Circular 1/91 para 2.

Any other costs were not to be brought into account. Specifically excluded was taking account of the costs of paying out frozen holiday pay and the long term effect on prices of there being no DSO. Nor were authorities to be permitted to apply higher supervision costs for outside contractors than DSOs. The costs of accommodation, storage or central administration that might not be immediately saved when work was contracted out were also excluded. These were said to represent either opportunities for future savings or costs that the authority would continue to bear irrespective of the outcome of competition.

The attitude of the courts

There has been little case law on CCT in general and on this area in particular. Proper judicial scrutiny has been largely placed off-limits by the decision in *R v Secretary of State for the Environment ex parte Knowsley MBC and Others*.[28] In that case, the Times law report records from Popplewell J's High Court judgement, the following:

> "If it had been for his Lordship to lay down the proper approach on principle it would be that the local authority was entitled to take into account the overall cost to the ratepayer as a result of the contract going outside, that is, those costs that properly flowed directly from losing the contract. However that was not his function which was to decide whether the Secretary of State was unreasonable."

As was seen in Chapter 1, this is a very high hurdle to jump. The Scottish case of *In Re Colas Roads* (unreported 1991) is interesting because it concerned the judicial review of a local authority's decision rather than that of the Secretary of State. After carrying out CCT for street lighting maintenance, the authority had decided to award the contract to its DLO. The DLO had submitted a bid of £6.5 million as opposed to a private contractor's bid of £5.97 million. However following adjustments the figures were £7.3 million and £7.7 million respectively and so the DLO won as the "lowest net cost tender". The adjustments included inflationary uplift for both bids and additions to the price of the outside bid to reflect the costs of redundant employees and assets. The contractor challenged the decision by way of judicial review on the ground that in making these adjustments, the authority had acted anti-competitively contrary to section 9(4)(aaaa) LGPLA 1980 (the equivalent of section 7(7) in the LGA 1988). Because the case did not involve the Secretary of State, what was at issue was the reasonableness of the local authority's conduct, specifically in taking account in the tender evaluation of the wider costs of awarding the contract to an outside tender. Lord Prosser came down very clearly on the side of the local authority, saying:

---

28   The Times, 28 May 1991 (High Court); The Independent, 25 September 1991 (Court of Appeal). Transcript available on LEXIS.

"... if the placing of a contract with an outside contractor would lead to the local authority incurring major liabilities, I cannot regard taking notice of the fact, and giving weight in the decision making process, as within the category of actings covered by sub-section (4)(aaaa). A responsible regard for the truth does not seem to me to be something which can be said to restrict, distort or prevent competition, unless one has decided that competition is more important than both truth and the interests of citizens for whom the local authority are responsible. I can see nothing in the language of the statute which indicates such a pre-eminence for competition over all else, nor am I prepared to assume that Parliament intended local authorities to enter into contracts regardless of perhaps disastrous, if indirect consequences. In principle it appears to me that the respondents were well entitled to have regard to the type of liabilities which they took into account, and I am satisfied that the fact they did so entails no breach of s.9(4)."

That is a powerful espousal of the argument for a wider approach to the consideration of extraneous factors in tender evaluation. However, if the contractor had chosen to complain to the Secretary of State and if he had acted using sections 19A and 19B of the LGPLA 1980 (equivalent provisions to sections 13 and 14 LGA 1988) the result would almost certainly have been different.

The Court of Appeal in *Knowsley* delivered a "double whammy" to the wider approach. The facts were outlined in Chapter 1. Essentially they were that Knowsley (and Leicester) councils had adjusted the price of outside tenders, which were on their face lower than the competing DSO bids, so that they were more expensive and could be rejected. The adjustments were considered to be anti-competitive in effect by the Secretary of State. In a long judgement Ralph Gibson LJ largely upheld the Secretary of State's position because he had not acted illegally, irrationally or unreasonably in law.[29] However the other two appeal judges held that the Act itself prohibited the wide approach to tender evaluation. In Parker LJ's words:

"The opening words of the Long Title refer to undertaking or doing work competitively. This appears to me to indicate that what is aimed at is a comparison between the amount of the DSO bid for doing the work and the amount of the outside tender so as to ensure that authorities only do the work themselves if their own DSO's bid competes favourably with that of the rival tenderer.

The approach of the authorities is in my view the reverse of this. They say that if they make a bid which properly sets out the price for doing the work they do not compare this with the outside tender but they take out of the bid

---

[29] He did say that any notional "profit" made by the DSO (above the required rate of return on capital employed, or presumably any other required financial objective) could be deducted from the price of a DSO bid, because it was a purely accounting figure not related to the cost of the work.

before comparing it the costs of not doing the work and the notional profit that they will lose (but would never have made) as a result of not doing the work.

That this distorts competition appears to me to be beyond doubt..."

In a similar vein, Leggatt LJ said:

"I endorse the suggestion made in argument by Lord Justice Parker that when the Act requires the fulfillment of a condition that an authority in deciding to do work did not act in a manner likely to have the effect of distorting competition, it is seeking to ensure equality in the elements that each tender has to include. In my judgement competition is distorted if elements which are included in the DSO's bid for the purpose of comparing it with those of other tenderers are therefore deducted on the pretext that if an outside bid were accepted there would be resultant costs to the chargepayers which would not be incurred if the work were done by the DSO."

This was a rejection of the wide approach in favour of a straight comparison of "price for the job". Both judges acknowledged that extraneous costs were a relevant factor. But the place where they were to be taken into account was in the local authority's response to a section 13 notice, admitting that it had acted anti-competitively but giving reasons why the Secretary of State should not go on to issue a section 14 direction.

From the above cases it can be seen that where it is relevant to the issue (and bearing in mind the effects of the *Knowsley* decision it usually won't be) judicial opinion is somewhat divided on the question of the financial evaluation of tenders. However the weight of opinion would appear to favour of the strict approach.

It is interesting to note that the government's new proposals for a strict "price for the job" evaluation of tenders followed hard on the heels of Parker and Leggatt LJJ's judgements in *Knowsley*.

The watershed

Because many local authorities were not following the guidance issued in Circular 1/91, the government decided to tighten the rules further. Its reasoning and proposals were outlined in the "Competing for Quality" consultations over 1991–92. The following passage, taken from the initial Consultation paper of November 1991, reveals the depth of its frustration and its determination to champion private sector competition:

"1.7 It is clear that authorities have been able to cushion their workforces against the full force of competition by using conventions for evaluating tenders which take account of cost items extraneous to the price for performing the work, to the disadvantage of the external tenderer. In policy statements and guidance circulars issued since the passage of the 1988 Act, the Government has hereto accepted that it is appropriate for some extraneous

factors to be considered. In principle, however, the effect of taking account of any items other than the direct price for the work is, in itself, to distort competition, and to deny the opportunity for efficiency gains. Innovative approaches by external contractors to traditional tasks have often been rejected because, although the tendered "price for the job" has been well below the price tendered by the in-house workforce, the tender evaluation process has increased the external price to the point where it is assessed as more expensive.
1.8 The Government believes that, in the medium to long term, it is vital that a healthy market for the provision of local authority services is fostered. It views with concern the possibility that external competition will become more restricted because of conventions of tender evaluation which the Government has, hereto, accepted. It is determined that local communities should not be denied the opportunity for better services more efficiently delivered which competition can bring. Of course, the Government recognises that, if a local authority awards a contract to an external tenderer, there may well be additional one-off costs, such as redundancy payments, so that in the immediate short term the overall cost to the authority of accepting the external tender could be higher than if the in-house workforce continued to provide the service. The Government is therefore looking to balance the short-term costs against the long-term benefits."

The "Competing for Quality" consultations mark a clear watershed in the government's attitude to extraneous costs in tender evaluation. Before it had been prepared to accept all those wider costs that "inevitably" flowed from the award of work to an external tenderer. There was room for argument over what constituted an inevitable cost, but such arguments were being fought over common ground, with the DOE simply taking a more restrictive interpretation. The new position was to be based on the ideological assertion that consideration of anything beyond the price for the work, was a distortion of competition and as such anti-competitive behaviour. The government conceded that "short-term costs" existed in going to an outside contractor. It saw the consultations as an exercise to establish which extraneous cost items should be admitted into the tender evaluation, and how they should be compared with potential long-term savings. The goal was to be a "healthy market for the provision of local authority services".

The 1993 Competition Regulations

The consultations resulted in section 9 of the LGA 1992 and the 1993 Competition Regulations,[30] which came into force on 10 May 1993. The Regulations removed local authority discretion over the financial evaluation of tenders by setting out a series of steps and calculations for authorities to follow. Failure to follow the prescribed stages and methodology was treated

---

30   S.I 1993 No. 848.

as anti-competitive conduct (Regulation 5). By doing so, it would be possible for an authority to rank the outside tenders and DSO bid in terms of cost, and so identify the lowest priced tender.

The Regulations permitted local authorities to take account of only two sorts of cost. These were called allowable costs and prospective costs.

Allowable costs were a concession to a local authority's wider social role. They reflected the costs of employing disabled people (Regulation 9) and trainees (Regulation 10). As was the case in previous guidance, the costs counted were the additional costs of such employees. The definition was tightened in that the amount of any government grant aid had to be used to offset the amount in costs.

Prospective costs were those wider costs that an authority might incur if the work were to be awarded to an outside contractor, which in the DOE's view were significant, unavoidable and outside the authority's control:

- redundancy costs (Regulation 12);
- payments to staff during period of notice of dismissal (Regulation 13);
- the cost of terminating contracts for hire and other contracts (Regulation 14);
- the cost of any reasonable indemnity required of a local authority by a contractor, bidding on the basis that TUPE did not apply, against the eventuality of TUPE being subsequently found to be applicable (Regulation 14A).[31]

The first stage: calculating allowable and prospective costs

The calculation of prospective costs had to take place before the opening of any tenders (Regulation 5). There was no similar requirement in the case of allowable costs, but practical reasons would have dictated that they be calculated at the same time.

The second stage: identifying "qualifying tenders"

On opening the DSO bid and other tenders, the local authority had to establish the "price for the work" under each. Regulation 7 then required that the amount of the DSO bid be adjusted by subtracting the total amount of allowable costs, and then adding back on the value of the "notional premium". This was defined in Regulation 1 as an amount equal to the lowest of the performance bonds offered by the outside contractors. Any outside tender that could offer savings on the amount of the adjusted DSO bid was termed a qualifying tender.

---

31   S.I 1995 No. 1336.

The third stage: comparison of costs/savings between DSO bid and qualifying tenders

Regulation 8 required an authority to compare the "present value of savings" with the total amount of prospective costs. The present value of savings was to be calculated in accordance with a formula set out in the Schedule to the Regulations. Essentially the saving offered by a qualifying tender in the first year of the contract was projected into the future (over a 10 year period), then discounted and brought back be expressed as a present value.

If the local authority wished, it might at this point subtract the total amount of all prospective costs from the price of the DSO bid (already adjusted by the deduction of allowable costs) and compare this with the present value of savings.

At the end of this stage it would be possible to rank all the tenders and the DSO bid in terms of cost and so identify the lowest tender. The Regulations did not expressly require a local authority to accept the lowest bid. It should therefore have been possible for an authority to evaluate all or any of the tenders on the basis of other financial or non-financial criteria provided that this was not otherwise anti-competitive or infringed the curtailment of non-commercial considerations in Part II LGA 1988.

5.5   Summary

Through the exclusion of non-commercial considerations and the development of the concept of anti-competitive conduct, the discretion of local authorities over contract tendering has been drastically curtailed. The contraction of local discretion has been matched by the extension of power in the hands of central government and the Secretary of State. The courts have showed little willingness to interfere with this creeping centralisation of power.

Chapter Six

TUPE and its Implications for CCT

Contents

6.1 The Acquired Rights Directive and its Implementation by TUPE
6.2 Identifying a TUPE Situation
6.3 The Consequences of TUPE
6.4 Summary

Competitive tendering, whether of the compulsory or voluntary kind, has implications for the employment rights of local authority employees, because competitors will often bid for work on the basis of reduced labour costs. The loss of contracts will leave employees previously assigned to that work facing three options:

- redeployment to another post within the authority;
- redundancy with the possibility of being re-engaged by the successful contractor (perhaps on changed terms and conditions of employment); or
- in a transfer of an undertaking situation, being transferred over to the employment of the successful contractor on the same terms and conditions enjoyed with the local authority.

The transfer of undertakings law is a new area of British law that stems from EC Council Directive 77/187 of February 1977.[1] The Directive was implemented in the UK by the Transfer of Undertakings (Protection of Employment) Regulations 1981,[2] which is otherwise known simply as TUPE. Despite this history, not until the 1990s (following a series of decisions by the ECJ) did it become apparent that the provisions of the Directive and TUPE were relevant to CCT and the contracting out of public services. This has had important consequences for employee rights, the commercial strategy of potential contractors for council contracts, and for councils themselves in the way that they plan and carry out the tendering process.

6.1 The Acquired Rights Directive and its Implementation by TUPE

The Acquired Rights Directive required the member states to introduce certain minimum measures for the protection of workers' rights where there had been a change of employer resulting from a transfer of an undertaking. The origins of the Directive can be traced to the early 1970s and the belief that there should be a social dimension to a common market that had seen an increasing number of business take-overs and mergers. It was considered

---

1 O.J. (1977) L61/26.
2 S.I 1981 No.1794.

unfair that employees should bear the brunt of these changes through redundancies and reduced terms and conditions of employment. Therefore legislation was prepared to preserve terms and conditions of employment through a change, and to give employee representatives some say in the fate of their businesses.

Initial proposals were noted by the Council of Ministers in January 1974,[3] and the Commission placed proposals for a directive before the Council later that year.[4] The proposed directive would have been very wide reaching. It would even have caught take-overs by share purchase where the formal identity of the employer (the company) would have remained the same. It also gave workers' representatives broad consultative rights and provided for compulsory arbitration in situations where workers and management could not reach agreement. These proposals were whittled down in the course of the legislative process, until a more limited directive was approved by unanimity in February 1977.[5]

The revised Directive was limited to transfers of undertakings where the identity of the employer changed (excluding situations where the share ownership of a business changed). Workers were to be protected by two devices:

- an automatic cross-over of obligations arising under an employment contract or relationship (including collective agreements) from the transferor to the transferee;
- a right to protection from dismissal solely by reason of the transfer (except for economic, technical or organisational reasons entailing changes in the workforce).

The remaining Articles preserved the status and function of employee representatives and imposed on employers the duty to inform and consult with such employees' representatives in the event of a transfer. The Directive permitted member states to implement rules that were more favourable to employees' rights if they wished. The period allowed for implementation was two years.

In order to appreciate the full implications of the Directive, it is necessary to consider the previous state of UK law concerning employee rights on the transfer of a business or an undertaking. This will of course still be the law in circumstances where the Directive and TUPE do not apply (see 6.2). There are three principal differences.

- employee rights to information and consultation are limited to situations where the employer had voluntarily recognised a trade union for these purposes.

---

3   O.J. (1974) C13/1 (12 February 1974).
4   O.J. (1974) C104/1 (9 September 1974).
5   For an overview of the proposals in the draft directive see "Workers Rights in Mergers and Takeovers: The EEC Proposals." by Bob Hepple (1976) 5 ILJ 197. For consideration of changes in the final version, by the same author, see (1977) 6 ILJ 106.

- the common law does not recognise a continuity of employment through a change of employer, so a contract of employment is terminated whenever there is a change in the identity of the employer.[6]
- there is statutory recognition of continuity of employment on the transfer of a business in cases where an employee is re-engaged by the new employer. An employee's period of service with the transferor will count as if it were service with the transferee for the purposes of an employee's entitlement towards statutory redundancy and unfair dismissal rights, where two years qualifying service is often required. However there is no continuity in relation to purely contractual rights.

Implementation of the Directive by the UK was slow. The Labour government failed to make much progress before it lost power in 1979. The new Conservative government was unsympathetic towards this inherited obligation. It was not until December 1981 that the Transfer of Undertakings (Protection of Employment) Regulations (TUPE) were laid before Parliament.[7] On being asked whether he was recommending the Regulations to the House, a Minister replied that he was recommending them with a remarkable lack of enthusiasm.[8]

TUPE did the minimum necessary to carry out the requirements of the Directive.[9] Undertakings that were not in the nature of a commercial venture were specifically excluded. This appeared to rule out the application of TUPE to public sector bodies such as local authorities. As well as this, the duty of employers to inform and consult representatives of employees was limited to situations where the employer had voluntarily recognised a trade union for such purposes.

Following a review of the measures taken by member states to implement the Directive, the EC Commission decided in 1991 to bring enforcement proceedings against the UK under Article 226 of the Treaty (see *Commission v UK*).[10] When the case was underway, the government introduced a number of amendments to TUPE through section 33 of the Trade Union Reform and Employment Rights Act 1993 (TURERA 1993). These amendments were said to clarify the existing state of the law. In particular they removed the exclusion of undertakings not in the nature of a commercial venture. These measures correctly anticipated the final decision of the ECJ in most areas, but not on the matter of employee representatives. Following the decision further amendment of TUPE proved necessary through the Collective

---

6   *Nokes v Doncaster Amalgamated Collieries* [1940] AC 549.
7   H. C. Deb. (1981/82) Vol. 14 cols. 677–698 (7 December 1981); H. L. Deb. (1981/82) Vol. 425 cols. 1482–1501 (10 December 1981).
8   H. C. Deb. (1981/82) Vol. 14 col. 680 (7 December 1981).
9   An overview of the original provisions of TUPE is provided by Bob Hepple in 1982 ILJ 29.
10 Case C-382/89 [1994] IRLR 392; [1994] ICR 664.

Redundancies and Transfer of Undertakings (Protection of Employment) (Amendment) Regulations 1995.[11]

6.2   Identifying a TUPE Situation

According to Article 1(1) the provisions of the Acquired Rights Directive apply wherever there is "the transfer of an undertaking, business or part of a business to another employer as a result of a legal transfer or merger". This has been implemented through Regulation 3 of TUPE as "a transfer from one person to another of an undertaking" or a part of an undertaking as a result of a sale or by some other disposition or by operation of law. The transfer may be effected by a series of two or more transactions and may take place whether or not any property is transferred to the transferee by the transferor. An undertaking is defined in Regulation 2 as including any trade or business (but those "not in the nature of a commercial venture" were excluded before 1993).

The Directive was originally seen as applying only to business take-overs and mergers in the private sector, hence the original exclusion of non-commercial undertakings by TUPE. However a series of ECJ decisions in the 1990s extended the Directive's scope and therefore that of national implementing measures such as TUPE to include transfers of public sector undertakings and in particular the contracting out of public services. This was accompanied by great controversy in the UK because of the implications for the government's policy of market testing the provision of public services including, in the case of local government, CCT. In identifying a TUPE situation, the courts and all concerned parties have to focus on two issues, the nature of the transfer, and whether what has been transferred is an undertaking. The impetus behind addressing these issues has come from the ECJ. This Part of the Chapter will consider the European case law that has created and driven events in this field, the reaction of the British courts to the European developments and finally the attitude of the British government.

6.2.1   The European Case Law

(i)   The nature of the transfer

The English translation of Article 1(1) of the Directive speaks of a "legal transfer" but other language versions of the Directive use different terminology. Because of the difficulties this raises, the ECJ has preferred to give the term the widest possible meaning in order to give effect to the purpose of the Directive, an approach that was first seen in *Abels*:[12]

---

11   S.I. 1995 No. 2587 see Reg. 8-14.
12   *Abels v Bedrijfsvereniging voor de Metaalindustrie en die Electrotechnische Industrie* Case No. C-135/83 [1985] ECR 469; [1987] 2 CMLR 406.

"the scope of the provision at issue cannot be appraised solely on the basis of a textual interpretation. Its meaning must therefore be clarified in the light of the scheme of the Directive ... and its purpose."

That purpose is protecting of the position of the workers in the transferred undertaking by enabling them to remain in employment with the new employer on the terms and conditions agreed with the transferor. Therefore where the facts show that an undertaking has retained its identity through a change in employer (see below), the ECJ has not allowed technicalities about the precise nature of a "legal" transfer, to stand in the way, if to do so would compromise employees' rights. True to this approach the ECJ has found a legal transfer to be present in a variety of situations.

In *Ny Molle Kro*[13] a legal transfer was found where the lease of a restaurant was terminated and the owner lessor took over the running of the restaurant herself. The crucial factor was that the owner had taken over the responsibilities as employer from the leasee. It did not matter that there had been no change in ownership or that there was no direct "agreement" between owner and leasee about the termination of the lease (although there was a termination clause in the lease).

In *Daddy's Dance Hall*,[14] a restaurant owner terminated the first lease on his premises and then re-let them to a new leasee, who continued to run the business with the staff previously dismissed upon the termination of the original lease. This was found to be a transfer, and the fact that it took place in two stages (from the original leasee to the owner, then from the owner to the new leasee) did not affect the applicability of the Directive.

Then, in *Berg*[15] the ECJ found a legal transfer in circumstances where a bar run under a lease-purchase agreement was restored to its owner by way of a court order.

Finally, in *P Bork International*[16] the lease of a factory was rescinded by the owners who subsequently sold the premises to a third party who in turn brought the factory back into operation with a little over half the former staff. The ECJ held this to be a legal transfer, taking place in two stages.

However it was not yet apparent whether decisions by non-commercial public sector bodies could amount to legal transfers, nor whether decision to contract out a service could amount to the same. These questions became particularly relevant in the late 1980s and 1990s as the privatisation of public services took hold across Europe, especially in the UK, and as the contracting out of non-core activities, spread in the private sector. The ECJ decisions in the

---

13 *Landsorganisation i Danmark v Ny Molle Kro* Case No. C-286/86 [1987] ECR 5465; [1987] CMLR468; [1989] IRLR 37; [1989] ICR 330.
14 *Foreningen af Arbejdsledere i Danmark v Daddy's Dance Hall* Case No. C-324/86 [1988] IRLR 315.
15 *Berg and Busschers v Besselsen* Case No. C-144 and 145/87 [1989] IRLR 447.
16 *P. Bork International v Foreningen af Arbejdsledere i Danmark* Case No. C-101/87 [1989] IRLR 41.

cases of *Redmond Stichting*[17] and *Rask*[18] in 1992 and 1993 respectively, brought the Acquired Rights Directive and TUPE clearly into the CCT arena.

The *Redmond Stichting* case concerned a decision by a Dutch local authority to switch the payment of a subsidy from one non-commercial body operating for the relief of drug dependency to another such body with similar (but not identical) aims. The ECJ held that transactions arising out of the grant of subsidies to non-commercial bodies were not excluded from the scope of the Directive, which applied to all employees who were covered by protection against dismissal under national law however limited. The fact that the decision to switch subsidies was taken unilaterally by the local authority rather than by agreement did not affect the outcome because it was comparable to a unilateral decision to change a leasee, which had been held in previous cases to fall within the Directive.

The circumstances in *Rask* involved a firm's decision to contract out the running of its staff canteen. The question arose as to whether this constituted a legal transfer to which the Directive was applicable. Under the terms of the contract, the catering contractor would be paid a fixed monthly fee to cover costs relating to management, wages, insurance and the provision of work clothing. The canteen premises, equipment and other facilities were made available to the contractor free of charge. In return the contractor agreed to take on the existing staff at the same pay. The dispute arose after the contractor made minor and non-detrimental changes to the conditions of employment, and dismissed the plaintiff and another when they refused to accept the changes.

The contractor argued that the contract did not constitute a legal transfer within the meaning of the Directive. It neither conferred full responsibility for the provision of services (the service being provided exclusively for the transferor at prices fixed by the contract) nor transferred ownership of the assets needed to provide those services. To find a legal transfer in those circumstances would give an excessively broad scope to the Directive, and would discourage and hinder the growth of privatisation and subcontracting in general. The ECJ disagreed and again it reaffirmed its previous case law. The crucial factor was that the contractor had assumed the responsibilities of employer in respect of the canteen staff and that meant that the transaction was capable of being a legal transfer.

Following these cases it is likely that there will be a legal transfer for the purposes of the Directive and TUPE in any CCT or contracting out situation in relation to local authorities. Attention must therefore focus on the nature of the entity or "undertaking" that is the subject of the transfer.

(ii)   The nature of an undertaking

Article 1(1) of the Directive simply refers to the "transfer of an undertaking, business or part of a business" without elaborating any further. TUPE is simi-

---

17   *Redmond Stichting v Bartol* (Case C29/91) [1992] ECR I-3189.
18   *Rask and Christiansen v ISS Kantineservice* (Case C-209/91) [1992] ECR I-5755.

larly brief, with Regulation 2 speaking in terms of "any trade or business" or part of such. Again it has fallen to the ECJ to develop the meaning of an undertaking through its case law.

The case of *Spijkers v Gebroeders Benedik Abattoir CV*[19] must stand centre-stage in this discussion. The transferor company owned and operated a slaughterhouse, but on running into financial troubles and was forced to sell all of its assets (the slaughterhouse and appurtenant premises and goods) to the transferee respondents. At the time of the sale, the slaughterhouse had closed and all goodwill in the business had dissipated. After a gap of six weeks, the transferee resumed the operation of the slaughterhouse for completely new customers and having re-hired the old workforce except the appellant and another. The appellant argued that the circumstances demonstrated a transfer of an undertaking, and that his employment contract was still subsisting with the transferee. This question was referred to the ECJ by way of the preliminary reference procedure.

It was clear from the Opinion delivered by the Advocate-General, Sir Gordon Slynn, that a broad and purposive approach would be adopted, for example (at the 9th paragraph):

"...in deciding whether there has been a transfer...all the circumstances have to be looked at. Technical rules are to be avoided and the substance matters more than the form. The essential question is whether the transferee has obtained a business or an undertaking (or part thereof) which he can continue to operate."

In its judgement, the ECJ went on to declare:

"[11]...that the Directive aims to ensure the continuity of existing employment relationships in the framework of an *economic entity*, irrespective of a change of owner. It follows that the decisive criterion for establishing the existence of a transfer within the meaning of the Directive is *whether the entity in question retains its identity*."

Therefore, the idea that lay behind the words "undertaking, business or part of a business" in Article 1(1), was one of an economic entity, performing economic activities with some sort of organisational structure. This point was developed in the succeeding paragraphs, as follows:

"[12]...it is necessary to determine whether what has been sold is an economic entity which is still in existence, and this will be apparent from the fact that its operation is actually being continued or has been taken over by the new employer, with the same economic or similar activities.
[13] To decide whether these conditions are fulfilled it is necessary to take account of all the factual circumstances of the transaction in question, including the type of undertaking or business in question, the transfer or otherwise

---

19   Case No. C-24/85 [1986] ECR 1119; [1986] 2 CMLR 296.

of tangible assets such as buildings and stocks, the value of intangible assets at the date of transfer, whether the majority of staff are taken over by the new employer, the transfer or otherwise of the circle of customers and the degree of similarity between activities before and after the transfer and the duration of any interruption in those activities. It should be made clear, however, that each of these factors is only a part of the overall assessment which is required and therefore they cannot be examined independently of each other.

[14] The factual appraisal which is necessary to establish whether there is or is not a transfer as defined above is a matter for the national court, taking account of the detailed interpretation which has been given."

In *Spijkers*, the ECJ passed over the opportunity to define a transfer of an undertaking, choosing instead to provide broad guidelines within which the national courts would decide the issue in each individual case. This left a number of conceptual uncertainties to be resolved in future cases.

One of these was whether the provision of services could constitute an undertaking under the Directive. The facts in *Redmond Stichting*[20] were concerned with a Dutch foundation called the Redmond Foundation that provided services to drug addicts, particularly those of Surinamese or Antillean origin. It also provided a social and recreational function for its clients, and all these services were wholly funded by means of a subsidy from a local authority. The local authority unilaterally decided to terminate this subsidy and switch it to the Sigma Foundation, a similar entity that provided general assistance for drug dependency but no social or recreational services.

The question was whether the undertaking carried on under Sigma was the same as that formerly carried on by Redmond despite the cessation of the social and recreational function. The ECJ said that the cessation of an activity, even one that may have been an independent enterprise, did not preclude the applicability of the Directive. The Directive applied not only to the transfer of undertakings but also to the transfer of businesses or parts of businesses to which activities of a particular nature may be regarded as comparable. So where an undertaking provided services, and some but not all of these were transferred, the identity of the part of the undertaking responsible for the transferred services could be retained.

The *Rask*[21] case concerned the decision by a company to contract out the operation of a staff canteen. The defendants argued that these services could not constitute an undertaking within the meaning of the Directive because they were ancillary to the company's activity. If successful this argument would have excluded most contracted out services from the scope of the Directive. Private companies are not prone to contract out their core operations, and most of the services covered by local authority CCT can be seen as ancillary to other statutory functions. The ECJ refused to accept any such exclusion. The Directive applied in situations where some of the activities of the transferor had been transferred (transfer of part of an undertaking) and

---

20 See footnote 17.
21 See footnote 18,

another person had taken on the responsibility as employer of the persons previously assigned to carry out those activities. The two plaintiffs had both previously been assigned to work in the canteen and so were covered by the provisions of the Directive.

The interpretation given to the transfer of an undertaking appeared to reach its zenith in the *Schmidt*[22] case. The applicant was employed as a cleaner at a bank. She was the only person employed for this purpose. When the bank decided to contract out its cleaning service to an external contractor, the applicant refused to work for them and claimed she had been unfairly dismissed by reason of the transfer of an undertaking. The questions referred to the ECJ were whether the contracting out of such cleaning operations could fall under the Directive, and if so, whether it mattered that a single employee carried out the operations? A particular feature of the case was that there were no tangible or intangible assets involved in the operations.

The Court applied its decision in *Rask* to hold that these facts did bring the transfer within the Directive. The cleaning operations constituted a part of an undertaking and the protection of the Directive extended to all employees assigned to it. The fact there was only one employee was immaterial. Further, the absence from the transfer of tangible assets did not preclude the applicability of the Directive:

> "[16] The fact that in its case law the Court includes the transfer of such assets among the various factors to be taken into account by a national court to enable it, when assessing a complex transaction as a whole, to decide whether an undertaking has in fact been transferred does not support the conclusion that the absence of these factors precludes the existence of a transfer. The safeguarding of employees rights, which constitutes the subject matter of the Directive ... cannot depend exclusively on consideration of a factor which the Court has in any event already held not to be decisive on its own ...
> [17] ... the decisive criterion for establishing whether there is a transfer for the purposes of the Directive is whether the business in question retains its identity. According to [the] case law, the retention of that identity is indicated inter alia by the actual continuation or resumption by the new employer of the same or similar activities. Thus, in this case ... the similarity of the cleaning work performed before and after the transfer – which is reflected moreover in the offer to re-engage the employee in question – is typical of an operation which comes within the scope of the Directive."

This decision pushed the scope given to the term "transfer of an undertaking" further than ever before. Significantly, the Court did not feel the need to recite the full *Spijkers* criteria and reached its own conclusion that on the facts the Directive was applicable, rather than leaving this to the national court. The retention of identity as indicated by the similarity of activities carried out by the undertaking before and after the transfer, was considered

---

22 *Schmidt v Spar und Leihkasse der fruherer Amter Bordesholm, Keil und Cronshagen* (Case C-392/92) [1994] IRLR 302; [1995] ICR 237.

paramount. Some commentators argued after *Schmidt*, that the Directive applied to most contracting out situations provided the essential nature of the activity remained the same. This was certainly the approach taken in the British courts (see later). An alternative view is that the decision can be explained in terms of the *Spijkers* criteria and its own peculiar facts, in particular that there were no tangible assets to speak of, which may explain the Court's willingness to discount their absence. In the light of the social purpose of the Directive, once the Court had found an economic entity in the cleaning operations, it could hardly refuse protection because there was only a single employee.

The ECJ's rather broad brush treatment, contrasted with the more cautious stance of the Advocate General's earlier Opinion, which sought the identity of the undertaking in organisational terms, that is to say "an organised whole consisting of persons and tangible and/or intangible assets by means of which an economic activity is carried on having a specific, even ancillary, objective of its own". The Court judgement made no mention of this, but the idea was to resurface in the next significant case, that of *Rygaard*.

The applicant in the case of *Rygaard*[23] had been employed as a carpenter apprentice by the transferor (Pederson) who had agreed to carry out work on the construction of a canteen for a firm called SAS Service Partner A/S. Pedersen notified SAS that it wanted part of the work relating to ceilings and joinery to be completed by another firm Stro Molle. SAS agreed and Stro Molle submitted a tender for the work. At this time, Pedersen and Stro Molle entered into an agreement for the handing over of the relevant works according to which the applicant was transferred to the employ of Stro Molle for a period of 3 months. Also transferred was a quantity of materials for carrying out the work in question. The applicant was subsequently dismissed by Stro Molle and in the course of a wrongful dismissal action, the question whether these facts could constitute a transfer of an undertaking, was referred to the ECJ.

This case differed from those that went before because a single works contract or job limited as to time formed the basis of the transaction, rather than a contract to carry out an on-going activity. The Advocate-General took the view that the transfer of even an isolated activity limited as to time could fall within the Directive so long as there was an "organisational underpinning". This would be shown by "a certain autonomy of organisation in the sense that in carrying on that activity one or more workers together possibly with materials have been assigned thereto, though that factor does not necessarily constitute a decisive criterion in that connection".

However the ECJ did not take such a broad view, holding that its previous case law had presupposed the existence of "a stable economic entity" whose activity was not limited to the performance of one specific works contract. In this case the assets transferred were strictly related to the completion

---

23 *Ledernes Hovedorganisation, acting for Rygaard v Dansk Arbejdsgiverforening, acting for Stro Molle Akustik A/S* (Case C-48/94) [1996] IRLR 51

of the works in question, and therefore there was no transfer of an undertaking.

The requirement that the undertaking transferred be a stable economic entity underlines the need for a degree of permanence in its activities. The facts of the *Rygaard* case are unusual and not to be found in any of the other cases considered. It is unlikely to have held any relevance to local government activities subject to CCT under the terms of the LGA 1988 because those were subject to specified minimum contract periods. That would have provided the necessary degree of permanence. *Rygaard* might possibly have been relevant to CCT of construction and maintenance work under the LGPLA 1980 where there were no such minimum contract periods.

Nevertheless Rygaard did mark the turning of the tide. The ECJ was beginning to rein back the scope given to the Directive. This was carried further by the Court's judgement in the Suzen case.

The *Suzen*[24] case was concerned with the change of cleaning contractors at a school following a competitive tender. The plaintiff worked for the outgoing contractor and was not offered reemployment with the new contractor. One of the questions referred to the ECJ was whether there could be a transfer of an undertaking even though no tangible or intangible assets had been transferred. The circumstances were similar to those in Schmidt, but although the Court did not depart from its earlier decision, it did put it into a more restrictive context.

The Advocate-General's Opinion argued that the concept of a transfer of an undertaking should be better defined. He noted that the general criteria established by the Court in the Spijkers judgement could be applied broadly as they were in Schmidt to bring the circumstances of the present case within the scope of the Directive, but expressed unease because this course ignored the competitive circumstances surrounding the transaction.

> "I fail to see how there can be any justification for the transferee of the service being required to keep on such staff of the undertaking as provided services of that kind in the past, if it has been excluded or, in any event, whose tender, submitted on that occasion, has been unsuccessful."

While the Spijkers approach allowed for a suitable degree of flexibility in applying the relevant criteria to the different circumstances of particular transactions, it was now necessary to identify the essential content of a transfer of an undertaking. This case was symbolic of this necessity: it was one thing to terminate a contract with an undertaking and subsequently award it to another undertaking; it was quite another to effect a transfer. The Advocate-General suggested that at the very least a transfer of an undertaking must involve the actual transfer of tangible or intangible assets. This must apply even in the services sector where the presence of such assets might be minimal.

---

24 *Suzen v Zehnacker Gebaudereinigung Gmbh Krankenhausservice* (Case C-13/95) [1997] IRLR 255.

The ECJ did not go as far as this, but its judgement did strongly reaffirm Spijkers and redirect the emphasis away from the broad brush "similar activities" test apparent in Schmidt, towards a more detailed evaluation of the transaction in terms of all the criteria mentioned in that case.

It held that there was no transfer of an undertaking on a change of contractor unless there was also a concomitant transfer of significant tangible or intangible assets or the taking over by the new employer of a major part of the workforce (in terms of numbers or skills) assigned by the previous employer to the performance of the contract.

For the Directive to be applicable the transfer had to relate to a stable economic entity whose activity was not limited to one specific contract. The term "entity" is used to encompass an organised grouping of persons and assets facilitating the exercise of an economic activity that pursues a specific objective.

In order to determine whether there had been a transfer of a stable economic entity, it was necessary to consider all the facts characterising the transaction, including those outlined by the Court in the Spijkers decision. Each of those relevant facts is merely a single factor in the overall assessment that must be made and cannot be considered in isolation. The Court restrained some of the wider interpretations put on the Schmidt decision by clearly stating that the mere fact that the service provided by the old contractor and the new is similar does not by itself mean that an entity or undertaking has been transferred. An entity, it said, cannot be reduced to the activity that has been entrusted to it.

However (and this is where Schmidt is reaffirmed) the absence of a transfer of assets does not necessarily preclude the existence of a transfer. Where an economic entity can function without significant tangible or intangible assets, the maintenance of its identity cannot logically depend on their transfer. Therefore where an activity is labour intensive a group of workers engaged in a joint activity on a permanent basis may constitute an economic entity. This entity may retain its identity after it has been transferred where the new employer continues to carry out the same or similar activities and takes over the major part, in terms of numbers and skills, of the employees assigned by his predecessor to that work.

6.2.2 The British Case Law

The early British cases on TUPE were influenced by the existing case law on continuity of employment, which emphasised the need for a change of ownership on the transfer of a business or undertaking.[25] The correct approach is of course to look for a change of employer. More important from the local

---

[25] See for example *R Seligman Corpn. v Baker* [1983] ICR 770. A hairdressing concession in a department store was transferred from A to B with fixtures and fittings but without goodwill. The last point was crucial in the EAT deciding that there had not been a relevant transfer. A different conclusion is more probable now.

authority perspective was the exclusion of undertakings that were not in the nature of a commercial venture. This exclusion was generally considered to exclude public sector bodies from the scope of TUPE.

In *Woodcock*[26] the Court of Appeal considered the meaning of the phrase in relation to a school with charitable status. The school received income in the form of fees and rents and aimed to break even over the short term. May LJ said that the meaning of the words "not in the nature of a commercial venture" was very much a matter of first impression and impossible to define exhaustively. However, the dictionary definition of "commercial" included the phrase "interested in financial return rather than artistry" which provided a useful pointer. The decision was that it was a non-commercial venture.

With the implementation of CCT under the LGA 1988, some commentators argued that local authority DSOs were now commercial ventures because of the new requirements imposed on them. They had to win work in open competition, achieve financial rates of return, and local authorities were forbidden to take account of non-commercial considerations in relation to contracts and tender evaluations.[27] However the prevailing case law suggested that while public sector bodies might be able to contract out certain activities as a relevant transfer of a commercial undertaking, everything would depend on how the contracted work was packaged.

In *Hadden*[28] the EAT gave some indication of how this could be done. The case involved a Student Association that wanted to contract out its catering services operation. The EAT said that if the contractor employed its own staff and controlled the prices, that arrangement could amount to a relevant transfer of a commercial undertaking. On the other hand, if the contractor merely provided the management and was remunerated on a fixed fee and/or percentage basis, without overall control, that would not qualify. In the later case of *Stirling*[29] the EAT drew a similar distinction between running an undertaking and taking over a contract for services. There was not a commercial venture within the meaning of TUPE in circumstances where a contractor took over a contract for the provision of specified services in return for recovery of expenses and a fixed fee. The effect of this was that TUPE remained inapplicable to most cases of local authority contracts under CCT.

The position in the UK changed because of three factors. One was that section 33 of TURERA 1993 amended TUPE, removing the "not in the nature of a commercial venture" restriction and clarifying the definition of a relevant transfer to make it clear that changes of ownership were not necessary. Another was the House of Lords decision in *Litster*,[30] which required

---

26 *Woodcock v Committee for the time being of the Friends School, Wigton* [1987] IRLR 98.
27 Stephen Cirell and John Bennett Solicitors Journal Volume 134 No.17 469 (27 April 1990).
28 *Hadden v University of Dundee Students' Association* [1985] IRLR 449.
29 *Stirling v Dietsmann Management Systems Ltd.* [1991] IRLR 368.
30 *Litster v Forth Dry Dock & Engineering Co. Ltd.* [1990] AC 546; [1989] 2 WLR 634; [1989] ICR 341.

the courts to give a purposive construction to TUPE in accordance with decisions of the ECJ. The third was the judicial activism of the ECJ. The influence of the *Redmond Stichting* and *Rask* decisions was felt from 1993 onwards. In a series of cases, the courts absorbed the purposive interpretation approach of the ECJ and in many respects applied it more radically.

The leading case that marked the change was *Dines*.[31] The case concerned a hospital cleaning contract that was switched after competitive tendering from the Initial Health Care Services Ltd to Pall Mall Services Group Ltd. The new contractors provided their own management, equipment and supplies, but re-engaged the majority of the former contractor's staff. The appellants were all former employees of Initial who had been dismissed on grounds of redundancy and started employment the next day with Pall Mall on lower pay. They brought proceedings against Initial for unfair dismissal. The industrial tribunal rejected their claims because there had not been a transfer of an undertaking:

> "...when one company enters into competition with a number of other companies to obtain a contract as happened in this case and a different company wins the contract from the company that was previously providing the services then this is a cessation of the business of the first contractors on the hospital premises and the commencement of a new business by the second respondents when they are awarded the contract."

The EAT held that the tribunal had not erred in law in reaching its conclusion. The European cases showed that it had to look for first an identifiable economic unit and second a transfer of that unit. Reaching a conclusion to both questions was always more difficult in cases involving three parties as here. The fact that the same activity was being carried out by the same employees at the same place of work was not sufficient in itself to constitute a transfer. The similarity had to be attributable to a transfer. This was essentially a question of fact and in this case the tribunal had considered and weighed a number of factors and could properly reach the conclusion it did.

The case went to the Court of Appeal, which reversed the earlier decision and held that the tribunal had misdirected itself in law. The decision was given by Neill LJ who said the European cases demonstrated that when another company took over the provision of certain services as a result of competitive tendering, this did not necessarily mean that the first business or undertaking came to an end. On this point therefore (see passage quoted above) the Court of Appeal held that the industrial tribunal had misdirected itself in law. As a matter of European law, this finding was not strictly true as the Rask and Schmidt decisions were concerned not with a change of contractors but with the contracting out of operations previously carried out in-

---

31 *Dines v Initial Healthcare Services Ltd. and Pall Mall Services Group Ltd.* [1993] ICR 978 [1993] IRLR 521 EAT; [1995] ICR 11 [1995] IRLR 336 CA. Also of interest are *Kenny v South Manchester College* [1993] ICR 934, [1993] IRLR 265; and *Wren v Eastbourne BC* [1993] ICR 955, [1993] IRLR 425.

house. Nevertheless the finding would accord with the purposive approach of the ECJ, and doubtless the Court of Appeal felt that this was how the ECJ would have applied the law in the same situation. The Court of Appeal also found that a transfer could take place in two phases, as in the case of Daddy's Dance Hall.

Normally a case such as this would be remitted to the industrial tribunal to be decided on its particular facts. However in this case the Court of Appeal decided that the facts were sufficiently clear and undisputed for it to resolve the case by itself. It found that there had indeed been a transfer of an undertaking because the cleaning services were being carried out by mainly the same staff on the same premises for the same authority. This was in stark contrast to the view of the EAT on the same point. The difference may be explained by the fact that the Court of Appeal had had the benefit of the decision of the ECJ in Schmidt, which was generally seen as widening the applicability of the Directive. This transfer took place in two stages, from the previous contractor back to the health authority, and the next day from the health authority to the new contractor.

This decision opened the way for a broad, purposive approach to the interpretation of TUPE and the Directive in subsequent cases such as *Kelman*.[32] A local authority organised the cleaning of school buildings through its DSO on the basis of area contracts. The applicant was a school cleaner. In 1992 the DSO lost the contract for the area in which the applicant worked to an outside contractor. Under the new arrangements the contractor recruited 60% of its staff from the existing council cleaning staff, replaced the council's equipment and materials with its own, and made significant changes to working patterns. The council retained a large measure of overall control under the terms of its contract. The applicant declined an offer of employment (on lower pay) with the contractor and was dismissed for redundancy by the council. The industrial tribunal, before the outcome of the Schmidt and the Dines cases was known, decided there had been no transfer of an undertaking, but the EAT hearing the case after those decisions found otherwise. The European cases showed that the crucial test was whether an undertaking had retained its identity in the hands of the new employer. The emphasis was on comparing the actual activities and employment situation in an undertaking before and after an alleged transfer. The transfer of assets was not essential.

> "The theme running through all the recent cases is the necessity of viewing the situation from an employment perspective, not from a perspective conditioned by principles of property, company or insolvency law. The crucial question is whether, taking a realistic view of the activities in which the employees are employed, there exists an economic entity, which despite changes remains identifiable although not identical after the alleged transfer. Although concepts of identity, change and continuity may pose difficult phi-

---

32 *Kelman v Care Contract Services* [1995] ICR 260.

losophical problems, the law, adopting a pragmatic approach, is well able to grapple with the notion that even important changes in constituent parts or attributes may not affect the persistence of identity of an economic entity. If, despite the changes resulting from the alleged transfer, jobs are still there to be done, though for a different employer, the Directive and the Regulations may apply."

Other decisions in a similar vein were *Council of the Isles of Scilly v Brintel Helicopters*[33] (where the council resumed the in-house provision of services, taking over employees from the previous contractor; so called "contracting in") and *BSG Property Services v Tuck*.[34] That case concerned the contracting out of council housing maintenance services, and was decided after the ECJ had given its decision in Rygaard. The EAT held that the continuing and recurrent maintenance work carried out in that case, satisfied the Rygaard requirement that what was transferred be a stable economic entity.

If *Schmidt* represented the high water mark for the Directive in the ECJ, the High Court decision in *Betts*[35] was its equivalent in the UK. The transferor operated helicopter services, transporting men and equipment to North Sea oil installations for Shell UK. In 1995, the transferor lost the contract for one of the North Sea sectors following competitive tendering to the transferees, who decided that they would operate from a different airport and without taking on any of the transferor's employees. Following the now well trodden purposive route, the High Court held that the same service was being performed before and after the alleged transfer in most of the core features. In particular, the service was being provided for the same person, to the same destinations, via similar routes, carrying the same sort of personnel and equipment and with the same mode of transport (helicopters, albeit with different aircraft, pilots and support staff). There was therefore an economic entity that had retained its identity. The fact that no employees were transferred did not negative this finding. The transferees had themselves decided not to take on any of the transferor's staff in order to reduce the chance of TUPE applying.

Before the case reached the Court of Appeal the ECJ had issued the *Suzen* decision. Giving the Court of Appeal's decision, Kennedy LJ said that *Suzen* represented a shift in emphasis or at least a clarification in the law and that as a result some of the reasoning of earlier decisions, if not the decisions themselves, might now have to be reconsidered. The proper approach was to consider all the circumstances of the transferor's operation and whether it amounted to an economic entity or undertaking; then to consider whether this had been transferred across to the transferee so that it retained its identity. In answering these questions the full width of the test propounded in

---

33 [1995] IRLR 6; [1995] ICR 249.
34 [1996] IRLR 134.
35 *Betts v Brintel Helicopters Ltd and KLM ERA Helicopters (UK) Ltd.* [1996] IRLR 45 [HC]; [1997] IRLR 361 [CA].

Spijkers was tending to be overlooked. There was a distinction between labour intensive undertakings such as those in *Dines* (and the other cleaning cases like *Schmidt* and *Kelman*) in which a court might safely conclude that the identity of an undertaking is retained where a service continues or is resumed with substantially the same staff, and other types of undertaking to which a more wide ranging inquiry was more appropriate. That was the case in *Betts*. The transferor's undertaking was found to consist of helicopters and infrastructure including the landing strip and buildings, pilots, maintenance and support staff, and the Shell UK contract together with the right under that to land on and use the facilities available on oil rigs. When defined in this manner it was clear that not enough had been transferred to say that the undertaking had retained its identity. Betts therefore marks the retreat from the high-water mark of TUPE in the UK, in the same way that the decision in Suzen is at European level.

6.2.3 The approach of the government to the applicability of TUPE

On 11 March 1993 the Chancellor of the Duchy of Lancaster issued general guidance on the relevance of TUPE to the market testing of public services. The scope of TUPE is considered over the course of paragraphs 2–9. The guidance is based closely on the criteria established by the ECJ in the Spijkers case, and while this may have begun to appear overly restrictive in the climate that followed the decision in Schmidt, the ECJ's more recent decisions in Rygaard and Suzen have restored its credibility. In particular, the 1993 guidance gives examples of circumstances that may or may not come under TUPE, and this is quoted below:

> "[8] Some circumstances in which the Regulations are likely to apply are as follows:
> – where the new employer employs substantially the same staff to do the same work as before, using the same premises and the same equipment for the work;
> – where the new employer is unable to do the work without keeping on a group of key employees who can be regarded as an essential asset;
> – where the new employer takes on substantially the same employees as recognisably the same organisational unit;
> – where the former employer makes it a condition of the contract, or there is an understanding between the parties, that the new employer will continue to use the same employees for the same work (it is the Government's policy that public sector organisations that invite tenders for the performance of public services should not impose such conditions except for reasons strictly related to the performance of the service in question);
> – where, whether or not any employees are taken on, the new employer takes over the management or control of premises, assets or equipment which:
>   (i) were used by the previous employer to carry out the activity in question;

(ii) are significant in relation to that activity; and,
(iii) are managed or controlled by the new employer for the purpose of carrying on that activity.

[9] In the Government's view the Regulations are unlikely to apply to instances of market testing:
- where the new employer conducts the operation substantially differently, without making significant use of previous staff, key employees, premises or equipment;
- where the identity of the previous undertaking is substantially changed and any staff taken on by the new employer are incorporated into a different organisational structure.'

However, the main thrust of the government's approach was to try and ensure that local authorities did not act in a manner that distorted, restricted or prevented competition in the tendering process. This important area has been considered in Chapter 5.

6.2.4 Summary

The scope of the Directive and TUPE remains wide even after cases such as Rygaard, Suzen and Betts. It is more likely than not to apply in contracting out situations. Specifically, its likely applicability in CCT situations is summarised below.

DSOs as economic entities

Most local authorities would have instituted internal reorganisations in order to implement a client–contractor split under CCT. Therefore, it is likely that a local authority operation would have had the organisational coherence to qualify as being an economic entity or undertaking for the purposes of TUPE. The requirements for minimum contract periods that existed under CCT strengthen the likelihood that these would have been stable economic entities.

Retention of identity after transfer

Local authority undertakings responsible for carrying out many defined activities were likely to consist of people and activities but minimal assets. This was likely in the case of building cleaning, management of sports and leisure facilities, housing management, vehicle management, construction and property services, legal services, financial services, personnel services and I.T services. The test for retention of identity would have been easier to satisfy in these cases (see *Dines* and *Betts*).

In the case of other defined activities, assets were more likely to constitute a significant part of the local authority undertaking and this would be brought into account in considering whether the undertaking had retained its identity after an alleged transfer (the wider ranging *Spijkers* inquiry referred to in *Betts*). In all cases the applicability of TUPE would have depended on the precise proposals behind any particular tender.

6.3 The Consequences of TUPE

This Part will consider the consequences where TUPE applies to a contracting out situation whether compulsory or voluntary competitive tendering is involved. Under CCT, in addition to the matters below, local authorities had to ensure that their conduct in relation to questions associated with TUPE was not anti-competitive. That issue is dealt with in Chapter 5.

6.3.1 Identifying employees covered by a TUPE transfer

The employees covered by the Directive and TUPE are those assigned to work in the undertaking or part of the undertaking that is transferred unless they object to being so transferred.

In *Botzen*[36] a company facing insolvency transferred to a new company, specifically formed for the purpose, certain of its departments, with the intention of saving as much of the business as possible. The plaintiffs worked in departments that had not been transferred, but their jobs did involve carrying out a variety of duties for the benefit of the transferred parts. The ECJ held (at paragraph 15) that the employment relationship on which the protections of the Directive were based, "is essentially characterised by the link existing between the employee and the part of the undertaking or business to which he is assigned to carry out his duties".

The ECJ mitigated the effects of imposing an automatic transfer of contracts by allowing individual employees a right to object to their own contracts being transferred. It did this in the case of *Katsikas*,[37] where it held that Article 3(1) did not oblige an employee to work for an employer that he had not freely chosen. The Court said that it had not intended to imply such an obligation in earlier cases such as *Daddy's Dance Hall* (see below), which would have undermined the employee's fundamental rights. However, the fate of the employee's contract with the transferor, in the event of such an objection, was a matter for the national law to determine.

In response to this decision, the government amended TUPE through the TURERA 1993 so that individual employees could object to their employment contracts being transferred by informing either the transferor or the transferee (amended Reg.5(1) and new Reg.5(4A)).[38] *Katsikas* left the fate of

---

36 Case No. C-186/83 [1985] ECR 519; [1986] 2 CMLR 50.
37 Case No. C-132/91 [1993] IRLR 179.
38 In *Senior Heat Treatment Ltd v Bell* [1997] IRLR 614 the respondent accepted a severance package with the transferor stating that he did not wish to transfer while on the same day signing a contract of employment with the transferee. The transferor became aware of this before the transfer took place. The EAT upheld the finding of the industrial tribunal that there had not been a valid objection for the purposes of Regulation 5(4A).

the employment contract with the transferor, to the laws of the Member States. This matter was settled by Regulation 5(4B) under which the transfer of the undertaking terminates the contract of employment, without the employee who notified the objection being treated as having been dismissed by the transferor. This has the effect of depriving the employee of any entitlement to a redundancy payment from the transferor.

To be covered by the Directive and TUPE, an employee must have been employed in the undertaking or part of the undertaking immediately before the transfer. This requirement has caused difficulties in cases where employees of the transferor have been dismissed shortly before the transfer. The leading authority in this area is the Court of Appeal decision in *Spence*.[39] That case involved dismissals taking effect at 11am, followed by a transfer of the business at 2pm the same day. The workforce was re-engaged by the transferee the next day, but eighteen employees sought redundancy payments from the Secretary of State (in lieu of the insolvent transferor) on the ground that they had not been employed immediately before the transfer. The Court of Appeal said that TUPE applied only to those employed by the transferor at the moment of the transfer. There was no room for a gap between dismissal and transfer.

Spence must be considered in the light of the House of Lords decision in *Litster*.[40] In that case the employees were dismissed one hour before the relevant transfer occurred. However, on the facts, the dismissals were clearly carried out to prevent the transferee bearing liabilities for the employees under the provisions of TUPE, so in effect taking advantage of the decision in *Spence*. The House of Lords held that regulations enacted to implement obligations under EC law should be interpreted so as to fulfil the purpose of that law. Consequently, Regulation 5(3) should be read as if, after the words "immediately before the transfer", there were inserted the words "or would have been so employed if he had not been unfairly dismissed in the circumstances described in Regulation 8(1)".

6.3.2   Consequences for individual contracts of employment

(i)   The transfer

Article 3 of the Directive provides that the transferors' rights and obligations arising from a contract of employment or from an employment relationship existing on the date of a transfer are, by reason of the transfer, transferred to the transferee. The ECJ has held in *Berg and Busschers v Besselsen*[41] that the transferor is discharged of his obligations by virtue of the transfer alone (unless a member state exercised its option under the Directive to legislate for joint liability, which the UK did not). There is no requirement for an employee to consent.

---

39   [1986] IRLR 248; [1986] ICR 651.
40   [1990] AC 546; [1989] 2 WLR 634; [1989] 1 All ER 1134; [1989] IRLR 161.
41   Case No. C-144 and 145/87 [1989] IRLR 447.

Regulation 5 of TUPE implements this by providing that a relevant transfer will not terminate a contract, which will instead remain in force as if made between the employee and his new employer, the transferee. Furthermore, anything done before the date of the transfer by the transferor regarding a contract or a person employed in the undertaking will be deemed after the transfer to have been done by or in relation to the transferee. A single exception is made for criminal liabilities, which are not transferred.

Effectively the completion of a transfer leaves the transferee standing in the transferor's shoes, responsible for any aspect of the employment contract or the employment relationship for which the transferor was responsible the moment before the transfer occurred. The significance of the transfer of the "employment relationship" is shown in the case of *DJM International Ltd v Nicholas*.[42] The respondent was dismissed by the transferor and subsequently re-employed on a part-time basis. After a relevant transfer under TUPE, the respondent was allowed to bring an action against the transferee for sex discrimination regarding her original dismissal. The EAT held that liability for a claim of sex discrimination was transferred to the transferee notwithstanding the fact that the contract to which the claim related had been terminated prior to the transfer. The claim related to something done before the transfer by the transferor in respect of a person employed in the undertaking

Therefore, the transferee must maintain existing terms and conditions of employment, make redundancy payments to staff dismissed by the transferor whose period of notice is current at the moment of the transfer, and assume liability for any outstanding grievances such as equal pay claims, arrears of wages, and claims for unfair dismissal. He will likewise have all the transferor's former rights under the contract to require performance by the employee, to negotiate changes to the contract or to make dismissals.

(ii) Variation of terms and conditions

The ECJ has held that the rights and obligations that switch from transferor to transferee at the time of the transfer, are of a mandatory nature and cannot be varied at the time, even by consent of the parties. This was established by the ECJ in the case of *Daddy's Dance Hall A/S*[43] in which the lease of a restaurant-bar was determined by the owners, who subsequently re-let the undertaking to the respondents. All the employees of the first leasee were dismissed but afterwards re-engaged by the respondents. One employee negotiated a different contract to that he had held before, waiving certain rights conferred by the Directive but being compensated in other ways so that overall he was in no worse a position. Nevertheless, the ECJ held that this was impermissible. The protections conferred in the Directive were a matter of public policy and as such outside the control of the parties to the contract.

The extent to which the transferee can introduce variations in the terms

---

42 [1996] IRLR 76.
43 Case No. C-324/86 [1988] IRLR 315.

and conditions of transferred employees is an area of legal uncertainty. The ECJ considered this question in Daddy's Dance Hall and also in *Rask*.[44] In the latter case it said:

> "[27] ...the Directive is intended to achieve only partial harmonisation, essentially extending the protection guaranteed to workers independently by the laws of the individual Member States to cover the case where an undertaking is transferred. It is not intended to establish a uniform level of protection throughout the Community on the basis of common criteria. Thus the Directive can be relied on only to ensure that the employee concerned is protected in his relations with the transferee to the same extent as he was in his relations with the transferor under the legal rules of the Member State concerned.
> [28] Consequently, insofar as national law allows the employment relationship to be altered in a manner unfavourable to employees in situations other than the transfer of an undertaking, in particular as regards their conditions of pay, such an alternative is not precluded merely because the undertaking has been transferred in the meantime and the agreement has therefore been made with the new employer. Since by virtue of Article 3(1) of the Directive the transferee has subrogated to the transferor's rights and obligations under the employment relationship, that relationship may be altered with regard to the transferee to the same extent as it could have been with regard to the transferor, provided that the transfer of the undertaking itself may never constitute the reason for that amendment..."

Therefore it would appear that the transferee is free to vary the terms and conditions of transferred employees by imposition or with consent, provided that the transfer of the undertaking itself is not the reason for the variation. This will be a question of fact for determination by the industrial tribunal.

If the transfer is the reason for the variation, then even a consensual variation will not be valid (per *Daddy's Dance Hall* and *Wilson v St Helens DC*).[45] In this situation an employee may choose to remain in the transferee's employment while seeking an appropriate remedy before an industrial tribunal or resign and use the unlawful variation as the basis of a claim for constructive dismissal.

6.3.3   Protection from dismissal by reason of a transfer

Article 4(1) of the Directive, provides that a transfer of an undertaking does not in itself constitute grounds for dismissal by the transferor or the transferee, but this does not prevent dismissals that take place for economic, technical or organisational reasons entailing changes in the workforce. This part of the Directive was implemented by Regulation 8 of TUPE, through a link with the unfair dismissal provisions in Part V of the Employment Protection

---

44   See footnote 18.
45   [1996] IRLR 320 EAT; [1997] IRLR 505 CA.

(Consolidation) Act 1978. These confer on an employee with two years of qualifying service the right not to be unfairly dismissed.[46] There are three stages to a claim for unfair dismissal which, if it is successful, will lead to an order for compensation, reinstatement or re-engagement:

- the employee must have been dismissed within the meaning of s.55 of the 1978 Act (which includes constructive dismissal at s.55(2));
- under s.57(1) the employer must show the reason for the dismissal, and then that the reason is potentially fair either because it falls under one of the grounds in s.57(2) (capability/qualifications, conduct, redundancy or illegality) or because it is some other substantial reason of a kind such as to justify the dismissal of an employee holding the position which that employee held;
- finally, having regard to the actual reason for dismissal, the employer must have acted reasonably in treating that reason as a sufficient reason for the dismissal.

Regulation 8(1) cuts through these stages, deeming a dismissal by reason of a transfer to be automatically unfair:

> "Where either before or after a relevant transfer, any employee of the transferor or transferee is dismissed, that employee shall be treated *for the purposes of Part V of the 1978 Act* ... as unfairly dismissed if the transfer or a reason connected with it is the reason or principal reason for his dismissal."[47]

The employer is provided with a defence under Regulation 8(2) where "an economic, technical or organisational reason entailing changes in the workforce of either the transferor or the transferee before or after a relevant transfer is the reason or principal reason for dismissing an employee...". If this is made out, the dismissal is deemed to be for some other substantial reason of a kind such as to justify dismissal. In that case it will still be necessary for the employer to show that the dismissal was reasonable in all the circumstances.

The first issue raised by these provisions is whether the transfer or a reason connected with it is the reason or principal reason for any particular dismissal. In *P Bork* the ECJ said that account should be taken of the objective circumstances in which the dismissal occurred, including the proximity of the dismissal to the transfer and whether the workers concerned were re-engaged

---

[46] Section 54 confers the right not to be unfairly dismissed and section 64 imposes the qualification of 2 years service.

[47] The words "for the purposes of Part V of the 1978 Act" are an economical reference to the fact that there is a right to compensation, reinstatement or re-engagement awarded on the footing that the employee concerned has been dismissed and that the dismissal is to be *treated* as unfair, so that there is no need to consider the detailed requirements of s.57 (per EAT in *Milligan v Securicor Ltd.* [1995] IRLR 288).

by the transferee. This is a question of fact for an industrial tribunal, and something that may be difficult to determine in circumstances where employees are dismissed for economic, technical or organisational reasons (etc) on the occasion of the transfer.

The words "economic, technical or organisational reason" are copied straight from the Directive. Being an exception to the general thrust of Regulation 8(1) they will probably be construed narrowly. The Government's guidance of March 1993 gives the following reasons as examples:

- unprofitability (economic reason).
- introduction of new technology (technical reason).
- relocation of operations (organisational reason).

An economic, technical or organisational reason must also entail changes in the workforce. The Court of Appeal considered the meaning of this requirement in *Berriman*.[48] The transferees had sought to standardise the terms and conditions of employees transferred under TUPE with those of their existing workforce. The respondent resigned and brought an action for constructive dismissal against the transferee. The transferee claimed that it had a defence under Regulation 8(2) because the dismissal was occasioned by an organisational reason. The Court rejected this argument. While the imposition of standard terms might lead to the dismissal of employees who did not fall into line and their replacement by others, this was not enough to constitute a change in the workforce. Changes in the identity of individuals within the workforce did not constitute changes in the workforce itself so long as the overall numbers and functions of the employees as a whole remained unchanged. The word "workforce" connoted the whole body of employees as in "entailing changes in the strength of the workforce".

A related issue that has been the subject of dispute, concerns the correct implementation of Article 4(2). This allows member states to exclude from the protection of Article 4(1) "certain specific categories of employees who are not covered by the laws or practice of the Member States in respect of protection against dismissal". In the UK persons without 2 years of qualifying service are excluded from protection against unfair dismissal under Part V of the 1978 Act. In *Milligan*[49] the EAT ruled that this exclusion was unlawful under the Directive. The effect of the ruling was swiftly reversed by new secondary legislation.[50] The Court of Appeal has since confirmed that the 2-year qualifying service requirement is lawful under the terms of the Directive.[51]

---

48   *Delaboe Slate Ltd. v Berriman* [1985] IRLR 305.
49   *Milligan v Securicor Cleaning Ltd.* [1995] IRLR 288.
50   Regulation 8 of the Collective Redundancies and Transfer of Undertakings (Protection of Employment) (Amendment) Regulations 1995 S.I 1995 No. 2587.
51   *R v Secretary of State for Trade & Industry ex p. UNISON* [1996] IRLR 438.

6.3.4 Consequences for collective agreements and trade union recognition

Regulation 6 ensures that the transferor's rights and obligations under collective agreements are transferred under a relevant transfer to the transferee. This provision is without prejudice to the general rule that collective agreements are unenforceable unless specified by agreement of the parties to be legally binding.[52] In a similar way Regulation 9 ensures that trade union recognition agreements will cross over to bind the transferee where the undertaking or part of the undertaking transferred retains an identity distinct from the remainder of the transferee's undertaking. In the case of collective agreements and/or trade union recognition agreements, the transferee will have the same rights enjoyed by the transferor to vary or rescind the agreements.

In cases where the terms of a collective agreement have been incorporated into individual contracts of employment, those terms are not affected by any abrogation of the collective agreement on the part of the transferee. In the case of *Whent*,[53] the appellants' contracts of employment with Brent LBC contained a clause linking various terms of their employment including rates of remuneration, holiday and sickness payments to agreements made from time to time by a National Joint Council (NJC) of local authorities. The appellants carried out street lighting maintenance work for the council until 1994 when the work was contracted out to the respondents. They withdrew from the NJC agreement. The EAT held that the appellants were still entitled to increases in pay in accordance with the subsequent NJC agreements because the relevant link in their individual contracts had not been severed by the transferee's abrogation of the NJC agreement alone. Regulation 5 meant that the transferee would continue to be bound until the contract itself was varied or terminated.

6.3.5 Consequences for occupational pensions

The rights that employees earn under occupational pension schemes are a form of deferred pay, accrued throughout employment with the transferor up to the moment of the transfer. They are generally more favourable in the public sector because of the advantages that the superior credit of public bodies can command. The Local Government Superannuation Scheme is a case in point, offering employees more generous terms on, for example, index linking, partly because it can take advantage of profitable tax breaks offered to local government and charitable bodies on US investments, an advantage denied to commercial organisations. However this aspect of employee remuneration is less well protected because Article 3(3) of the Directive excluded employees' rights to certain benefits under these schemes from the general transfer of rights and obligations. This was implemented as TUPE Regulation

---

[52] s.179 of the Trade Union and Labour Relations (Consolidation) Act 1992.
[53] *Whent v T Cartledge Ltd.* [1997] IRLR 15.

7, which excludes from the general transfer, so much of a contract of employment or collective agreement (or anything arising from either) as relates to old age, invalidity and survivors benefits within occupational pensions schemes. Other rights that may be provided under occupational pension schemes can be transferred where they do not relate to old age, invalidity or survivors' benefits. Examples of such benefits are the payment of lump sums on redundancy or early retirement.

The effect of Regulation 7 is that rights and obligations in respect of the pension scheme are lifted from the transferor but are not transferred over to the transferee. In order to protect already accrued pension rights, the second limb of Article 3(3) requires the member states to adopt the measures necessary to protect the interests of employees and ex-employees of the transferor in respect of rights conferring immediate or prospective entitlement to benefits under occupational pension schemes. In the UK this protection is conferred by the social security legislation rather than by TUPE. Under this "early leavers" of pension schemes are protected by the conferment of entitlement to a deferred pension.

This arrangement was considered inadequate by the industrial tribunal in *Perry*.[54] The tribunal held that TUPE did not correctly implement the Directive. A transferred employee could lose out on the enhancement of benefits already accrued and chance of receiving future benefits as well, thereby leaving a gap in the protection of employee rights to deferred pay existing at the time of the transfer. The tribunal suggested that additional words should be read into Regulation 7 so that any contract of employment transferred across would be deemed to contain comparable pensions rights to those the employee enjoyed before. However this approach was rejected by the EAT in *Walden Engineering Co. Ltd. v Warrener*[55] and by both the High Court and the Court of Appeal in *Adams*.[56] Both cases make it clear that the requirement imposed in Article 3(3) is in respect of pension rights accrued up to the time of the transfer.

On this reading of Article 3(3) of the Directive and Regulation 7 of TUPE there is no reason why a transferred employee should be entitled as against the transferee to a comparable pension to that enjoyed previously through the transferor. As Morritt LJ said in *Adams*, since an employer is not obliged to establish a pension scheme for the benefit of his existing workers, there is no good reason to suppose that the Directive ever intended a transferee to be subjected to such an obligation in respect of transferred workers. That would discriminate between employees simply on the basis of the identity of their previous employer.

However the exclusion of pensions rights from the transfer-over provisions of TUPE may be affected by the preservation of an employee's right to resign

---

54 *Perry v Intec Colleges Ltd.* [1993] IRLR 56 [I.T].
55 *Walden Engineering Co Ltd v Warrener* [1993] IRLR 420.
56 *Adams v Lancashire County Council and BET Catering Services Ltd.* [1996] IRLR 154 [HC]; [1997] IRLR 436 [CA].

and claim constructive dismissal under TUPE Regulation 5(4). Because in the public sector pensions are generally more favourable to employees than those in the private sector, the contracting out of work is likely to leave employees with less favourable pension provision than before. Therefore the probable effect of Regulation 7 is to leave the transferor exposed to claims for constructive dismissal from employees whose contracts have been transferred in circumstances where the transferee has not provided a broadly comparable pensions package. In such a situation, an employee may be able to establish that this constituted a substantial and detrimental change in working conditions.

This is the view taken by the government, as expressed in The Government's Guide to Market Testing 1993 at p.26:

> "5.18 ... If pension rights overall in the new employment are to be worse there may be grounds for claims of constructive dismissal against the department or agency. To avoid the risk of this, pensions in the new employment should be broadly comparable to the PCSPS (government scheme) or the employee should be compensated."

This advice is equally applicable to the local government CCT situation, a point confirmed in a DOE letter to local authorities on TUPE, dated 15 March 1995. (This was primarily concerned with the handling of pension matters in the tendering process so as to avoid charges of anti-competitive conduct)

6.3.6   Rights to information and consultation

Regulation 10 imposes on the transferor and the transferee, duties to inform and to consult either elected representatives of the employees or representatives of a recognised trade union where there is to be a relevant transfer. This provision has had a chequered history (see 6.1) and the current wording was introduced through the Collective Redundancies and Transfer of Undertakings (Protection of Employment) (Amendment) Regulations 1995.[57] It is not specified how representatives of employees are to be elected. This is left for individual workplaces to determine.[58] The representatives of employees are also conferred the same protections and privileges already enjoyed by trade union representatives, such as protection against dismissal and time off with pay to perform their functions.

The employees who are relevant to these duties are known as "affected employees". This term is widely defined as any employees of the transferor or the transferee (whether or not employed in the undertaking or part of the undertaking to be transferred) who may be affected by the transfer or measures taken in connection with it.

---

57   S.I. No.2587/95. see Reg. 8-14.
58   *R v Secretary of State for Trade & Industry ex p. UNISON* [1996] IRLR 438.

The duty to inform must be discharged "long enough before a relevant transfer to enable consultations to take place". The information that is to be divulged covers a range of matters: the details of the transfer; its legal, economic and social implications for affected employees; and, any measures to be taken in relation to those employees. Where the information to be divulged is not factual, but is based on appraisal or judgement, the duty is only to communicate the results of the employer's deliberations, not the information, calculations or assumptions behind it. Therefore intended steps to reduce staffing numbers in line with manpower projections, should be divulged, but not necessarily the manpower projections on which those steps were based.[59]

The requirement to consult is narrower, arising wherever measures are to be taken in relation to affected employees. The nature of the consultation is expressly defined. The employer must consider and reply to any representations made, giving reasons for rejecting any of them. Consultations must be entered into "with a view to seeking agreement".

6.3.7 Provision for sanctions

Regulation 11 provides for the imposition of sanctions on employers in breach of their duties to inform and consult under Regulation 10. Like that provision, this one has had a chequered history. Complaints must be brought before an industrial tribunal within 3 months. The tribunal is empowered to award "appropriate compensation". As originally enacted, there was a financial ceiling on compensation of up to 2 weeks pay per employee. Also, in situations where an employee received damages for breach of contract or a protective award (made in relation to an employer's failure to comply with the statutory requirements for consultations over proposed redundancies)[60] this amount had to be set off against any compensation received under TUPE. The EC Commission considered the level of these sanctions to be ineffective and contested them (successfully) in *Commission v UK*. Before the ECJ had given judgement, the government amended Regulation 11 through the TURERA 1993. The setting off rules were abolished and the financial ceiling on compensation doubled to four weeks pay per employee.

6.3.8 Anti-competitive conduct in handling TUPE

The Conservative government was particularly concerned that TUPE (and its handling by local authorities) might deter private contractors from bidding. As it became increasingly clear that TUPE would indeed apply to local

---

59 *Institution of Professional Civil Servants v Secretary of State for Defence* [1987] 3 CMLR 35; [1987] IRLR 373; (concerned the Dockyard Services Act 1986 which applied TUPE with a modified Reg.10 to the transfer of dockyard undertakings).

60 Now contained in the Trade Union and Labour Relations (Consolidation) Act 1992.

authority transfer of undertakings, the government again resorted to that all-purpose workhorse of CCT enforcement, the prohibition of anti-competitive conduct. Guidance on TUPE first appeared in DOE Circular 10/93 and has been present in all its successors. The DOE has also separately released Issues Papers in relation to the handling of TUPE in the tendering process[61] and in relation to pensions matters.[62] The principal points of DOE guidance on the avoidance of anti-competitive conduct in handling TUPE matters were as follows:

(i) the applicability of TUPE was not to be pre-judged by an authority. It was required to wait and examine the particular circumstances of each tender. However authorities were allowed to refer potential contractors to the regulations and state a preliminary view of their likely applicability.

(ii) where the authority and a contractor disagreed over whether TUPE applied to a particular tender submitted, every effort was expected to be made to reach a mutual agreement. Other tenderers had to be given an equal opportunity to revise their own tenders. If the disagreement could not be resolved, then the authority was permitted to reject the tender on that ground but it had to be able to clearly demonstrate its reasons for doing so.

(iii) an authority could ask contractors for a reasonable indemnity against the following contingency: a contract, entered into on the basis that there was no transfer of an undertaking, being at some later date found to be subject to TUPE. The indemnity would be in relation to claims based on a failure to consult affected employees.

(iv) a contractor could likewise ask an authority to provide an indemnity against the same contingency. The authority was permitted to treat such an indemnity as a prospective cost in any financial evaluation of tenders under the 1993 Competition Regulations.[63]

(v) an authority was required to make available to all of the contractors that it invited to tender enough information about the existing workforce to enable them to establish the cost of a TUPE-based tender, should they choose to submit one. The DOE listed the sorts of information that it expected authorities to disclose. It stated its view that this did not involve information of a personal nature that it would, if held on a computer database, be prevented from disclosing by the Data Protection Act 1984. The information that should be disclosed included the principal terms of employment (including pensions arrangements), collective agreements, the number of staff who would transfer and in relation to each their age, sex, salary, hours, regular overtime, redundancy entitlement and any outstanding claims for industrial injury etc. The disclosure of this infor-

---

61 January 1994.
62 15 March 1995.
63 S.I. 1993 No. 848.

mation was without prejudice to a contractor's freedom to submit a tender on the basis that TUPE did not apply (or indeed to hedge its bets and submit two tenders, one based on TUPE and the other, not).

(vi) where it was agreed that TUPE applied to any tender, prospective redundancy costs were not be brought into account in any financial evaluation of that tender.

6.4 Summary

The Acquired Rights Directive and TUPE have had significant implications for the conduct of the CCT process and the contracting out of local government functions in general. The activism of the ECJ, combined with the willingness of the UK courts to follow its lead, have been important factors behind this. The uncertainty engendered by the phenomenon of developing case law has also had a significant effect in practice. However the Directive and TUPE were never, as has sometimes been believed, a deadly threat to contracting out or to CCT itself, because market competition is not exclusively based on labour costs and conditions.

PART THREE

CASE STUDIES

Chapter 7
Resbrough Borough Council

Chapter 8
Greenbrough Borough Council

CHAPTER SEVEN

A CASE STUDY: RESBROUGH BOROUGH COUNCIL

CONTENTS

7.1 Local Authority Profile
7.2 The Results of CCT
7.3 Management of Service Provision under CCT
7.4 Case Studies of CCT Tenders
7.5 Summary and Conclusions

This Chapter presents the results of case study research into a single local authority. Unless otherwise indicated, the presentation reflects the law and events up to May 1997. In the interests of confidentiality, the authority has been identified throughout by the pseudonym of Resbrough. The research methodology is outlined in Appendix 1 of this book.

7.1   Local Authority Profile

Resbrough is a small English local authority covering an area of 3,411 hectares and a population of 70,000. It is located on the edge of a metropolis. The area is predominantly residential consisting of some 27,000 properties of which 75% are detached or semi-detached houses, the remainder being divided evenly between terraced houses and flats. The level of home ownership is high at 80% with council-owned housing and privately rented accommodation at about 10% each.[1] As would be expected, many residents commute to work in the city but the local area does host a significant business presence. This consists chiefly of professional services and retailing firms (indeed the town holds the headquarters of some notable companies). There is no significant manufacturing industry. Levels of unemployment are low in national terms, standing at 4.4% but are still higher than the average for the local county area, which is 3.9% (according to February 1996 figures). This is partly because the area has been relatively slow to recover from the 1990/91 recession. Nevertheless this is an affluent part of the country.

The local authority has the functions of a non-metropolitan or shire district council. It therefore operates as the lower tier of a two-tier system of local government for its area, the upper tier being the county council. Its specific functions include local planning, building regulations, housing, highways (maintenance of certain urban roads and off-street car parks), environmental health, refuse collection, cemeteries and crematoria. It carries out other functions concurrently with the county council such as recreation (parks, playing

---

1   1993 figures

fields, swimming pools), museums, and the encouragement of the arts, tourism and industry.

Although the Parliamentary seat is a Conservative stronghold, the area has a longstanding non-political tradition in its local government. A network of resident's associations controls the council, each sponsoring its own candidates in elections. A Standing Committee of Resident's Associations coordinates the concerns of the associations, and their councillors in relation to the business of the council itself. The independent resident's association group enjoys a massive majority on the council against small Liberal Democrat and Labour opposition groups. The non-political tag given to this group is probably justified. While it is true that the Conservatives do not run against them, the fact that two-thirds of households are members of resident's associations would indicate a broad movement and appeal. In most of the wards, the resident's association is the only forum for local political activity. It is notable that this form of local representation has retained majority support while the neighbouring local authorities have fallen to the mainstream party political machines.

7.2 The Results of CCT

This Part of the Chapter will consider the outcome of CCT for direct service provision in all areas and the resulting balance between direct and contracted service provision.

7.2.1 Record of voluntary contracting out

The voluntary efforts of local authorities to contract out the provision of services before the advent of compulsion have been tracked in other published sources.[2] Resbrough was not among the few authorities that enthusiastically engaged in this form of "privatisation". Contractors were used to supplement in-house provision where the workload was too large or there were skills shortages, but this remained marginal. So when the Local Government Bill was passing through Parliament in 1987–88, most construction and maintenance work (already covered by the CCT provisions of the LGPLA 1980) and almost all of the new proposed defined activities were still being provided by direct labour. The services covered by the new Act alone, cost the council 20% of its annual gross revenue expenditure and directly employed a third of the staff overall and three quarters of the manual workers.

If Resbrough had shown no political enthusiasm for the principle of contracting out, there existed other circumstances that might have gradually pushed it in that direction. Being a small local authority, it is especially vulnerable to financial pressures, in part because of the limited scope it has for

---

[2] K. Ascher "The Politics of Privatisation" (1988) and surveys published by the Local Government Chronicle 1982–87.

achieving economies of scale. Contracting out offers the potential for cost savings and greater flexibility. Essentially, the problem is that the workload for many of the council's services (an example would be electrical engineering support) can only support one or at most a handful of employees. This causes problems in relation to work skills (is the employee(s) able or willing to retrain to upgrade skills?) and sickness/holiday cover. In such a situation there is greater flexibility and backup in relying on the services of a contractor.

Nevertheless when considering these pressures from the standpoint of 1988, no observer would have envisaged them bringing about significant changes in the short to medium term. Compulsory competition would have significant implications for the levels and methods of in-house service provision.

7.2.2 The results of CCT: An overview

The LGPLA 1980, which came into force in relation to Resbrough in 1982, had a limited effect on the council's building maintenance and highway maintenance work in the following years. It has been the LGA 1988, including the amendments to its predecessor that has brought about far-reaching change. Under the 1988 Act, the council was required to implement CCT by dates specified by the Secretary of State in regulations. These are shown below in Table 1.

Table 1

Defined Activity	CCT to apply from...
Vehicle maintenance & repair	1 August 1989
Ground maintenance	1 January 1990
Refuse collection	1 January 1990
Street cleansing	1 August 1990
Building cleaning	1 January 1991
Other catering	1 August 1991

The council anticipated that the new Act would have significant implications for its existing arrangements for service delivery. It reacted by establishing a separate Direct Services Organisation (DSO) that would carry out most of the services covered by the legislation, and would prepare to make competitive bids to retain the right to carry on the work when the time came.

The DSO was successful in the first CCT tenders during 1989, although there were signs of trouble ahead. The award of the vehicle repair and maintenance contract was made conditional on a financial performance review, while the refuse collection contract was won only because council members overruled a recommendation by the chief officers that the contract should go to a lower priced private tender. After that the DSO hit a long losing streak. The vehicle maintenance and ground maintenance contracts were terminated early (in 1991 and 1992 respectively) because of financial losses, and the DSO failed to win either when they were retendered. The DSO also lost the CCT tenders for street cleansing (1990), building cleaning (1991) and building maintenance (1991). A further blow came in 1992 when an in-house bid failed to win leisure services management. This left the DSO in a parlous state by 1993, with responsibility for just refuse collection and highways maintenance.

The corner was turned in 1994. The retendering of the refuse collection contract that year was the decisive moment in the DSO's life. Loss would have meant closure. Losing was anticipated and so the council, on the advice of its external auditor, decided to offer the DSO for sale. Previous undertakings given to staff and the desire for a fall back position if the trade sale fell through, ensured that the DSO was allowed to submit a bid under CCT. The trade sale and CCT options were pursued in tandem. The trade sale option ultimately proved unsatisfactory, and in the CCT tender the DSO secured its future by the narrowest of margins, beating its closest rival tender by a few thousand pounds. In a strange twist to the tale, the DSO then went on to recapture the street cleansing contract shortly afterwards, so putting itself on a firm financial footing for the years ahead.

The extension of CCT into new areas and in particular into white-collar services has had less of an impact on the authority, largely because the dates for implementation of many of the activities have yet to be reached. In preparation for white-collar CCT a system of internal trading accounts was established. However there was no organisational change because of uncertainty over the eventual form of the new regime, and because few of the new activities were believed to be large enough to face a competition requirement. A CCT Steering Group oversaw the Council's preparations. The relevant dates for implementation are shown below in Table 2.

7.2.3 The results of CCT: Service by service

The outcome of CCT in each of the service areas is considered next.

Table 2

Defined activity	CCT to apply from...
Housing management	1 April 1996
Security work	1 April 1997
Vehicle management	1 April 1997
Parking management	1 April 1997
Legal services	1 October 1997
Construction and property services	1 October 1997
Financial services	[1 October 1998]
Personnel services	1 April 1998
Information technology services	1 April 1999

Building maintenance

Manual workers in the Borough Engineers Department carried out a number of low value building maintenance jobs on the council's own housing stock. When the 1980 Act came fully into operation in 1982 it had only a limited effect because the council was able to keep its work within the competition free allowances set out in regulations. The changes that did come were in the field of financial management. A separate trading account was established for building maintenance in order to comply with the accounting and required rates of return provisions of the Act. Schedules of rates were also introduced for the first time to further improve financial management. However the absence of serious competition meant that costs remained very high, with rates of return being achieved by charging high prices, not by improving productivity.

This problem was recognised by the council as it was preparing to implement the changes brought about by the LGA 1988 and the LGPLA Competition Regulations of 1989. In 1989, the council's building maintenance work was tendered on the basis of 10 trades, each with its own schedule of rates, against which approved contractors were invited to submit prices for individual jobs in each category. The result was a mix of in-house and contracted out provision. In 1991 the situation changed again. This time bids were invited on the basis of a single schedule of rates contract. The DSO lost. In 1994 with the voluntary transfer of the council's housing stock to a housing association (see below), the responsibility for building maintenance passed with the houses. The DSO has not tried since then to win works contracts from the housing association to do this work.

Highway maintenance

Staff from the Borough Engineer's Department carried out highway and winter maintenance work under an agency agreement for the local county council. Following the LGPLA 1980, the work was organised into a Highway DLO (still within the department) operating by a separate trading account. The DLO was believed to be high cost, although reliable measures of costs were not available. As a result of the 1988 Act the county council was expected to demand more competitive pricing. The DLO was absorbed in 1988 by the new DSO and has since then succeeded in retaining the right to carry out highways maintenance for the county council.

This is a small area of work but it has generally been a profitable one. The Highway DSO's greatest moment of danger was during 1994 when the council was considering the option of a trade sale of the DSO. There was then a serious danger that it would be shut down (because the council performed this work as an agent of the county council rather than "of right", it could not have been sold on), but with the rejection of this option it has successfully operated ever since.

Ground maintenance

The council decided to let a contract for 75% of its ground maintenance work from 1 April 1989, well in advance of the deadline. The DSO submitted the lowest priced bid and the Recreation Committee awarded it the contract. Unfortunately the DSO then proved less successful at running the contract than winning it. It ran into financial difficulties because of ageing equipment, which the council could not afford to replace. Proven unable to meet the required rate of return, the council decided to terminate the DSO's contract early and to invite tenders for a new contract beginning in 1993. The DSO was allowed to submit a bid but lost the work this time to a lower priced tender from a private firm.

Since then ground maintenance work has remained in the hands of an outside contractor. No firm decision has been made on whether the DSO will submit a bid for this work when the contract is let in 1998. If it were to submit a bid, limitations in the DSO's management capabilities and expertise mean that it could only bid for part of the available work. The decision would be contingent on the manner in which the next contract is packaged.

Vehicle repair and maintenance

This contract was first put out to tender early in 1989 to commence on the 1 April again in advance of the statutory timetable. Apart from the bid by its own DSO, bids were also received from the County Council DSO and a private contractor. The in-house bid was the lowest priced, although some concern was expressed as to its financial viability. In the end it was awarded the contract subject to continued financial monitoring of its performance and the prospect of early termination if it failed to break-even in the first year. The DSO sub-committee expressed concern about these terms, believing that a higher performance was being expected of the DSO than would have been the case for an outside contractor, because it was reasonable to expect a contract to run for some time before assessing its commercial success. The DSO did make a loss over 1989/90 which it was projected to repeat in 1990/91.

In January 1991 the Council terminated the contract and retendered vehicle repair and maintenance work as two 3-year contracts, one for heavy vehicles and the other for light vehicles. Financial pressures had forced the council to sell part of its depot site in 1990 in order to raise a capital receipt, and so the DSO only had the facilities to bid for the light vehicles contract. It did bid but without success. This time the County DSO succeeded, and was awarded both contracts commencing in October 1991.

When these contracts expired in 1994, the council considered an externalisation option: the trade sale of its transport fleet to the private sector on a sale and hire-back basis. At the same time the council was also considering a trade sale of the DSO itself, so this was a part of a serious externalisation prospectus. Unable to get a good deal from private firms, the council received an offer from the County DSO that was "so low it couldn't be rejected". The sale and hire-back went through and was considered a good deal. In contrast, the trade sale of the DSO was not followed through.

Refuse collection

Refuse collection was the council's flagship service; the one that was the most visible, and the one whose efficient running the members especially prized. Its fate under CCT has been the subject of controversy. On each occasion the contract was tendered, the DSO was ultimately successful. The issues surrounding these tenders are considered in case studies at 7.4.1 and 7.4.3 respectively.

Street cleansing

The scope of the street cleansing contract was broadened to include all non-highways related cleansing, apart from building cleaning, and "winter maintenance" (gritting roads and snow clearing, which fall under the LGPLA 1980 provisions). What was called the "borough cleansing" contract was to run for 4 years from 1 August 1990. Because the contract work crossed the responsibilities of more than one council committee, the final decision on awarding the contract was taken jointly by the Environmental Services Committee and the Policy and Resources Committees. Only two tenders were submitted, one the in-house tender and the other from the county council's DSO. The County DSO was the cheaper and was awarded the contract.

The contract ran smoothly. When the Environmental Protection Act 1990 brought about new standards for litter clearance, the necessary variations to the service specification were agreed between the parties. In preparation for the re-letting of the contract in 1995, the council prepared a new service specification to incorporate more output-based criteria. The incumbent contractor was however facing difficulties in relation to bidding to renew its contract. Since the passage of the Environmental Protection Act 1990, county councils had lost the right to undertake street cleansing work except through arms-length entities known as local authority waste disposal companies (LAWDC status, known as "LAWDAC's"). LAWDACs were authorised to carry out "waste related activities", which could include street cleansing operations as well as refuse collection. The County DSO had constituted itself on these lines but at the time had yet to achieve the approval of the Secretary of State to LAWDC status.

These legal uncertainties meant that the County DSO, the incumbent contractor, was not invited to tender. An in-house bid was made and despite six other private firms being invited to tender, it was the only one submitted. The DSO's success, following soon after the retention of the refuse collection contract, was a very significant boost to its future viability.

Building cleaning

In the first round of competition, building cleaning work was let as a single 4 year contract from 1 January 1991. Cleaning work carried out at the council-run leisure centre was excluded so that it could form a part of a separate contract. As had been the case with the borough cleansing, the work cut across the responsibilities of several committees, but in this case the final decision was to be taken on their behalf by the Policy and Resources Committee. The DSO lost to a cheaper tender by a private contractor.

When the contract became due for renewal at the beginning of 1995, the DSO decided not to bid. Building cleaning was considered a cut-throat low wage market where the DSO stood little chance of success. The incumbent contractor bid again but lost to a rival. The absence of an in-house bid allowed the contract manager more freedom outside the CCT rules to evaluate the quality of different contractors. The new contractor was considered to offer greater quality than its predecessor had.

Other catering

This work includes catering for staff at the Town Hall, and operating catering facilities at other council run locations. The value has remained de minimis for CCT purposes. While this has meant that it does not have to be subject to competition, the council must still comply with other requirements of CCT, such as the need to maintain a separate trading account. In fact much of this work is voluntarily contracted out.

Management of sports and leisure facilities

Resbrough owned and managed a leisure centre and a number of smaller facilities (tennis courts, cricket pitches and bowling lawns etc). The management of the leisure centre was let in 1992 under CCT. A private firm was awarded the contract. The evaluation process in this case was distinctive for the more structured consideration given to the quality of service offered (considered in the case study at 7.4.2). The smaller facilities were contracted out by the end of that year with no in-house bid. When the leisure centre contract was retendered in 1996, no in-house bid was submitted so CCT did not apply. A different firm was awarded the contract.

Housing management

During 1994 the council carried out with the approval of the Secretary of State a large scale voluntary transfer of its housing stock with sitting tenants to a local housing association. In accordance with the relevant provisions of the Housing Act 1985[3] the tenants were balloted before the transfer and a majority gave their approval.[4] The housing association owns the housing stock, not the council, and therefore it is now responsible for matters such as

---

3   s.106A and Schedule 3A; see also DOE Circular 6/88.
4   The Minister must withold consent to the transfer if the majority of the tenants are opposed to it.

housing management and maintenance, and a limited amount of ground maintenance and building cleaning at some of its properties. Because housing associations are not defined authorities under the 1988 Act, it is not subject to CCT in any of this.

The new blue-collar services

None of the new blue-collar activities face CCT. Vehicle fleet management was externalised by way of the sale and hire back arrangement of 1994 and so falls outside the CCT regime. The authority has not been given responsibilities for the supervision of parking by the Secretary of State. The value of security work undertaken is de minimis for the purposes of CCT.

Financial services

The council's competition requirement for financial services work was estimated at the beginning of 1997 at £320,000. In accordance with DOE guidance in Circular 5/96 the council formally consulted the market on contract packaging options in January 1997. Subject to clarification of CCT requirements by the new government, the council decided in July 1997 to prepare the following areas of work for CCT:

- administration, collection and recovery of Council Tax and the National Non-Domestic Rate;
- administration and payment of Housing Benefit and Council Tax Benefit.

The intention is to prepare these as three separate contract packages including associated I.T requirements, to be offered either separately or amalgamated as considered appropriate.

Other white-collar services

The remaining white-collar defined activities will be largely unaffected by CCT. The value of legal services work and personnel services work falls within the de minimis credit of the statutory formula. The competition requirement for construction and property services has been met by voluntary outsourcing. A marginal competition requirement for I.T services remains, which will be satisfied by further voluntary outsourcing if necessary.

7.2.4   State of contracted services in May 1997

In Table 3 shows the balance between the different forms of service provision at the time of the general election of May 1997. The implementation deadlines in respect of legal services, construction and property services, financial services, personnel services and IT services had not fallen due by that date.

This shows a picture of a mixed economy in local service provision. Of the 12 services to which CCT applied on that date, 5 were being performed in-house while 7 were being performed by outside organisations. Of those 7 services, Resbrough retained client-side responsibilities for the service in 3 cases, while in the remaining 4 the service provision was wholly externalised. This is considered below.

The level of in-house provision shown in Table 3 is firmly entrenched. Other catering and security work are both de minimis for CCT purposes and likely to remain so. The DSO has won contracts for the remaining services lasting at least until 2000. It appears to be well suited in terms of management and expertise to the work it holds and is in financial terms making a success of its contracts. Its position is secure, certainly for the next few years. In the longer term, what happens when its principal contracts expire in 2000–2001 will not be clear until the new government has fully worked out its approach to replacing CCT. This is also true for the de minimis services.

A careful distinction must be drawn for the remaining services between those that are contracted out but for which the local authority retains client-side responsibility, and those that are truly privatised or externalised.

The cleaning of buildings, the management of leisure facilities and ground maintenance services are all contracted out services. The council still owns the buildings, leisure facilities and parks (etc) but relies on private contractors to clean, manage and maintain them. It retains the client role of setting the service specification and managing the contract. Because the DSO has consolidated its operations into a position as a niche service provider, it is likely that these arrangements will be permanent. Indeed leisure management and building cleaning, after initial capture from in-house provision in first round CCT have both since been retendered with a consequent change of contractors without an in-house bid.

In contrast, the areas of housing management, building maintenance, vehicle fleet management and vehicle maintenance have been fully externalised or privatised. Complete responsibility has passed into the private or voluntary sector. The council contracts like any other body in order to satisfy its requirements. For example, the council has transferred its housing stock to an independent housing association, which is fully responsible for the

Table 3

In-house	Contracted out	Externalised
Refuse collection	Leisure management	Housing management
Street cleansing	Ground maintenance	Vehicle management
Highway maintenance	Building cleaning	Vehicle repairs etc.
Other catering		Building maintenance
Security work		

management and repair of that housing stock. The council's statutory duties towards the homeless are now fulfilled through contractual arrangements with the housing association. In a similar way the sale and hire-back of the council's vehicle fleet means that matters relating to that fleet fall for determination in accordance with ordinary contract law. These arrangements are likely to be permanent.

7.3 Management of Service Provision under CCT

The management of service delivery under CCT has raised a number of new challenges for local authorities. This Part will consider how Resbrough has approached some of these challenges.

7.3.1 The effect of corporate initiatives on CCT

The council has tended to avoid the development of over-arching corporate themes in its handling CCT. A degree of centralisation has occurred over time but it has yet to fundamentally shift the balance of influence from the departments to the corporate centre, as will be seen in subsequent sections on tender evaluation policies and contract management. This may be due to a number of factors. Being a relatively small local authority there has been less need for a systematic approach in order to control the bureaucracy. Personal relations have more room to be effective. Furthermore the council is essentially non-political and so has tended to stand aside from ideological approaches.

The council's official policy on CCT is that services should continue to be provided by direct labour wherever possible within the constraints of the CCT legislation. In practice the council has paid more attention (quite properly) to complying with the constraints of the legislation. This caution has meant that it generally has not cut corners in a bid to save direct service provision.

At a corporate level, the council has adopted some modern management trends, such as the development of a "Vision and Values Statement" setting out the organisations' aims and guiding values, and an internal market (see below). It has also achieved the "Investors in People" certification, while individual departments and sections have been encouraged to apply for Chartermark awards. At the same time it has avoided the adoption of quality assurance management systems on the lines of the ISO 9002 series, which have been regarded as overly bureaucratic.

Vision and Values

The Vision and Values Statement sets out the council's aims and guiding values. Some clues to the council's attitude can be found here, despite the somewhat clichéd and bland tendencies of such documents.

"Vision Statement
[Resbrough] believes that the local community is best served by local people making decisions locally. It will continuously improve the service it provides by responding to those it represents in order to enhance the quality of life in the Borough and to secure a thriving community.

Values
We recognise that the achievement of our vision is *constrained by the financial restraints within which we operate* and we will prioritise the use of the resources available to us in order to maximise their impact. We will work in partnership with residents and businesses to achieve the vision through action based on the following values:
Open and accessible local government
The importance of local identity
Excellence in customer care and quality of service
The importance of cost-effective use of resources
A commitment to enhance the environment
A commitment to reduce crime
Economic prosperity
The importance of caring for vulnerable sections of the community.

Business Strategy
In order to secure the survival of the Borough as the agency best able to achieve the vision the following strategic aims will form the basis of our business planning:
- ensure services are delivered in the most cost-effective way.
- become a unitary authority.
- project a positive image.
- *have a local tax level at or below the median for [the other districts in the county]*.
- enable staff to feel proud of their performance and that of the Council."

Three things stand out. The desire to contain costs and improve efficiency is clearly discernable. This reflects general financial constraints and a political goal to contain local taxes. The aim of enhancing the environment reflects government policy (the achievement of 25% recycling of waste materials by 2000) and general trends in public opinion. In fact, the council adopted an Environmental Policy Statement in 1992. This declares policy aims such as the promotion of recycling, but has had only a limited impact on tendering issues.[5] The aim of achieving unitary authority status arose out of the Local Government Review from 1992 to 1994. The Local Government Commission examined the feasibility of replacing the two-tier structure with a smaller number of unitary authorities. The council proposed its own enlargement as the basis of one of these new unitary authorities, but the Commission and Secretary of State rejected this in favour of retaining the status quo.

---

5   See case study at 7.4.3.

The internal market

Between 1992 and 1994 Resbrough established a system of internal trading accounts between cost centres, known as the internal market. This has improved the financial management of the Council's operations because it has made transparent the actual cost of central support services. Before the internal market central costs (legal, financial, management, IT support etc) had been recharged to the costs of other departments as overhead costs. The level of recharges was determined by the "provider" of services without reference to the "customer" department and without any systematic basis for ascertaining the nature, quality or quantity of the services consumed. This affected both the frontline departments like the DSO and also other central service departments (which provided support services for one another and recharged those costs in the same way). Greater transparency of central costs was important for 3 reasons. The first was that the level of costs compromised the competitive position of services facing CCT. This could not be addressed without greater knowledge of the cost of central services. Second, the government proposals for white-collar CCT indicated its intention to legislate for internal trading accounts. Although this was afterwards dropped in favour of a requirement to publish statements of support service costs (SSSCs), this happened late in the day and in any case the same information was still required. Third and finally, Resbrough suspected that the value of most of its white-collar services would be too small to face a competition requirement under the new regime, but to be sure a clarification of its central costs was needed.

The purpose of the internal market is to make costs transparent and by imitating a market situation to exert a downward pressure on costs. The authority has been divided into over 20 cost centres. These do not necessarily mirror departmental structures. For example, the two cost centres of Legal Services and Land Charges, both come under the Chief Solicitor's management. Each cost centre is assigned a budget at the beginning of the financial year and will charge fees for the services that it provides to other cost centres throughout the year in accordance with the terms of bilateral service level agreements (SLAs). Cost centres will similarly incur costs throughout the year, made up of direct costs (salaried employees) and overheads (rent, recharges from other cost centres etc). Each will aim to break-even at the end of the financial year.

Service Level Agreements (SLAs) and time recording systems form the basis of the relationship between the different cost centres. SLAs are negotiated agreements between a provider and a customer that specify the services that will be provided, to what standard, and the fees to be charged. Intended to improve providers' accountability to customers, the SLAs are nevertheless still provider-driven. Different cost centres use slightly different methods of charging for work done. Legal Services has been among the most adventurous in this, utilising a mix of retainer fees and fixed fees for certain jobs as well as the usual hourly charging rate. Accurate time-recording ensures that customers only pay for services they use (chargeable hours) and enables managers to accurately keep track of other time used up by their staff (non-chargeable hours).

Financial data from each cost centre is collected on a monthly, quarterly and annual basis. The data is used to monitor charge rates against coverage of costs and against comparable market rates. Information on costs is exchanged with other local authorities through the Inter Authority Group. The aim is for each cost centre to break-even, and cost centres that show a year-end profit or loss will come under pressure to either cut their charges or their costs. However the annual figures are mainly used for monitoring purposes and no direct or punitive action follows from them.

The general perception of the internal market has improved over time. The need to collect and monitor financial data relating to the cost of central support services remains, but some of the more bureaucratic features like the paper invoicing of costs between cost centres for services rendered has been discontinued.

7.3.2   Changing internal management structures – the client and contractor roles

Before the onset of CCT all the relevant services had been carried out by works units within the council's existing departments with no formal separation of client and contractor roles. This was also the case for the committees that oversaw the activities of the departments. The division of responsibilities is shown in the Table 4 below.

The council responded to the 1980 Act by establishing Direct Labour Organisations (DLOs) within the Borough Engineer's Department for building maintenance work and highways maintenance work. This is an example of what is known in the jargon as a "soft split"; that is one that occurs within an existing organisational structure such as a council department. Because the legislation required the council to keep a separate trading account in respect of each category of work, the formation of a dedicated in-house contractor

Table 4

Service	Responsible department	Responsible committee
Highway maintenance	Borough Engineer's	Highways
Building maintenance	Borough Engineer's	Housing etc Services
Vehicle maintenance	Borough Engineer's	Highways
Ground maintenance	Borough Recreation	Recreation
Refuse collection	Borough Engineer's	Environmental health
Street cleansing	Borough Engineer's	Environmental health
Building cleaning	Various	Various
Other catering	Various	Various
Leisure management	Borough Recreation	Recreation

for each was a logical step. It was not pursued in any other area of operations where there was no such requirement.

However the Local Government Bill of 1987/88 raised the prospect of much wider organisational change. In January 1988 the chief officers presented a report to the council on the organisational implications for the authority. Clear recognition was given to the differences between client and contractor roles under the proposed legislation. The report made four working assumptions:

- that the council would wish to retain direct provision wherever practicable;
- that competition would fundamentally change the working environment in a number of highly visible services;
- that for the health of the organisation it was essential that the inevitable conflicts of interest were seen to be resolved in a fair and open manner;
- and therefore, this required the separation of client and contractor roles at both member and officer level coupled with clear procedures for arbitration and co-ordination.

The chief officers were divided on the question of whether this separation was best accommodated within existing departments (further "soft splitting") or by the creation of a free standing contractor department covering all of the services subject to CCT (a "hard split"). The majority favoured the latter option. The council agreed.

Departmental arrangements

A decision was taken in January 1988 to establish a free standing Direct Services Department (DSO) by amalgamating the respective works units for refuse collection, street cleansing, ground maintenance, building cleaning, vehicle repairs and maintenance, together with the existing DLOs for highways and building maintenance. For different reasons other catering and the management of sports and leisure facilities were left outside the new DSO. In the case of other catering the reason was that it was de minimis for CCT purposes. With the management of sports and leisure facilities the principal reason was that the expertise demanded for it was not compatible with any of the other operations for which the DSO was responsible. The remaining departments, shorn of any contractor-side functions (but for the exceptions mentioned), were left to concentrate on the client-side role of contract management.

While this was going ahead, the management and staffing of the authority were more generally reviewed over the course of 1988–89 by management consultants. Titled as a "Review of the Structure and the Recruitment and Retention of the Staffing Resource" this produced a number of changes to the departmental and committee structures of the authority, and to the employment conditions of its staff. The changes resulted in a new 4-departmental structure, which was put into place over 1990–91, based around the following:

- Planning and Engineering Department
- Community Services Department
- Treasurer's Department
- Town Clerk and Chief Executive's (TCCE) Department.

Because the DSO had lost so many contracts by this stage, it was placed under the wing of the Community Services Department (losing its status as a free-standing department). Nevertheless, this arrangement has preserved the hard split except in the two instances of other catering services (which are de minimis) and leisure management (and even then only up to 1992 when this work was lost to an outside contractor). The fact that the DSO has lost responsibility for carrying out so many services (to outside contractors) as a result of CCT has significantly reduced the likelihood of any challenge by the Secretary of State to the authority's organisational arrangements. Indeed since 1992, the DSO has only had responsibility for refuse collection, highways maintenance and (from 1995) street cleansing work, the client function for all of which is located in the Planning and Engineering Department.

As part of the organisational response to blue-collar CCT, the central support services function was constituted as a separate division of the TCCE Department under an Assistant Chief Executive. This encompassed I.T services, management support, legal services, office services and property management services. There was no separation of client and contractor roles in these cases, despite the publication at the end of 1991 of the government's proposals for white collar CCT. Most of these services were small and likely to be de minimis under any white collar CCT regime, so it was considered unnecessary to take this course.

Committee arrangements

The council's committee structure was reviewed with the help of management consultants in 1989–90 alongside the departmental review. Before this was completed, as a short term measure, a DSO Sub-Committee to the Policy and Finance Committee was set up to deal with contractor-side issues. To ensure that these issues were considered and reported separately, members of service committees were excluded. When the review was completed, the sub-committee became a full DSO Committee, although one that continued, like other committees, to report to the (renamed) Policy and Resources Committee. It was later renamed itself as the Management Services Committee, although its role is essentially the same. The remaining committees were left to concentrate on client-side issues.

The next sections will look in greater depth at each side of the client-contractor split.

7.3.3   The Direct Services Organisation

The DSO was established in April 1988 by bringing together in a single new organisation a number of the works units previously located in different departments. This created a client – contractor split at departmental level in line with the perceived requirements of the 1988 Act. Its chief objective was to submit winning bids to perform defined activities for the council. The DSO's track record has been mixed. Beginning life as an all round service provider, it lost a series of contracts to teeter on the brink of extinction in 1994, before recovering to secure a place as a niche supplier of refuse collection, street cleansing and highways maintenance services (a progression that is tracked in greater detail in 7.2). This section will focus on the internal operations of the DSO.

Management structure

The competitive record of the DSO has over time had significant repercussions on its size and management. When it was formed the DSO provided all of the CCT services for the council: it was then a much bigger organisation (although still small by the standards of most local authorities) with 137 employees, of whom 22 were support staff. The management structure was more extensive in those days, although made up of no more than four levels between the General Manager and operatives on the ground. The DSO management was all recruited from within the authority. A Deputy Chief Executive and Head of Legal and Administrative Services was moved across to become the DSO General Manager with a fixed 2-year contract (and a guarantee to be redeployed after that time, although not necessarily to the same post). The Deputy Borough Engineer was appointed as his Assistant General Manager. There was also Grounds Maintenance Manager and a Head of Finance and Administration who were similarly appointed from within the authority. Below this level were five supervisors of the former departmental works units who were also redeployed to the new organisation to take charge of the five sections of Transport, Refuse, Cleansing, Highways, and Parks. The DSO operated from a council owned depot for which it paid a rent. The council paid to refurbish office accommodation for its use on-site.

After the loss of so much work from 1989–94, the DSO is a lot smaller and leaner. At the end of 1996 there were around 40 staff of who at any one time 30%–50% were agency staff. This allows the DSO the flexibility to employ enough full-time staff to cover troughs in work levels, and to "top-up" with agency staff to meet peak demands. The current management structure is correspondingly lighter, consisting of the General Manager supported by a Cleansing Manager, a Highways Manager, and 2 working supervisors. There is also one part-time administrative manager but no other support staff.

It still operates from the same council depot, but part of the site was sold in 1990.[6]

---

6   See 7.2 for the effect the sale had on the retender of the vehicle maintenance contract in 1991.

Operational autonomy

The DSO exercises a high degree of operational autonomy with the General Manager being in charge of most operational matters. The powers of the General Manager are set out in a formal contract of employment with the authority. Under the authority's management structure, the General Manager is responsible to the chief officer in charge of the Community Services Department.

The DSO relies heavily on the "Town Hall" for its support services. This is provided chiefly through the Borough Treasurer's Department, which acts as the DSO's banker. The relationship is intended to be similar to that between a private business and its bank. The "bank" assesses the financial viability of the "business" and its plans, and gives appropriate support and/or direction. However the "business" operates day-to-day as an autonomous entity. Therefore, the DSO has a very high degree of decision-making freedom over matters such as procuring supplies, staffing, and the services it offers. Decisions on sub-contracting work also lie with the General Manager, subject to the approval of the relevant client officer.

The DSO Manager reports on behalf of the DSO to what is now the Management Services Committee, which in turn reports to the Policy and Resources Committee. Trading accounts for each service are submitted to this committee every quarter, and this provides the main basis of DSO accountability to the authority. Inter alia, the committee's terms of reference (revised in 1997) give it responsibility, within the overall policy of the council, for:

- supervising business plans for the delivery of all council services subject to CCT, and support services.
- exercising control as contractor over those services operating trading accounts under the 1980 and 1988 Acts (and over any other service that is subjected voluntarily to competition).
- directing the work of the [DSO] in respect of its revenue budget, capital programme and business plan.
- determining policy for the recruitment, appointment, appraisal, promotion, transfer, conduct, discipline and termination of employment of staff.
- determining policy regarding industrial relations, equal opportunities, health and safety, and the welfare of employees.

With regard to CCT, its particular responsibility is one of:

> "...ensuring that the [DSO] tenders in a professional and business like manner by quoting the keenest price commensurate with the standard of service required."

Staff and industrial relations

DSO employees have their own terms and conditions, which are separate from those in the rest of the authority. They are also subject to a separate disciplinary procedure.

Negotiations with employees are generally conducted at the depot between them and the General Manager directly. Typically, an official union representative and another employee representative from each of the Cleansing or Highways Sections of the DSO negotiate with the General Manager, as needed. The General Manager is also based at the depot and so is closely involved with the interests of the staff. There tends to be little involvement from "Town Hall" management or the local UNISON branch secretary.

The General Manager considered management – staff relations to be "very good", this being the case with both full-time and agency staff. In this respect, matters had considerably improved since the mid-1980s, when trade union strength was "unrealistic for the work we were trying to do". Another change over this period was in the closeness of different sections of the workforce to one another. Prior to CCT and continuing into the formative years of the DSO, different sections tended to remain aloof from each other. Now there was a greater sense of common identity. This is no doubt a product of time but also of necessity. The range of services carried out by the DSO has since 1992 been so limited that the consequence of losing even a single area of work would bring the survival of the entire DSO into question. The workforce will stand or fall together.

Quality management issues

The DSO has not gone down the road to implementing quality assurance standards such as ISO 9002. This reflects the reluctance at corporate level to get involved in this area. As has been noted, service quality has not to date played a formal role in tender evaluation practices. However, in common with the rest of the authority, the DSO has achieved "Investors in People" certification. It has also sought on its own for the Chartermark award. Although "highly commended" the first application was turned down. It is intended to reapply in 1997.

Relations with the client-side

The DSO is responsible for the running of its contracts to client managers in the Planning and Engineering Department, namely:

- the Contracts Management Section (for refuse collection, borough cleansing and recycling work).
- the Highways Engineer (for highways maintenance work).

Contact takes place on a daily basis, with more formal meetings happening once a month. The service contracts provide for the referral of disputes between the DSO and clients to the Town Clerk and Chief Executive, and ultimately to binding arbitration. In the case of refuse collection work this would be an arbitrator appointed through the Institute of Waste Management. Matters had never gone as far as binding arbitration, and the General

Manager said that they never would because the DSO remained an integral part of the authority.

Changing service standards and practices during the life of a contract had not been a problem. The client-side had simply introduced variations to the service specification as needed (in accordance with a variation clause).

DSO values, political support and future

The General Manager saw the DSO as being halfway to a commercial entity, saying that it was:

> "...more of a business than any other part of the authority ... more of a service than any other private contractor."

The DSO, he said, had community values and involvement that a private contractor would not share. By way of examples, he cited instances where they would work beyond the specification for free, and school visits to explain their work.

The members of the council were, he said, very supportive of the principle of the council having a DSO. This did not extend to uncritical support: members were critical and enquiring and demanded high standards which was very proper. He made every effort to keep them on-side, for example, by annual tours of the depot to outline their operations.

The General Manager saw the Local Authorities (Goods and Services) Act 1970 and the prevailing uncertainties about the legality of cross-boundary tendering as the main limitations on the ability of the DSO to behave in a true business-like manner. Being a small local authority, the limited opportunities to spread overhead costs over a greater volume of work were a real concern.

The future of the DSO appears to be fairly safe. It has found a niche market and is servicing it effectively. There may be scope for expansion when the ground maintenance contract is re-let in 1998. The General Manager said that the decision would be up to him and would depend on whether the DSO had the management expertise and experience to handle the work offered. It was not a line of work that could be added on like an appendage to the DSO's existing activities. The hope was that the work would be let as at least two contracts, perhaps dividing between conservancy work, and parks and open spaces. If the work were to be tendered in this way, the DSO would feel confident of making a competitive bid for the smaller workload of the conservancy contract. However a single contract package was likely to be beyond the DSO's capability.

7.3.4   Approach to tender evaluation

The relevant client-side officers who act in the role of contract managers generally drive the tender evaluation process. They are responsible for all of the early stages of tendering such as preparing and drafting the service specification, advertising the work, preparing the pre-qualification questionnaire, and selecting those firms that will be invited to submit tenders to carry out the work. In doing so they may choose to draw on the support of central services professionals in the Management Support Unit (MSU) or the Legal Services Section. This support is voluntary, informal and happens only on an "as needed" basis. Some client managers prefer to seek this support at an early stage while others do not feel the need.

The MSU forms part of the Town Clerk and Chief Executive's Department. It consists of six people including two I.T support staff to handle a contracts management data base, and is headed by the Management Services Officer. The MSU is commissioned by the Chief Executive or other departments to examine management issues as they arise. In CCT situations, the earliest point at which the MSU tends to become involved is in the selection of those invited to tender, when it may assist client officers in assessing the suitability of firms expressing an interest in the work.

Once the deadline for the submission of tenders has passed, the tender evaluation process becomes somewhat more standardised. From the outset, the council has adopted a standard format for tender evaluation reports presented to committee. This has formed the basis for the process of tender evaluation itself. The standard format requires evaluations to be reported in two parts, a technical evaluation and a corporate evaluation. All of the tender documents are available for both of the evaluations.

The technical evaluation must be presented by the relevant client-side contract manager, and examines the commercial price of each tender and the technical ability of each of the tenderers to carry out the contract in accordance with the specification. Historically, the lowest priced tender that is technically viable is recommended.

The corporate evaluation is the joint responsibility of the Chief Executive and the Borough Treasurer. The purpose of their report is to remind the committee of the CCT rules and the legal and financial implications for the council as a whole of accepting any of the tenders. Three matters are of particular relevance here:

- the financial viability of the DSO bid from the perspective of the council's role as the DSO's "banker". The CCT regime requires a DSO to make a specified rate of return and the council is at risk of sanction from the Secretary of State if this is not made.
- the affordability of tenders with regard to current budgetary estimates.
- where the price of an outside tender is cheaper than that of the DSO bid, the extraneous costs to the council of awarding the contract to an outside contractor.

These evaluations are both carried out for the purposes of reports to be presented to committee by named officers, and nobody else is formally involved except those officers. In practice, the MSU will normally carry out the corporate evaluation on behalf of the Chief Executive and with the help of members of the Borough Treasurer's Department, but may also advise the contract manager regarding the technical evaluation. Both reports are normally considered by a meeting of all chief officers before finally being presented to committee. In every case, the technical and corporate reports have agreed on which tender to recommend to the committee, and only on one occasion have members rejected that recommendation.

Throughout the evaluation process, the tendency is for the client contract manager to call the shots. He will form a view as to the best tender and the "corporate" side, while still making a full assessment, will tend to focus on that. If there is a difference of view, or if the contract manager is unsure, then matters will be resolved eventually by the chief officers group.

So far the council has operated on the basis that service standards will be secured by the specification, and so long as a tender looks reasonably certain to meet these, the council will thereafter look simply to secure the best price for itself. The council has to date avoided more formal evaluations of the quality of service offered by different tenders. It has been left to the contract manager to consider quality in the technical evaluation, and the emphasis is placed on whether the lowest priced tender can meet the specification. If it can, then it will go through subject to the corporate evaluation. Indeed formal evaluation models are wholly absent from this council's practices.

7.3.5 Contract management arrangements

The authority's client-side or contract management arrangements have been handled on a departmental basis from the beginning. The Management Services Unit (MSU) carried out a review of the council's arrangements in 1991 and noted a range of different "cultural" attitudes among contract managers within and between departments to the management of contracts and in particular towards direct service providers. These ranged from sympathy towards in-house provision, regarding DSO staff almost as part of an extended council family, to a strict and neutral stance of seeking fulfilment of the specification for the cheapest price possible whatever the contractors colours. It was not possible to identify a common style amidst these different approaches, although the equilibrium point would have appeared to lie closer to the second approach than to the first. This made it difficult for the DSO and other in-house providers to know where they stood in respect of different areas of work.

In 1991 the MSU's recommendations only tinkered with the existing system, which was broadly considered to be working satisfactorily given the new conditions. By 1993 when the DSO had lost every contract of significance bar refuse collection, a new review was called for. At this point the council was facing a very real prospect of becoming an "enabling council" reliant on contractors for the provision of all its blue-collar services. The cost and effectiveness of the council's contract management was seen to be crucial to its ability to deliver services.

The 1993 contract management review

The review covered all the principal centres of contract management expertise within the authority and a number of smaller contracts (some non-CCT) as well. What follows is a synopsis of the principal findings.

Service specifications

In general contract managers saw their role as ensuring that the contractor performed the defined activities to the standards set down in the specification. However a pro-active approach to setting and developing service standards was not common. The report noted pointedly that "some" contract managers did not see it as their role to actively identify the needs or seek the views of their customers, and ensure that the services were designed and delivered to meet those needs. Naturally, contract managers did try to design services to meet customer needs but their judgements were a reflection of past experience and informal contact with customers, and furthermore were informed by knowledge of resource constraints. There had been few systematic attempts to define, record and monitor user requirements. The chief exceptions to this were the surveys of residents that had preceded and accompanied the introduction of wheelbins for refuse collection.

Customer views were generally being ascertained through complaints, but while this was a typical procedure it had a number of shortcomings. Most complaints were made by telephone but these were not recorded. Where complaints did get through, attention tended to be given only to those concerning service delivery where officers felt that they could do something, rather than complaints about policy where they (directly) could not. In other cases the contract documentation was ambiguous about the responsibility for complaints, client or contractor, so complaints fell between two stools. Finally many complaints were not reported to members on the relevant service committees. This lack of reporting was particularly bad where clients acted as agents for other departments or committees. On a more positive note, the review could acknowledge the planned introduction of a computerised telephone system to handle complaints in the Planning & Engineering Department, and the use of a contract term in the recent Leisure Management contract to require the contractor to undertake research into customer needs.

Overall the review found that contract management emphasised service delivery rather than service specification. Managers who were previously in charge of directly delivered services had had little or no training for their new client role. Individual contract managers had then developed their own philosophies and methods without corporate guidance. There were few opportunities for support and the exchange of ideas on good practice. The lack of customer involvement was also disturbing in the light of the council's public commitment to listen and respond, and the Citizens' Charter.

Approaches to contract monitoring

There were a wide variety of approaches to the monitoring of contracts, giving rise to different styles of client-contractor relations and different degrees of enforcement of contract conditions. Monitoring through customer complaints was the norm with refuse collection and vehicle maintenance, while inspections were favoured for street cleansing, building cleaning, ground maintenance and leisure services.

Monitoring costs

The council's contract monitoring costs were above the average for local authorities on Audit Commission figures and in many cases lay in the upper quartile of local authorities. This is shown in Table 5 below. However allowance should be made for the absence of time recording procedures for client-side officers, which probably obscured the true level of contract management costs. The introduction of time-recording procedures was one of the matters addressed in the review's recommendations, something that was also urged by the council's auditors.

The reason for these relatively high costs was partly a reflection of the small size of the local authority, which made it difficult to achieve economies of scale generally. Another explanation was the current structure of contract monitoring, which was based on three principal contract-monitoring sections.

Monitoring structures

The council's contract management structure had developed in an ad hoc fashion, based on the existing departments. There were three principal centres of contract management expertise within the authority, which were the:

- Planning and Engineering Department, with either the Contracts Management Section (responsible for refuse collection and street cleansing), or the Highways Engineer (responsible for highway maintenance).

Table 5: Contract Monitoring Costs as % of annual contract value

Contract	Resbrough	Average of local authorities	Upper quartile of local authorities
Leisure management	3.8	1.5	1.7
Refuse collection	4.5	3.8	5.6
Building cleaning	5.1	4.4	5.4
Street cleansing	7.1	5.6	7.3
Ground maintenance	8.3	5.7	7.1
Vehicle maintenance	2.5	12.5	16.7

- Community Services Department, Recreation Division (responsible for leisure services management and other catering).
- TCCE Department (responsible for remaining defined activities).

Recommendations

The review concluded that the essential requirements for effective contract management were good specification writing and the effective management of the contractor and the monitoring process. Depending on the type of contract this might need to be supplemented to a greater or lesser extent by technical expertise. The implication that good contract management was made up of a number of differing skills was that larger client teams should offer greater flexibility to deploy the relevant skills than smaller teams. A single dedicated client unit might provide the council with this flexibility.

Balanced against this were a number of other factors. The transfer of skilled employees to a new unit would risk weakening the existing service departments and through that the local authority as a whole. The creation of a dedicated client unit would also have implications for the career structure in the authority. Technical or professional staff who had done a bit of contract management would be forced, if they wanted advancement, to concentrate on contract management in future, something which might have put many off joining the authority. The other consideration was the uncertainty surrounding the government proposals for white-collar CCT. It was felt to be more prudent to carry out organisational change in reaction to this rather than in anticipation of it. In the end the most beneficial option was considered to be the retention of the existing department based structure supplemented by an inter-departmental working group.

The Policy and Resources Committee acted on the recommendations of the MSU in November 1993, giving approval to a number of measures:

- training seminars for officers and members involved in contracted services;
- time-recording systems for contract management staff;
- improved procedures for the reporting of complaints to committees, and the use of contract conditions to ensure that the council's contractors have a complaints handling procedure, the records and reports to which the council has access;
- creation of the recommended inter-departmental officer group to exchange ideas, good practice, organise training events and maintain links with experts in the field of contract management.

The Contracts Management Working Group

The Group, which met for the first time at the beginning of 1994, is a consultative forum involving the principal contract managers and representatives of the "corporate" interests, namely the Chief Solicitor and sometimes the Borough Treasurer. It has met an average of 5 times a year and reports to the Chief Officers Group (COG). Its deliberations share some ground with the CCT Steering Group, which also reports to the COG but is concerned more with forward planning. The Contracts Management Group has tended to focus on current practical issues. It has been involved in three main areas, which are outlined below.

Pushing forward a corporate agenda

The Group has been responsible for implementing a limited range of corporate or centralising measures: a standard format for contract documents, the agreement of a number of standard contract clauses, and a computerised contracts database. However the balance of influence still lies on the side of departmental autonomy. The prevalent view is that most contracts still require professional expertise, which is located in the departments.

Informing and co-ordinating responses to legal developments

The Chief Solicitor has led the Working Group in this area. It has covered legal developments regarding TUPE, European public procurement law and Health and Safety law. Where legal problems have arisen that could rebound on the council as a whole, the Group has been a means of checking that individual contract managers are informed of these and kept in-line. In the case of race relations, in April 1994 the Commission for Racial Equality wrote to the council to see whether it was properly exercising its responsibilities to ensure racial equality etc within supplies and works contracts in accordance with section 18 of the LGA 1988. Accordingly, the Chief Solicitor checked that all the contract managers were sending out an appropriately worded questionnaire at the pre-tender stage.

Promoting the discussion and exchange of best practice

The Group has been a forum for the contract managers to relate their experience of tendering and managing contracts, seek advice and exchange ideas. This has been on a range of issues including the balance that can be struck between price and quality in tender evaluation, and the dangers of being drawn into "cosy" relationships with contractors.

Overall the performance of the Contracts Management Working Group has been considered a success, and that by getting to grips with these issues on a informal inter-departmental basis, the council has avoided the need to take more radical centralising measures such as the establishment of a Central Client Unit.

7.4 Case Studies

The following case studies have been included to illustrate some of the problems faced by the council in the implementation of CCT and its attitudes towards overcoming them.

7.4.1 CCT for refuse collection 1989

The 1988 Competition Regulations required Resbrough to have subjected its refuse collection work to competition by the 1 January 1990. On the advice of the council's external auditor, it was decided that commercial and household waste collection would be tendered in a single contract. In the interests of securing greater value for money, the tender documents required prospective contractors to price their bids for the work on the basis of 3 separate Bills of Quantity. These related respectively to domestic refuse collection, commercial refuse collection, and dayworks/general items. The Council reserved the right to award the work comprised in each bill to a different contractor, and to require a discount on the price if domestic and commercial refuse collection were awarded together to the same contractor.

The work was tendered on the basis that it would be carried out from the Council's depot. The necessary vehicles were to be hired from the Council's vehicle fleet, although parking spaces for them would be free. While it was not considered appropriate to offer proper office accommodation to the successful tenderer, officers were also of the opinion that it would be anti-competitive behaviour to refuse to make available any office space at all. Therefore a portacabin was made available on site at a rent.

In this period the refuse collection service was going through a transition period, being based partly on the old-fashioned sack/dustbin collection method, and partly on the modern wheelbin system. The Council had plans to extend the wheelbin system across the borough, but it took the decision to base the contract documentation on the position as it stood on 17 April 1989 when only one quarter of the borough operated on wheelbins. Afterwards a decision was made to phase in wheelbins across the whole borough over the period of February to June 1990. This decision did not at first lead to any amendment of the contract documentation.

The CCT process

The contract was advertised in the local and trade press in the week ending 7 April 1989, as required by the LGA 1988. There was no need to send a notice to the European Journal (OJEC) as the EC public procurement law did not yet extend to cover contracts for services. The specification was made available for inspection at the Town Hall for a period of four weeks from the 17 April 1989. Copies were available to purchase for £40. Interested parties were required to notify their interest in being invited to bid by completing and returning a pre-qualification questionnaire by the 19 May 1989.

At the close, appropriate notifications had come from thirteen private companies, one other local authority DSO, and the Resbrough DSO. The Council decided to invite tenders from six parties, including its own DSO, in the expectation (derived from the experience of other local authorities) that not all would submit tenders. The following criteria were used to whittle down the numbers:

- whether the firm was known to have inspected or bought the specification.
- the satisfactory completion of the questionnaire.
- the quality of supporting information and other considerations.

The considerations relevant to the tender included:

- size and trading record together with that of any parent company.
- experience of the type and size of contract work now being offered.
- experience of developing and operating wheelbin systems of refuse collection.
- Health and Safety policies, and Race Relations Act policies.

Invitations to tender were issued to the successful six parties on 17 July 1989 for return by 21 August 1989. They included the Resbrough DSO and Firms B, C, D, E and F, which were all private companies. Concurrently with the issue of invitations to tender, the Council took up the technical references supplied by the outside contractors. The referees for E professed no knowledge of them, while those for F did not reply. Satisfactory references were received for B, C and D.

The tendering period was marred by problems. First, there was an error in Bill of Quantity No.2 (commercial waste collection), which had to be revised. A post-invitation letter was sent to all parties on the 3 August 1989 containing the revised Bill. Second and more seriously, Firms B and C had been awake to the Council's policy on the introduction of the wheelbin method of refuse collection. They were known to have inspected the Council minutes for references to the refuse collection service. Both now queried the discrepancy between the tender documents, which were based on the April 1989 situation (one-quarter of the borough being covered by the wheelbin system), and the subsequent Council decision to phase in the wheelbin system over the whole borough between February and June 1990. A further post-invitation letter was sent to all parties informing them of the Council's new plans on 11 August 1989.

On the 15 August 1989, F indicated to the Council that it would not be submitting a tender, because the profusion of tender documents made it impossible for it to prepare one properly.

By the closing date, tenders had been received from the Resbrough DSO and Firms B, C and E. Firm D simply failed to return a tender. The DSO and Firm B had each submitted bids that were fully priced to take account of the extension of the wheelbin system. Firms C and E had covered this point with general information but no prices.

There was a particular problem with E, who had not priced Bill of Quantity No.2 (commercial waste collection) in accordance with the revisions contained in the letter of 3 August. When this was drawn to their attention they said that they had forgotten to include the revision. The Council then invited them to withdraw their tender. Firm E declined to do this, and instead submitted the revised Bill. As this was late, the Council disqualified the tender, having also taken into account the unsatisfactory position regarding Firm E's technical references.

Financial evaluation of tenders

That disqualification left the bids from the DSO, and Firms B and C still in the running. A financial evaluation was needed to establish the "bottom line" price for each. This was not straightforward because there were several different bases for making this calculation:

- each bid contained separate quotes for each of the 3 Bills of Quantity, and the work in each Bill could be awarded to a different contractor.
- the work in Bills 1 and 2 could be awarded together in which case the successful contractor was required to offer a discount.
- the work had been advertised as part-wheelbin, part sack and dustbin collection, but the Council had since decided to develop the service to a 100% wheelbin service.
- Firm C had given notice that it would not take any combination of work that did not involve domestic refuse collection, unless it was guaranteed a certain level of commercial refuse collection work. This could not be guaranteed so the Council would have to accept fewer options regarding C than with the others.

Taking the separate quotes, unadjusted for the planned phase-in of the wheelbin system, the DSO came out cheapest for Bill No.1 (domestic waste collection) but not on the others. However the greatest benefits for the Council were seen to come from combining the domestic and commercial work because of the discounts that were on offer. On this front, the DSO lost out to B who could offer a discount four times as large as its own. The DSO was also more expensive than C on this basis, although not by much. However when all the bids were adjusted to take account of the phasing-in of the wheelbin system, C lost ground, being unable to match the savings that its rivals could offer.

Therefore, on the basis of the work as advertised (one quarter of the borough on wheelbins), and combining domestic and commercial waste collection to take advantage of the discounted prices, the cheapest bid came from B, followed by C and then the DSO. When account was taken of the coming phase-in of the wheelbin system across the borough the two cheapest bids were those of B followed by the DSO. The Council chose to proceed on the basis that the cheapest bid was that of B, and that the next cheapest was that of the DSO.

Having established the two lowest proposed costs of the service, the next stage of the financial evaluation was to consider the true cost to the council of awarding the work to an outside contractor. This meant establishing the extraneous costs that it was permissible to take into account in assessing the true cost of an outside tender. This task was undertaken by the Town Clerk, the Chief Executive and the Borough Treasurer. They saw their responsibilities as ensuring that the Council avoided any behaviour that could be deemed to be anti-competitive and so bring about the intervention of the Secretary of State. They noted from DOE Circular 19/88 that "rejecting lower tenders from contractors in favour of the DSO's bid without good reason" was behaviour that was likely to be regarded as anti-competitive. Since B had the lowest bid, the officers clearly saw it as their duty to reject it only for "good reason".

The DOE had accepted in Circular 19/88 that potential redundancy costs could be taken into account, provided that they were spread over the life of the contract. On the basis of the bid from B there would be 19 redundancies in the DSO workforce. The potential redundancy payments to those employees could therefore be taken into account if they were unavoidable and spread over the five years.

The officers also had regard to Audit Commission advice contained in a letter to local authority chief executives on 9 August 1989. The letter was stated to give "their view" of the costs that could legitimately be taken into account in tender evaluation. The CIPFA Code of Practice for Compulsory Competition 1989 was also considered, but the officers noted that it differed from the advice given by the Audit Commission in a number of respects. The Audit Commission stance was generally the more restrictive. The Audit Commission line was preferred for 3 reasons:

- whereas the DOE had not endorsed the CIPFA code, it had in a letter to local authorities said that it viewed the legitimacy of certain costs in tender evaluation "very much eye to eye with the Audit Commission".
- the DOE Minister Christopher Chope had told a local government conference that the DOE would have similar considerations to the Audit Commission in mind when deciding whether to exercise its sanctions powers under the LGA 1988.
- the Council's own external auditors were appointed by the Audit Commission and so would consider its views in reviewing the award of any contract by the Council.

On the basis of the Audit Commission advice, the officers added on the following costs to the bid by B:

- the cost of redundancy payments to 19 DSO staff.
- the cost of certain pension enhancements.
- payments in lieu of notice.
- fixed costs not eliminated by the performance of the work outside the authority.

But even having taken all that into account, the bid by B was still the cheaper. The three officers therefore recommended to the Council that it would be in the financial interests of the Council to award the work to Firm B.

Chapter Seven

Technical evaluation of tenders

There remained the evaluation of non-financial factors. The tender from B was based on four combined domestic and commercial waste collection rounds per week. A Contract Manager would be in overall control, with an Area Manager below him exercising day to day control of operations. Below the Area Manager would be two full time supervisors with a role that encompassed quality control. B proposed to retain the existing service until the wheelbin system was fully implemented. Thereafter there would be redundancies because wheelbins were less labour intensive. B said that if it won the contract, it would consider employing the existing workforce and anticipated that the vast majority of its personnel on the contract would be existing council employees.

The first consideration was B's level of technical expertise. It was already operating one refuse collection contract with an English local authority. The Borough Engineer visited that local authority to inspect B's operations there. He found what was described as a competent organisation giving satisfactory service. B's technical expertise was considered to be adequate for the Council's requirements.

Another important consideration for the Council was the quality of B's management. Apart from the operation mentioned above, the company had won other local authority work through CCT, which was getting under way at that point. The senior management had considerable experience of local authority work. The quality of management was therefore considered to satisfy the Council's requirements.

The main reservations about B focused on its assumptions about work rates for employees throughout the life of the contract. These also applied to the DSO bid, although to a lesser extent because it proposed to operate four domestic waste collections per week with a fifth dedicated trade waste round. B assumed an average work rate of 6,800 wheeled bins per round per week. The experience of other authorities indicated that this was an achievable rate, but officers noted that it was "towards the upper end of reasonably achievable levels". The feeling was that B had left little margin for failure and so in the event of problems would be forced to recruit extra manpower, with consequent loss of profitability. Ease of recruitment could not be presumed, given the very low levels of unemployment in the borough. There were other concerns about the assumed work rate. It was feared that it would lead to a high turnover of staff and so to problems in maintaining service standards; also, that it would pressurise older and less fit members of the workforce; and finally that it would result in a need for higher supervision costs. There were further reservations about B's relative lack of local knowledge, which risked undermining some of the underlying assumptions on which the company had based its bid.

Overall, the Borough Engineer came down in favour of B, recommending it in the following terms to the Environmental Health and Control Committee:

"The Local Government Act 1988 does not demand that the lowest tender in financial terms should be accepted. However there must be clear and justifiable reasons for selecting a different bid. The Borough Engineer advises that in his opinion there are no reasonable grounds to disqualify the bid from [B] and recommends that they be awarded the contract for refuse collection for a period of five years from 1 January 1990."

The councillors reject the recommended tender

In this case, the councillors did not follow the advice of the officers. The Committee met on the 16 October 1989. As a measure of the importance attached to this meeting, all members of the Council were invited to attend and speak. Firm B and the DSO were each asked to make a short presentation and to answer questions.

The Committee found B's proposed arrangements for the division of the borough into workable rounds to be unacceptable. It went on to fault B's tender on a number of other grounds:

"It had failed to demonstrate the level of awareness which members had expected or to provide any analysis of local geophysical conditions.

The company had not demonstrated that it could establish and maintain its proposed operations under the employment conditions currently experienced in the Borough.

In particular the committee had regard to the expected performance levels of each tenderer and considered that insufficient regard had been paid by [B] to the implications of its proposals to combine domestic and commercial waste collections with possible adverse consequences for the domestic service."

Despite the opportunity for financial savings with B, the Committee concluded that it would be in the best interests of the residents of the borough for the work to go to be awarded to the DSO. In reaching this decision, the Committee minuted that it did not consider this course of action to be anti-competitive behaviour.

Therefore, the final outcome of the first round of refuse collection CCT was the award of the work to the DSO for a period of five years from the 1 January 1990.

A complaint was made to the DOE that resulted in the Secretary of State serving on the Council a notice under s.13 LGA 1988 (notice for further information) alleging anti-competitive behaviour. The matter was resolved when the Chief Executive wrote to the Secretary of State. The Secretary of State did not serve a direction in relation to the complaint pursuant to s.14 LGA 1988 and the contract proceeded without any further trouble.

7.4.2   CCT of sports/leisure facilities management

The council's Leisure Services CCT strategy was to let and contest a contract for the management of its only leisure centre, including the on-site cleaning and catering operations. This represented about 70% of the defined activity, with the remaining 30% being contracted out without in-house bids. The leisure centre contract would run for a period of 4 years and 3 months commencing on 1 January 1992. This period was chosen to bring the eventual renewal date into alignment with the financial year. Under the terms of the contract, the successful contractor would pay a management fee to the council based on projected income from the centre. It would in return be allowed to keep the actual income that was raised.

The tendering process

Responsibility for the CCT tender lay within the Recreation Section of the Community Services Department. This applied to both the client and the contractor role. The contractor role had not been placed with the DSO in this case because the expertise required was considered incompatible with any of the other work done by the DSO. The responsible contract manager was the Recreation Manager, who reported to the Recreation Committee.

The Recreation Committee approved the service specification in January 1991 and the work was advertised in the local and trade press the same month. A draft specification was available for inspection for four weeks over February and March (with copies available for £150). There were a total of 10 responses by interested firms to the advertisement, out of which 7 returned the pre-qualification questionnaire to the council by the end of April deadline. All of these were invited to tender. Invitations were dispatched at the beginning of July with a mid-August deadline for the submission of tenders.

By the close of tendering only the in-house team and one outside firm had submitted tenders. Three of the firms invited wrote to the council to withdraw from the process citing the workload imposed by other tenders as the reason (two were in fact awarded contracts by other local authorities at around this time). The rest simply failed to submit tenders. Out of the two submitted tenders, that of the outside firm "Firm A" was the cheaper. Each tenderer was interviewed as part of the evaluation process.

Tender evaluation

The technical evaluation of the tenders was conducted by the Recreation Manager, with the purpose "to ensure with reasonable certainty that the required volume of work will be done to the requisite standard as economically as possible". A number of indicators were used to assess each tender as either good/average/poor in relation to contract price and quality of service. While contract managers had undoubtedly used similar assessments before, this is the only occasion that a formal scoring model has been used for the purposes of a report to committee.

The assessment regarding the contract price looked at the consistency of a number of indicators with the contract price quoted: marketing plan, staffing levels, maintenance programme, operating costs, and income and usage projections. The indicators used to assess quality of service covered staffing structure, qualifications, training and flexibility, and levels of management support. The service specification covered matters such as quality control and standards of service but the council was looking for a contractor who would go beyond these over the life of the contract.

The tender submitted by Firm A was superior to the in-house tender on both of the bases (contract price and quality of service) used for the technical evaluation. Its overall scoring was good – average whereas the in-house tender was simply average. Firm A was able to score well because it was a large company that specialised in leisure services provision. In particular, its tender proposals were based on a more extensive management structure and greater numbers (and proportion) of full-time employees. This enabled it to score well on indicators such as staff structure, management support, and staff flexibility. The Recreation Manager was therefore satisfied that it was appropriate on technical grounds to award the contract to Firm A.

The tender price of Firm A was lower than that of the in-house bid, so the corporate evaluation was primarily concerned with identifying and calculating the extraneous costs to the authority of awarding the contract to an outside contractor. This was carried out by the Chief Executive and the Borough Treasurer and they acted having regard to the guidance contained the newly released DOE Circular 1/91 and the CIPFA Code of Practice (1991). The most recent guidance from the Audit Commission was that of August 1989 (see case study at 7.4.1), which was disregarded as being out of date.

The evaluation brought into account the cost to the council of potential redundancy costs (relevant to 14 employees) and also of contractually required pension enhancements (relevant to 2 employees). In previous CCT tenders the council had lacked the confidence to go against DOE guidance and bring pension enhancements into the evaluation. Under its Employment Stability Policy, the council had committed itself to exercise the maximum discretion available to it under the various Acts and Regulations governing superannuation and redundancy payments, but this commitment fell short of the contractual obligation to make payments to specific individuals that DOE guidance had insisted on. The omission was resolved in January 1991, when the council's Personnel and Performance Review sub-committee resolved to make the council contractually obliged to make these payments.

The other consideration was whether additional supervision costs would be incurred by awarding the contract to Firm A, and whether these could be brought into account. The Recreation Manager considered there would be no need for additional supervision costs, so avoiding the need for the authority to choose between the conflicting DOE and the CIPFA guidance on this point. No other costs were relevant to the evaluation. Having taken all this into account, the tender from Firm A was still the cheaper, and consequently its acceptance was recommended as being in the financial interests of the council.

Overall the evaluators had been persuaded to favour Firm A's tender for the following reasons:

- it had the backing of a large parent company that would be able to invest in the leisure centre to upgrade the facilities.
- the tender emphasised market research and translating customer needs into reality, something that the Council's Contract Management Review wished to see more generally promoted.
- the staffing structure also emphasised the promotion of the leisure centre.
- the firm would contribute to sports development through the operation of its Community Sport Grant Aid Scheme.
- its management were highly experienced and able to offer a 24 hour quick response to problems.

However they were also influenced by two factors that could not (officially) count in the evaluation because if admitted they would have qualified Firm A's tender. They were appended to the evaluator's report to the Recreation Committee with an explanatory note that:

> "...it is felt that it would be in the best interests of the authority for all known facts to be available to members determining the outcome of the contract."

The first was that Firm A had indicated at its interview that it would be willing to negotiate an over-performance clause with the council, that is an agreement to share with the council part of any income generated from the centre in excess of levels projected in the contract documentation. It had already negotiated such a clause with two other councils. Since the council was running a budget deficit, this was an attractive enticement. Also at interview, Firm A had indicated that it would be willing to endow a lump sum of money to the council to distribute as part of its Grant Aid to Sport. Bearing in mind the council's enabling role and the need for community funding this was again considered to be a tempting offer.

These considerations were not cited among the official reasons after the Recreation Committee met in September 1991 and awarded the contract to Firm A. The decision was taken on the basis that Firm A had submitted the lowest priced bid, one that had passed the technical evaluation, and with regard to the council's fiduciary duty to local taxpayers, the duty to act reasonably, and the considerations deemed relevant by the DOE and CIPFA.

This is to date the only area where the council has had to operate CCT in the context of a management rather than a manual activity. This was reflected in the tender evaluation, where a more objective stance towards the question of service quality was adopted, although still within the usual format. The case study also shows the weak position of a small in-house provider against competition from a large and specialist private firm, and the influence extraneous factors can have on the evaluation of tenders.

7.4.3 Refuse collection: CCT or trade sale – deciding the future of the DSO in 1994

At the beginning of 1994 the DSO had been reduced to a rump provider of refuse collection and highways maintenance services. The refuse collection contract was the mainstay of its business, without which it would have ceased to be viable. The expiry of that contract at the end of 1994 with the consequence that the DSO would have to go through CCT again, threatened the very existence of the DSO. Serious competition was anticipated and hopes of winning under CCT were not high.

The council's external auditor advised that a trade sale of the DSO might be a more beneficial option than letting a contract go under CCT. This would involve the sale of the DSO as a going concern to an outside buyer who would contract with the council to provide a refuse collection service for a set period. Two things followed from this, the first being that the council would no longer have a DSO and would have to rely on outside contractors to provide all of its LGPLA 1980 and LGA 1988 services in the future. However, as the DSO's chances of winning under CCT were not highly rated anyway, it was considered more relevant that better value for money could be obtained under a sale. The second was that a trade sale would be outside the CCT rules (although it would have to comply with the European public procurement regime and the usual fiduciary responsibilities regarding the use of local taxpayers' money). This was important because it would give the council more freedom in determining how and to whom it would entrust its future service provision and the welfare of its staff.

The Council accepted the auditor's advice in April 1994, but it decided to adopt a twin-track approach, going ahead with both CCT and a trade sale at the same time. This was seen as having a number of advantages such as:

- giving the Council access to competitive rates against which they could evaluate the trade sale and/or satisfy the external auditor.
- providing a contingency against any failure in the trade sale.
- honouring a pledge made to the DSO staff that they would be permitted to submit a bid.

Progress of the CCT option

The CCT process had already got underway when this decision was taken. The Council's Engineering Services Committee approved new contract documentation in January 1994 and the work was advertised in the local and trade press and in the European Journal (OJEC) the same month. It was planned to take the decision to award the contract in August, in order for the new contract to start on 1 January 1995. The decision to run preparations for a trade sale of the DSO in parallel with CCT did not significantly affect the process, beyond realignment of some of the timetabled stages. In particular, the dates for the submission of tenders were put back by a few weeks into

September 1994 so that they could be considered alongside tenders for the trade sale.

The Council had anticipated a high level of interest in the tender for refuse collection and this was fully borne out by events. A total of 14 organisations were invited to tender in the summer of 1994, and out of these 11 submitted bids. Apart from the DSO these included bids from the County Council DSO and a further 9 private companies.

Progress of the trade sale option

The council sought a trade sale of the DSO on the basis that tenderers would be invited to provide a refuse collection service taking over the DSO's vehicles, equipment and labour force. A Trade Sale sub-committee of the Policy & Resources committee was formed to oversee the process. It met towards the end of April 1994 to determine its terms of reference and to approve the use of a firm of management consultants to advise the council.

Many of the issues behind the proposed trade sale were considered in a report that the consultants prepared for the next meeting of the Trade Sale sub-committee in May 1994. This made a number of recommendations, which are discussed below.

(i) Contract Length: the consultants recommended a 5 year period in line with the duration of the proposed CCT contract. However they noted the council's interest in adding a waste recycling option to any new contract. This interest stemmed from two sources. The first was the council's recent adoption of an Environmental Policy Statement, which encouraged and promoted the use of recycled materials. The second was the government's own target of 25% recycling of waste materials by 2000. If the council wished to pursue a recycling option then they considered that a longer contract length could be justified (on the basis of allowing a longer period to pay-back investment made). The consultants still regarded a 5-year period as feasible especially if the contractor could use existing facilities outside of the local authority area, but recommended that the trade sale give the council an option to extend the contract.

(ii) Use of the council depot and vehicles: the depot provided space to park vehicles. Part of it was used to store (road gritting) salt for the county council. The consultants considered it unlikely that a contractor could make use of the whole facility just for the refuse collection contract. Therefore any contractor, if required to take over the depot, could be expected to insist on vacant possession so that it would have the freedom to use the depot for other purposes. If the council were willing to grant this, it would need to choose between doing so on the basis of a sale or a lease. Of these, a sale would probably realise less value because of the depot's limited development potential. If a lease were to be chosen it would have to be for a commercial rent and a further decision would be needed on whether it should be tied to the length of the contract or be for a longer period. In view of the age of the council's refuse collection vehicles, the consultants recommended that they be offered only as an optional part of any trade sale.

(iii) Employee terms and conditions: the council had taken the position that it wanted to see the existing terms and conditions of DSO employees maintained. For the purposes of the CCT tender, the council had indicated that it considered TUPE to be applicable. The consultant's report took the view that TUPE would apply to any trade sale but further that the council "may be able to negotiate to contractually secure greater protection for its employees". This is a surprising suggestion, considering the restrictions on the use of non-commercial considerations contained in Part II of the LGA 1988, and one which, as will be seen, the trade union representative also entertained. A stronger recommendation was that the council should closely examine any alternative arrangements for employee pensions proposed by contractors because these could turn out to be less advantageous. This might expose the council to potential claims for constructive dismissal by ex-employees.

(iv) The Highways Maintenance function: part of the DSO was engaged in carrying out highway maintenance work for the county council. The consultants considered that this work would attract little interest because the size of operations was considerable and the amount of work could not be guaranteed. Since the council was not under a legal duty to perform this work, the consultants recommended the closure of these operations and the redeployment of staff to refuse collection work.

(v) Recommended Evaluation Criteria: the report suggested a number of evaluation criteria that the council might use, apart from price. These were quality of service, location, investment plans, recycling plans, and staff welfare. It made no recommendation about the priority attached to different criteria.

The analysis and recommendations of the consultant's report were largely agreeable to the chief officers except that they wanted to keep the Highways DSO and the depot. They were against selling this partly for strategic reasons connected with the Local Government Reorganisation in England. Resbrough was hoping to become the core area of a new unitary authority, amalgamating with parts of two neighbouring district authorities. The retention of the depot would leave a new restructured council with the flexibility to adapt its operations to the new circumstances.

In May 1994 the Trade Sale sub-committee accepted the consultant's report. The contract to be offered would be for 5 years initially or for 7 years if suitable recycling proposals were agreed. There would be no fixed requirements for recycling but contractors would be invited to submit any proposals that would complement the council's existing plans. Parts of the council depot would be leased for a commercial rent to the successful contractor who would also be given the option to rent or purchase any of the relevant vehicles and machinery. A working party of trade unions, managers and councillors would consider any staff concerns.

More controversially, the sub-committee agreed a number and priority of evaluation criteria for the final tenders:

1. quality of service
2. staff welfare
3. price
4. investment plans, including any recycling proposals
5. location of depot

The tendering procedure then began to run. A restricted procedure notice was sent to the European Journal (OJEC) and by the relevant deadline, a total of 14 expressions of interest had been received. The interested firms were then evaluated by the council's consultants according to their financial robustness, relevant experience and number of similar contracts operated. Acting on the consultant's recommendations, a July meeting of the Trade Sale sub-committee selected 7 firms to be invited to tender.

While this was going on a rearguard action was being fought over the sub-committee's ranking of evaluation criteria in May, which had been criticised by consultants and chief officers. Following a meeting with the council's external auditor, the chief officers recommended and the July sub-committee meeting accepted a different approach:

> "The view is now taken that having established and secured the delivery of appropriate levels of quality of service through both the detailed specifications written into the service contract and the selection of a shortlist of suitable contractors (including their financial standing and the taking up of appropriate work based references) the overriding consideration must be for the council to secure value for money for itself. The largest single factor in determining value for money will be price, although other factors are likely to have a bearing on the overall position."

Out of the seven firms that were invited to tender, only four actually submitted tenders of which the council chose two for detailed evaluation. These came from Firm C and Firm S.

Consultations with DSO employees

At the beginning of April, after the decision to examine the trade sale option had been made, a staff – management meeting took place at the council depot. The management side reassured the staff that whatever option (trade sale or CCT) they wanted would be pursued by the council:

> "This was by way of "thanks" for the sterling service given by the refuse collection staff in the past."

The staff faced three future scenarios.

Scenario I – the DSO winning under CCT

In this case they would remain employees of the council under terms and conditions that were either negotiated or imposed by DSO management in order to win the contract. To be competitive these might be reduced terms and conditions compared to those previously in place.

Scenario II – the DSO losing under CCT

The council stated that it considered TUPE would apply in this situation. In this case staff would transfer across to the successful contractor on their existing terms and conditions. What happened after that would be a matter between them and their new employer. The length of the period for which TUPE protected the transferred terms and conditions, was unclear.

Scenario III – the trade sale of the DSO

Similar to Scenario II in that the council would consider TUPE to be applicable and so staff would transfer over to their new employer on existing terms and conditions. The tendering process could take place outside the CCT regime, leaving the Council with greater freedom to choose its preferred contractor and to negotiate the terms of sale. However the freedom to negotiate extra protections for transferring employees over and above TUPE would be constrained by the requirement to ignore non-commercial considerations under Part II of the LGA 1988.

Following the staff – management meeting in April, the UNISON branch secretary drew up a report for the Trade Sale sub-committee outlining her view of staff concerns. The stated minimum objectives for the staff/unions in the event of transfer to a new employer were:

- retention of existing terms and conditions of employment;
- the guarantee of this state of affairs for a set period through a contract clause;
- continuing trade union recognition.

It was suggested that a staff – management working party be created to oversee the trade sale. The report went on to put forward three proposals either as alternatives or supplementary to the trade sale process. In fact the three were wholly ill-conceived and never stood any chance of being seriously considered by the council.

    (i)   The creation of a joint venture company with the council holding 51% of the shares and putting in most of the management.
           – as a way of avoiding competition this would have been a non-runner. Such a company would be associated with the local authority for the purposes of s.33 LGA 1988 and as such the authority could only contract with it having previously taken

reasonable steps for the purpose of securing competition. While this requirement is less rigorous than the full CCT regime, it would be likely to be closely scrutinised by the DOE because of the transparent intent to avoid CCT. Furthermore the arrangement would amount to controlled company status under Part V of the LGHA 1989. Although in 1994 regulations had yet to be made, the government's stated policy was that where a company was effectively under the control of a local authority, the most significant controls that Parliament had laid down for the conduct of local authorities should also apply to that company. On a practical level, the question would arise why private investors would want to put their money in such a creature anyway?

(ii) The transfer over of current pension scheme arrangements to cut out "cowboy companies" and to give the staff a sign of the council's positive commitment.
- such a transfer of the current pension scheme would have been impossible. Commercial organisations are precluded from being granted the admitted body status that would enable a former local authority employee to continue in the Local Government Superannuation Scheme. This is mainly due to the profitable tax concessions available to local authorities and charitable bodies on US investments, which would be lost if commercial organisations were to be brought into the scheme. However the government has adopted the policy stance that comparable pensions schemes must be offered by transferee organisations in a TUPE situation, a view that was shared by the Council's consultants.

(iii) An option for the staff to be offered redundancy 12 months following a change-over to cut out companies that would want to change terms and conditions after the first 12 months and to encourage staff to stay on over the first 12 months transition period.
- the imposition of such a requirement would breach the prohibition of non-commercial considerations in tendering situations in s.17 LGA 1988.

None of these suggestions was taken up by the Trade Sale Sub-Committee when it met in May. However a staff – management working group was established to oversee future progress and it met twice before the next sub-committee meeting in July. There was considerable uncertainty about how effective a guarantee TUPE would be in the event of a trade sale or the loss of the contract by the DSO under CCT. The staff's preferred option was a DSO victory under CCT.

The trade sale tender evaluations

Both C and S had submitted two separate tenders, with and without recycling proposals. The "with recycling" tenders were both significantly more expensive than the council's budgeted provision for recycling schemes. The evaluation reports stated that if either were chosen, further discussions would be required. In reality, cost rendered both of these non-runners. Attention was therefore focussed on the "without recycling" tenders.

C's bid was the cheaper. It proposed to operate the contract from a depot outside the local authority area, which would have freed the council depot for an alternative use. However the firm had no previous experience of undertaking highways maintenance work. S proposed to carry out the refuse collection contract from the council depot and the highway work (for which it had previous experience) from an existing facility outside the local authority area.

On the staffing issues, both proposals were broadly similar. Both accepted that TUPE applied and did not envisage having to make any employees redundant. Neither firm had a policy of harmonising terms and conditions across their workforces, and so transferred employees could expect not to come under immediate pressure to alter their existing terms and conditions in the aftermath of any transfer. Both firms offered pensions schemes that were described by the government actuary as broadly comparable with the current local government scheme.

> "To summarise, C offers a cost advantage and the opportunity to use the [council depot] for another purpose, whilst S offers a more credible plan to preserve the viability of the Highways Section and the retention of an operational base at the [council depot]"

Price was however the chief factor, and C's tender was significantly cheaper. If the trade sale option was to be pursued, C was to be the preferred buyer.

The CCT evaluation

The tenders submitted as part of the CCT process ranged in value from £1.6 million to £3 million over the 5 years of the contract. From these, the four lowest priced bids (out of which the DSO was third) were chosen for further study. This resulted in the elimination of two of the four bids from contention.

One of these was the County DSO's tender, which although the cheapest, was excluded on legal grounds. Since the Environmental Protection Act 1990, county councils had not been empowered to collect refuse unless their contractor organisations had LAWDC status (Local Authority Waste Disposal Company). The county DSO was re-established to qualify for LAWDC status but was at this point still awaiting the Secretary of State's approval. Despite protests that this approval would be forthcoming, Resbrough decided in the interests of certainty to reject the bid. The other tender was eliminated following an analysis of its cost projections against likely future demand (in this case, a rising number of domestic collections, and a decreasing number of commercial collections).

The outcome of this evaluation left the DSO bid in close contention with one of the private contractors, Firm C, which was in fact the same firm that had submitted the preferred tender in the trade sale evaluation.

With both the bids being technically satisfactory, the winner would be the lower priced of the two, taking into account any extraneous costs to the council in awarding the work to an outside contractor. By 1994 such financial evaluations had to be conducted according to the rules of the 1993 Competition Regulations. However the application of these regulations did not produce a clear result.

They permitted the deduction of certain "allowable costs" and "prospective costs" from the price of the DSO bid. However, none of these costs seemed to apply. For example, there were no allowable costs because there were no trainees or disabled workers employed in the DSO. Nor were there many prospective costs to take into account. C was tendering on the basis that TUPE applied, which meant that there were no costs relating to redundancies that could be taken into account by the council (C was planning to take on all the existing staff on their current terms and conditions).[7]

In the end very little separated the two bids. Depending on the assumptions used in the calculations, the result could have gone either way within a margin of no more than £5,000 out of a total contract value of around £2 million or in other words 0.25%. The contract manager (responsible for the technical evaluation) sought the help of the Management Service Unit because he could not be sure of the correct result. The deliberations went to four meetings of the Chief Officers Group before a recommendation could be made.

The options

Ultimately, the council had been left with a choice between three options:

- selling the DSO to Firm C (without the recycling option) and contracting with them for the provision of refuse collection and highways maintenance services; or,
- awarding a contract under CCT rules to the same Firm C; or,
- awarding a contract under CCT rules to the DSO.

For the purposes of the final evaluation report to committee it was decided to present all of these options. However the one recommended by the chief officers was the third – awarding the contract to the DSO under the CCT rules. The recommendation was made on the basis that the DSO bid was sustainable, and that by making certain assumptions they could justify treating it as the lowest bid. It was also considered that it would not be worth the disruption of closing the DSO and changing to an outside contractor for the sake of at most a tiny financial saving (depending on the assumptions used for the financial calculations). In the background there was also political pressure to keep the DSO if possible and perhaps the chief officers were mindful of what had happened in 1989 (see 7.4.1).

---

7   Prospective costs could also include payments to staff in lieu of notice and contract cancellation costs but these did not apply in this situation.

The decision

The final decision was taken following presentations made by the respective tenderers, by the full council meeting in committee in October 1994. This time around the members followed the chief officer's recommendation. A 5-year contract beginning on 1 January 1995 was awarded to the DSO, so assuring its survival.

7.5   Summary and Conclusions

1. Resbrough is a small shire district council that exercises the functions of a lower tier authority in a two-tier system (the upper tier being the county council). It does not undertake the defined activity of schools and welfare catering. The local area is a prosperous part of suburban England, which although Conservative in Parliamentary terms has a strongly non-political tradition in local politics. The council is controlled by independents.
2. Resbrough had not previously shown any ideological leanings toward the contracting out of services. In 1988 all of the defined activities were carried out by direct labour and there was no local political will to change this situation. The authority was however small and in a stringent financial climate faced greater difficulties than most in cutting costs through the achievement of economies of scale. This circumstance dictated a pragmatic approach to service provision, which would in time prove receptive to the potential cost benefits and flexibility of contracting out services.
3. In response to the 1988 Act, the council adopted a policy of supporting the direct provision of services wherever possible within the constraints of the legislation. In-house providers have been helped to make competitive bids. However the council has practiced neutrality in the evaluation of tenders, and the aim has been for the council to get the best price for the service specified.
4. The results of CCT have been dramatic, as shown by the situation in May 1997. By that date and for this council CCT applied to work covered by the LGPLA 1980 and ten defined activities under the LGA 1988. If the LGPLA 1980 work is taken as two activities, namely building maintenance and highway maintenance that means that CCT applied to twelve of the council's services on that date. Of these, five were provided in-house (two because they were de minimis and the other three won in competition), three had been awarded to external contractors as a result of CCT, and another four had been externalised outside of the CCT regime. As a result the council has a mixed economy of service provision, with highly visible services such as refuse collection and street cleansing continuing to be provided directly by the council, but most others either contracted out or wholly externalised. The council's principal

competitor for many of the blue-collar services has been the county council DSO rather than the private sector.

5. The effects of white collar CCT have been seen largely in the preparations for it. Chief among these has been the establishment of an internal market between different cost centres in the authority. This is set to stay and has had an important influence on the way the council operates (although not necessarily a popular one). However by May 1997 no CCT tenders for white-collar services had taken place. Housing management CCT had been avoided by the voluntary transfer of housing stock to a housing association, and the implementation dates for the council's remaining white-collar services had yet to be reached.

6. The council has avoided a centralised corporate approach to CCT. The achievement of cost savings, efficient management of services, strict and cautious compliance with the legislation, and the avoidance of bureaucracy have all been important in the council's approach, but there has been no attempt to achieve wider political goals through the process. Therefore the individual departments have been left to take the lead in developing service specifications, evaluating the technical side of tenders and managing contracts. Corporate involvement has tended to be restricted to legal and financial concerns affecting the council as a whole.

7. The council has been concerned from the outset to achieve a visible separation of the client and contractor roles in CCT. That was why a free standing DSO was established as early as 1988 under the control of a chief officer of the council, to undertake and bid to retain defined activity work. Although the loss of contracts has meant its demotion to being a division of the council's Community Services Department, the DSO is still organisationally apart from the client-side of the contracts that it performs. A similar separation has been achieved at committee level, with a Management Services Committee taking responsibility for the DSO.

8. The DSO operates with a degree of commercial autonomy. It has its own manager who is responsible for operational matters and reports to a Management Services Committee of the council. That committee has a wide responsibility for the DSO and its workforce. They are employed under different terms and conditions to those in the rest of the authority. Agency staff are used to fill up peaks in demand. Staff – management relations are largely conducted on site at the council depot with little official in-put from UNISON. The small size of the workforce and the commitment of the DSO manager have ensured harmonious relations.

9. Contract management arrangements have assumed greater importance over time as more services have been contracted out. Responsibility has been decentralised, contracts being treated on a case by case basis within the departments (although becoming concentrated into three contract management sections). The Council has

recognised the disadvantages of an uncoordinated approach to contract management but has been unwilling to create a dedicated contracts management department. Instead an inter-departmental working group has been created, which acts as a forum for the exchange of experiences and dissemination of best practice. This has been considered a success.

10. In conclusion, CCT in conjunction with general cost constraints of recent decades, has had a significant influence on the provision of local services. It has pushed the council away from direct provision (although this is still important) towards a more enabling role. The arts of contract management have grown as this has taken place. The roles of service specifications, the separation of clients from contractors, and the rigorous examination of competing tenders in the provision of services are now deeply entrenched.

CHAPTER EIGHT

A CASE STUDY: GREENBROUGH BOROUGH COUNCIL

CONTENTS

8.1 Profile of Greenbrough
8.2 The Results of CCT
8.3 Managing Service Delivery under CCT
8.4 Case Studies of CCT Tenders
8.5 Summary and Conclusions

This chapter is based on the results of case study research on a single local authority. Unless otherwise indicated, the presentation reflects the law and events up to May 1997. In order to preserve confidentiality, the authority is identified throughout by the pseudonym of Greenbrough. The research methodology is outlined in Appendix 1 of this book.

8.1   Profile of Greenbrough

Greenbrough is an English suburban borough with a population of around 190,000 people. The local area is largely residential, with a strong retailing and service industries sector but very little manufacturing industry. The social make-up of the local population is broadly professional or managerial middle class. There are a number of parks and other open spaces in the borough with the south bordering on open countryside.

The council is a unitary local authority and so carries out the full range of local authority services including those as the local education authority.

In political terms, Greenbrough was a safe but moderate Conservative borough until the late 1980s. At that time it was captured by the Liberal Democrats whose majority has grown over subsequent elections, and who are now very strongly entrenched. The Conservative Group has steadily been reduced over the same period, so much so that the Labour Group has taken over as the principal Opposition.

8.2   The Results of CCT

Greenbrough was not an exponent of voluntary contracting out before the introduction of CCT. In the first half of the 1980s, the Conservative administration had considered contracting out services such as conveyancing, office and building cleaning, and grass cutting on highways verges but no action was taken beyond awarding a small contract for the cleaning of branch libraries to a contractor.[1] Nor did the CCT provisions of the LGPLA 1980

---

1   K. Ascher "The Politics of Privatisation" (1988) and surveys published by the Local Government Chronicle 1982–87.

have a big impact on the amount of construction and maintenance work carried out directly. Contractors were used in these areas but only to supplement in-house provision where it was lacking in skills or capacity. The principal effect of the LGPLA 1980 was the improved financial administration of the council's Direct Labour Organisation but little else.

When the government released its 1985 consultation paper "Competition in the provision of local services", the council's response was that compulsion was only suitable in the case of high spending councils. Greenbrough defined these as councils whose costs, on Audit Commission figures, were at least 25% above the average of comparable councils. Needless to say, this did not include Greenbrough itself. The Conservative group lost power shortly after that, but there were no new developments when the Liberal Democrats took over. When the LGA 1988 was passed the Council provided the overwhelming proportion of local services in-house and there was little prospect of that situation changing.

8.2.1 The results of CCT: An overview

The implementation of CCT for the original seven defined activities was governed by the 1988 Competition Regulations.[2] Greenbrough was required to have implemented CCT before the deadlines shown below in Table 1.

The response to CCT, which saw the creation of a number of Direct Service Organisations (DSOs) within the existing council departments, is traced in 8.3. Greenbrough let all of its defined activity work by the required dates. Indeed the school catering contract was let two years early, while refuse collection and street cleansing were combined in a single contract and let on the earlier of the two required dates. In this first round of competition, the DSOs were successful in winning most of the contracts on offer. The only work gained by outside contractors was an estates cleaning contract (part of building cleaning work) and some of the smaller other catering contracts, which were in any case voluntarily contracted out.

Table 1

Defined Activity	CCT to apply from...
Vehicle repair and maintenance	1.8.89
Ground maintenance	1.1.90–1.1.94
Refuse collection	1.1.90
Street cleansing	1.8.90
Building cleaning	1.1.91
Other catering	1.8.91
Schools and welfare catering	1.1.92
Management sports/leisure	1.1.92–1.1.93

2 S.I 1988 No. 1371.

The DSOs faced greater difficulties in carrying out the first round contracts. Particular problems were faced but overcome in relation to building cleaning work and school catering work. Failure to meet the required rate of return on the staff catering contract and more seriously on the building maintenance contracts led in each case to the early termination of those contracts in 1991 and 1994 respectively. The DSOs were not allowed to retender for the work in these cases.

However, despite these difficulties, those DSO contracts that had lasted their term were generally retained when they came up for renewal. The exception was building cleaning work, but in compensation the DSO did manage to win back the estates cleaning contract. Clearly the DSO has been successful in holding onto blue-collar work despite the pressures of CCT.

Being a unitary local authority, Greenbrough has been at the forefront of white-collar CCT. The government proposals were published and consulted upon from 1991 onwards. Greenbrough took early notice and began to develop the competitiveness of its white-collar services with the assistance of external management consultants. This included the development of internal trading accounts (an internal market) and the implementation of a client–contractor split into some professional services divisions. The necessary regulatory framework for white collar CCT (and three other new CCT activities) was settled over 1994–1995. Greenbrough was not subject to the English Local Government Review and so found itself in the first wave of authorities to be subject to the new regime. The implementation deadlines are reproduced below in Table 2.

8.2.2   The results of CCT service by service

The outcome of competition in each of the services is considered below.

Refuse collection and street cleansing

These activities were combined into a single contract to reflect the existing pattern of organisation. This meant that the contract had to be let from the

Table 2

Defined Activity	CCT to apply from...
Supervision of parking	1 January 1996
Vehicle management	1 January 1996
Security work	1 January 1996
Housing management	1 April 1996
Construction/property services	1 April 1996
Legal services	1 April 1996
Personnel services	1 October 1996
Financial services	1 April 1997
Information technology services	1 October 1997

earlier of the two dates prescribed in the Regulations, namely 1 January 1990. Despite the size of the contract that was being let, there was a high competitive response with ten firms being invited to tender of whom seven actually submitted tenders. The DSO was awarded the contract, having submitted the lowest priced tender.

For the second round of CCT and in furtherance of the council's environmental agenda, the service specification for the contract was redefined to take account of the council's waste minimisation policy. This meant that tenderers in the second round were required to submit for evaluation their proposals for minimising waste collection and disposal. The work was also let as five separate contracts to facilitate the tender evaluation process. When these waste minimisation contracts were tendered, despite early interest from a number of firms, only the DSO actually submitted bids. Following many weeks of negotiations over the financial provisions of the DSO bids, it was accepted as contractor by the Council in early 1996.

Building maintenance

This area is governed by the LGPLA 1980 regime, under which there is no formal regulation of the length of contracts. The previous time that building maintenance had been put out to tender, it had been divided into four contracts of which the DSO had won three. However it was found that the financial terms of its tender had been misjudged and the DSO could not make the required rate of return. To forestall action by the DOE the Council terminated the three DSO contracts in 1994 and did not allow the DSO to bid for the work when it was subsequently retendered. This work has since remained in the hands of outside contractors.

Building cleaning and estates cleaning

The cleaning of schools, council offices and other establishments was divided up and let as five contracts for CCT purposes. This was to encourage a reasonable competitive response from medium–large commercial companies while deterring small operators. The DSO won all five contracts (on price in four cases and as the only bidder in the other). However the contracts ran into immediate problems because most of the staff refused to work under new terms and conditions of employment. It took six months and a change of management to end the turmoil.

Building cleaning work was retendered in 1994 as three contracts (to reflect the loss of schools cleaning work as a result of LMS and opting out). The competitive response was intense with no fewer than 84 firms replying to the advertisement of the work. This time all of the contracts were won by outside tenderers, the DSO being soundly beaten on price. When contracts fell due for retendering in 1997, the DSO decided not to bid on commercial grounds.

The cleaning of the common areas in council run housing estates (halls, stairways etc.) was let separately to the rest of building cleaning work. The contract was won by an outside contractor in the first round of CCT. However the DSO won it back when it came up for renewal in 1995.

Other catering

This covered the operation of staff canteens and catering facilities at leisure centres, arts galleries, theatres and libraries. It has been largely left to outside contractors. In the first round of CCT, the DSO won the contract for operating staff canteens but was unable to carry it out profitably and early termination of the contract followed.

Schools and welfare catering

This defined activity was tendered as two separate contracts. A schools catering contract (covering 64 sites) was tendered in 1989–90 to commence from 1 September 1990. This was in advance of the statutory timetable and so ensured that the school catering arrangements were settled before the implementation of local management of schools (LMS). The DSO won against a single competitor having submitted the lower priced tender. The contract ran into mid-term financial problems in 1992 when the council had to withdraw the subsidy on secondary school meals in order to contain its costs. This forced the prices of meals to rise with adverse consequences for the take-up of school meals (and so for the profitability of the contractor). Despite these difficulties, the DSO was successful in retaining the contract in 1995.

Greenbrough tendered its welfare catering contract (for the provision of meals at day centres and the meals-on-wheels service) at the normal time on the statutory timetable (January 1992). The DSO tender was successful, narrowly defeating two other tenders on price. The DSO retained the contract in April 1997 in the second round of CCT. This is considered in greater detail in a case study at 8.4.1.

Vehicle repair and maintenance; Ground maintenance; Management of sports and leisure facilities.

The vehicle repair and maintenance contract was won in the first round of CCT by the DSO, which of four other competing bids, submitted the lowest priced tender. The contract continues to be operated by the DSO. The Council tendered its ground maintenance work in five separate tranches over the permitted period to the beginning of 1994. The contracts were won by the DSO and remain in its hands. The contract for Sports and Leisure management was also won by an in-house bid.

Supervision of parking; security work; vehicle management

Supervision of parking work was divided into two contracts covering off-street parking and on-street parking. The former was won by the DSO, and the latter by a private company. The on-street parking contract is due to be retendered in 1997 and there may be an in-house bid. Security work is de minimis for CCT purposes, as is vehicle management work.

Housing management

The housing management contract did go to CCT, but the in-house bid was not successful. A private contractor now runs the service on behalf of the council.

The remaining white-collar defined activities

The various Competition Regulations required a specified proportion of defined work to be subject to CCT, the precise amount being calculated in accordance with a statutory formula of T (total value of defined work) minus credits. This has led to a number of different outcomes:

(i) In the case of construction and property services a large and mixed package of work was tendered. The in-house provider unit was successful on both price and quality grounds against four outside bids. This is considered in a case study at 8.4.4.
(ii) For legal services the authority chose to put out to tender more than the specified proportion of work. However despite evidence of outside interest from a preparatory market testing exercise, no outside bids ran against the in-house provider in the real thing. This prompted an investigation by the Secretary of State regarding suspicions of anti-competitive conduct, but Greenbrough was able to rebut this suspicion and no further action was taken. This is considered further in a case study at 8.4.3.
(iii) In the case of financial services, Greenbrough tendered its revenue services work in satisfaction of the specified proportion. The contract was won by an outside contractor, who took over the existing staff assigned to this work in accordance with TUPE. A case study at 8.4.3 examines this tender further.
(iv) However the specified proportion of Personnel services work and Information technology services work is nil - both are de minimis for the purposes of white-collar CCT.

8.2.3   The current position of contracted services

CCT has left this authority with a mixed economy in local service provision, in which in-house provision is still very much dominant. Table 3 shows the balance between in-house and contracted out service provision in the case of blue-collar work, as it stood in May 1997.

Clearly the majority of services to which CCT applies are still provided directly by the Council. In a sense not much has changed from ten years earlier. However this would be to underestimate the extent of contracted out service provision. Although a minority proportion, it is nevertheless significant. What is noticeable, when compared to the experience of Resbrough BC (discussed in Chapter 7), is the fact that Greenbrough has not externalised any aspects of blue-collar service provision. This is possibly

Table 3: Blue-Collar Services

In-house	Contracted out	Externalised
Refuse collection	Building cleaning	
Street cleansing	Other catering	
School catering	On-street parking	
Welfare catering	Building maintenance	
Ground maintenance		
Vehicle maintenance		
Estates cleaning		
Off-street parking		
Leisure management		
Security work*		
Vehicle management*		

*value is de minimis for CCT

a reflection on the relative sizes of the two councils as well as their political composition.

The services that have been contracted out are likely to remain so into the foreseeable future. In particular, the DSO has no recent track record in building cleaning or other catering contracts. Only in the supervision of on-street parking contract, which is renewable in 1997, is there a possibility of swift return to in-house control. On the other hand the DSO and other in-house providers would appear to have a strong grip over the services they currently control. It is probable that the current pattern of service provision will remain unchanged into the next century.

The situation with white-collar services is similar. Table 4 shows the situation in May 1997.

Again there has been no attempt to externalise service provision (although some IT facilities are shared with a neighbouring local authority). The balance between in-house and contracted out provision is largely tipped towards the former, although the degree of contracting out is significant. The services that have been contracted out are likely to remain so into the foreseeable future. Housing management and revenue services work are both out on contract for the rest of the 1990s and in any case because of TUPE the Council lost its in-house staff when the contracts were awarded outside.

8.3   Managing Service Delivery under CCT

Managing services in the CCT environment has posed new challenges for local authorities. This Part will examine the way in which Greenbrough has responded to some of them.

Table 4: White-Collar Services

In-house	Contracted-out	Externalised
C&P services	Housing management	
Legal services	Revenue services	
Personnel services		
IT services		
Financial services		

8.3.1 Incorporating corporate goals into the CCT process

In the 1990s the council adopted a set of core values and developed certain corporate policies, especially in relation to the protection of the environment. It has sought to build these into all aspects of its service provision, while staying within the parameters of CCT.

Council core values, priorities and policies

Those of relevance to CCT include the community charter and core values, the policy towards in-house provision of services, and environmental policies including Local Agenda 21.

Corporate "Vision and Values"

The Community Charter is a general declaration of what the council sees as its purpose and role in the local community:

> "We aim to build a community in which all can take part and all can take pride. We believe that people have a right to be involved in running their communities. We will work for a sense of partnership and community in all areas of life. We will aim to disperse power, to foster diversity and to nurture creativity. We believe that the role of the Council is to enable all citizens to attain these ideals, to contribute fully to their communities and to take part in the decisions which affect their lives".

The associated Core Values set out a number of guiding principles by which the Council pledges to operate in all areas:

> "We are committed to:
> A. Working in PARTNERSHIP with the people who live or work in the Borough.
> B. Enabling and encouraging INVESTMENT in the Council's decision making processes.

C. Making our services open and ACCESSIBLE so that everyone should feel able to approach us with confidence, be listened to and treated with respect.
D. Providing HIGH QUALITY COST EFFECTIVE SERVICES which meet community needs in a changing environment.
E. Promoting EQUALITY where everyone is treated fairly but taking account of the special needs of people who lack resources or face disadvantage.
F. INVESTING WISELY FOR THE FUTURE, protecting and developing human and natural resources to ensure a healthy environment for present and future generations.
G. The Council also recognises that its MOST IMPORTANT ASSET IS ITS STAFF who have a key role promoting pride in our community through the adoption of these core values."

Greenbrough therefore sees itself as a progressive and "enabling" council with a distinctly "green" ideology and agenda.

The in-house provision of services

Greenbrough's official policy is that it values its staff and aims to keep service provision in-house provided that this offers the best value. In practice the emphasis is placed on the achievement of best value. Indeed if the wording is reversed it means that in-house provision is not preferred where it does not offer best value. A comment from an external consultant working for the council was:

> "The line seems to be they would be very pleased for the internal provider to win but they are not going to tilt the playing field to make it happen."

Environmental policies

Green issues are of considerable importance. In 1986, under the new Liberal Democrat administration, the Council adopted an Environmental Policy Statement. It consists of eighteen policies, which aim to achieve environmental improvement through balancing short-term economic requirements against the long term ecological needs of the community. Progress in all policies is reviewed and reported on annually and particular policies are targeted each year for special attention. In addition, the council standing orders require that all policy proposals and reports coming to council committees outline their environmental implications (even if just to say there are none).

Although framed before the LGA 1988, the Environmental Policy Statement touches on a number of activities that are subject to CCT. For example, particular policies aim:

- "to reduce and discourage litter as part of the Community Action Programme" (re street cleansing, ground maintenance).

- to "discourage waste and encourage the recycling of materials and use recycled materials wherever practicable" (re refuse collection).
- to "encourage the responsible and informed attitude to the use of artificial fertilizers, pesticides and herbicides on Council owned land and elsewhere and aim to minimise the use of artificial fertilizers" (re ground maintenance).
- to "encourage healthy eating and provide the widest circulation of information on the subject and discourage the use of unnecessary additives particularly within the Council services" (re catering).

On the basis of the Statement, the Council has developed a number of green policies and initiatives. The most significant of these, and relevant to the refuse collection service, is a waste minimisation strategy. The council plans to maximise the recycling and recovery of waste so as to minimise the disposal of waste by landfill or incineration. The target is to achieve a 50% recycling/recovery rate by 2000 with the potential to achieve 80% by 2005. Further examples, relating to catering services, are policies to promote healthy eating and avoid publicity of slimming foods.

Local Agenda 21

In the 1990s, the Environmental Policy Statement has been complemented by Local Agenda 21, the product of the international agreement at the Rio de Janeiro Earth Summit in 1992. Local authorities of the signatory countries were asked to prepare with their communities a local agenda for sustainable development in the 21st Century. This is defined as development that meets the needs of the present without compromising the ability of future generations to meet their own needs. The process involves the setting of local sustainability indicators against which the local authorities and communities can measure the outcome of environmental initiatives. The Council has actively pursued its own Local Agenda since 1994 and local service delivery is being progressively reviewed to ensure that it is consistent with sustainable development. One result of this has been a requirement for all contractors to work towards implementing an Environmental Management and Audit system (EMAS) by the end of their contract period. In-house providers such as the DSO are also required to adopt EMAS and to identify further areas of operation for environmentally friendly improvements as a part of Local Agenda 21. These initiatives are closely linked in practice, both being based on a progressive identification and adoption of environmentally sound practices. An example relevant to cleaning work is the environmentally safe disposal of used cleaning fluids.

Other relevant policies

There are a number of other policies that are relevant to CCT services. These include the imposition of relevant international standards of quality management, and others relating to the handling of customer complaints, customer care, health and safety, and equal opportunities.

Implementing council core values, priorities and policies

Where a local authority seeks to build its corporate policies into tendering and contractual arrangements, it must work within a broad legal framework and avoid a number of pitfalls:

- discriminating against other EC nationals contrary to the general principles of EC law.
- contravening EC public procurement rules as set out in the Public Works Contract Regulations 1995 or the Public Services Contract Regulations 1993 (and/or the originating EC directives).
- imposing a condition that may be considered by the Secretary of State to be anti-competitive under the CCT rules.
- contravening the prohibition of non-commercial considerations in Part II of the LGA 1988.
- imposing a condition that is irrelevant, unreasonable or otherwise ultra vires.

Also, where a local authority contracts on its standard terms and conditions, the courts will construe any ambiguity in those terms against it in accordance with the contra proferentem rule. Within these limitations, local authorities may still have the scope to impose their own policy priorities. Greenbrough has made full use of this scope.

Implementation of council values and policies through the tender evaluation process

The CCT regime prescribes many aspects of tender evaluation but stops short of laying down an overall framework. The Council has sought to create its own framework, making use of its parallel obligations under the EU public procurement rules, to condition its handling of CCT matters. In 1995, the Corporate Legal Adviser drew up a Guide to Tender Evaluation to assist officers and members involved in this area (see also 8.3.4). This establishes a framework through which the Council aims to identify the tender offering it best value. The Introduction to the Guide states:

> "Wherever possible, evaluation criteria must be drawn up to incorporate a requirement to comply with the Council's current policies, priorities and core values."

For the incorporation of its policies, priorities and core values to be effective, a council needs flexibility over the considerations that it can take into account in its evaluation of tenders, and in particular the flexibility not to be constrained into accepting the lowest cost tender.

CCT has never required councils to accept the lowest cost tender. In particular, it has nothing to say where a council rejects the lowest tender in favour of another if both come from outside contractors. Only where a lower tender is rejected in favour of an in-house bid, does anti-competitive behaviour become relevant and even then the council will be in the clear if it can show good reason for its decision. By adopting relevant policies, systematically incorporating them into the contract documentation and tender evaluation process, and rigorously documenting all decisions as they are taken, the Council believes that it can show good reason where it chooses not to accept the lowest tender.

Therefore, Greenbrough advertises, in accordance with the EU rules, that it will award contracts to the "most economically advantageous tender", on the basis of "quality, other criteria, and price".

Naturally therefore, Greenbrough uses its tender documentation especially the pre-tender questionnaires and method statements to elicit information from tenderers relating to its policies, priorities and core values. The example given below is taken from the environmental section of the pre-tender questionnaire sent out for Construction and Property Services CCT in 1995. Environmental issues are a priority for Greenbrough but not many other authorities. Indeed the "model" forms of pre-tender questionnaire published by organisations such as the Association of Metropolitan Authorities do not cover them, which makes the asking of these questions, a matter of particular interest:

"H1. The [Council] has an Environmental Statement which sets out the Council's Policies with regard to the protection and improvement of the environment. Would your firm be willing to work with the Council to further protection and improvement of the environment?
H2. Does your firm have an environmental policy or an environmental purchasing policy? [If so please attach a copy...].
H3. What action has your firm taken to implement your environmental policy if the answer to H2 is positive.
H4. Please give details of any practical measures your firm has taken in the last three years to improve the environment, reduce consumption of fuel and other natural resources or reduce pollution.
H5. Please give details on how your firm is dealing with environmental considerations in the design and maintenance of buildings and structures?
H6. Has your firm received any national/international awards relating to the service which recognises the environmental dimension of your work?
H7. Has your firm adopted an environmental purchasing policy? If so please attach a summary."

A similar use is made of method statements in the qualitative evaluation process (whether a particular tender meets the service specification), especially in white collar CCT. A method statement requires tenderers to describe in a set format the procedures and resources they will use to meet particular sections of the specification.

Incorporation of council values and policies through contract documents

The actual service contracts are also used to impose council goals and policies on a successful contractor. The following examples are drawn from the Leisure Facilities Catering contract documentation (provision of catering facilities at council run leisure outlets including leisure centres, libraries and theatres).

Conditions of Tender

An incorporation of the authority's ideological position is attempted by the recital of the Community Charter and Statement of Core Values in the Conditions of Tender, with the additional statement that:

> "In addition to whatever is contained in the rest of these documents the Contract requires the Contractor to be mindful of the Council's community charter and to take on board the core values and invites the Contractor to aspire with us towards promoting the best possible service to our customers."

This should achieve two things for the Council. Firstly, it is a clear statement that conformity with the council's values will be a part of the criteria used to evaluate tenders. This will forewarn tenderers and provide a defence against any subsequent challenge by the Secretary of State. Secondly it provides the basis (and justification) for a purposive interpretation of the contract in the event of a dispute.

The Service Profile

The service profile or specification (which is an integral part of the contract) is drawn up in general and output based terms: contractors are required to provide a hot and cold catering service (and/or bar facilities) at a specified leisure outlet to "high standards". This challenges tenderers to come up with their own proposals for satisfying the contractual requirements, and so widens the council's discretion in tender evaluation. The service profile also contains a general requirement that the successful contractor works within the council's policy statements:

> "The contractor shall conform, obey, and institute practices which are in accordance with all policies of the council insofar as these are relevant to the Contract [and its operation] and as are allowable under the 1988 Local Government Act. The Council reserves the right to change, modify and alter such policies as already exist and to add and adopt new policies as it sees fit and without the requirement for discussion or consultation with the Contractor. On agreement by elected members of any modifications or additions to policies which are relevant to the Contractor, the Contractor will be so notified and will accordingly make any modifications necessary to ensure that [the contract is performed] in accordance with such new policies."

The Conditions of Contract

The Conditions provide that the contractual agreement is enforced through the action of an "Authorised Officer" who is nominated by the Council to exercise its rights under the contract. The contract gives the Authorised Officer a wide discretion:

> "General Responsibilities
> The Contractor shall perform the services [and any authorised variation thereof] in accordance in all respects with the Contract in a proper, skilful and workmanlike manner to the satisfaction of the Authorised Officer and shall comply with and adhere strictly to the Authorised Officer's instructions on any matter connected therewith (whether mentioned in the contract or not)."

This discretion is especially significant when it is considered that the service profile contains a general requirement that the successful contractor works within the council's policy statements (see above). Other contract conditions go beyond this, either by clearly imposing specific requirements relating to individual policy areas or by inviting contractors to submit their own proposals for the Authorised Officer's approval. For example, the successful contractor is required to implement any relevant international standard of quality assurance (by the end of the contract period). Other examples relate to customer care and the environment:

> "Customer Care
> The Council requires the Contractor to submit to the Authorised Officer their own Customer Care Policy for approval. Failure to do so will result in the Council imposing its own Customer Care Policy..."

> "Environmental Issues
> The Council supports the reduction in use of packaging, the use of biodegradable products and energy conservation.
> A) In view of this, disposable cutlery and crockery will only be acceptable in emergencies and with the Authorised Officer's permission.
> The Contractors must adhere to its Environmental Policy annexed as Schedule 12. In the event that the Contractor does not have an Environmental Policy or alternatively wishes to he shall adhere to the Council's Environmental Policy annexed as Schedule 13."

The conditions allow for variations of the contract by written agreement between the Authorised Officer and a duly authorised representative of the contractor. They also permit variations to be made to the service specification:

> "...The Authorised Officer may from time to time require changes to the Service and accordingly upon given written notice to the Contractor may add

to or delete from or otherwise amend in any way the provisions of the Specification. The Contractor shall be bound by any such variation."

"...Where either the Contractor or the Authorised Officer consider that a variation has a material financial effect on either party the value of the variation shall be agreed by negotiation."

These examples show the extent to which a determined local authority with a genuine and properly worked out policy agenda can put its own stamp on the CCT process without necessarily straying into anti-competitive behaviour.

8.3.2   The separation of client and contractor roles

Before the passing of the LGA 1988, the council's departmental structure had been based around seven departments:

- Chief Executive's
- Finance
- Education
- Leisure Services
- Technical Services
- Social Services
- Housing, Health and Consumer Service.

Of these, the Chief Executive's and the Finance were relatively small central services departments, and the others were frontline service departments. There was no organisational separation of client and contractor roles within departments, and nor were defined activities necessarily the exclusive preserve of any one department. For example, the Education Department was responsible for grass cutting in schools, while Leisure Services had responsibility for grass cutting in parks. The departments were accountable to seven council committees that broadly shadowed their names and functions. The principal committee was Policy and Resources. Again the committees operated without regard to the separation of contractor and client roles.

1988–92 Client–Contractor splits within existing departments

In considering the implications of the LGA 1988, the council's chief officers were concerned that the existing organisational arrangements might be deemed anti-competitive by the Secretary of State. In a report to the Policy and Resources Committee in July 1988 they said that:

"It is not yet known whether the Secretary of State will consider the structure of the local authority's contract arrangements to be subject to this provision but it is possible that this provision could be used to ensure that 'client' and 'contractor' roles of a local authority are separately managed."

At this point the council considered but rejected the option of creating a free standing Contracts Directorate. The chief officers' viewed such a body as having three main advantages. The first was that it would have been the hardest of hard splits, achieving a very visible separation of client and contractor roles and thereby minimising the possibility of a challenge from the Secretary of State. Secondly, it would have made transparent the "client" and "contractor" nature of costs, and thirdly it would have ensured the development of what the report described as "acute" motivation among the staff on each side of the divide. However these advantages were considered outweighed by the "considerable" costs of establishing such a Directorate (which would in turn burden the services facing competition), the lack of time, and the dislocation involved in placing disparate staff and skills together in a new organisation.

Instead the chief officers came down in favour of a second option, which involved a client–contractor split within each department, with the relevant head of department (at chief officer level) remaining responsible for both elements. This was seen as a pragmatic response to the requirements of the new Act, separating the two roles while still fostering staff co-operation, which it was argued, would be greatest if the existing departmental structure were to be preserved. A number of DSOs were created within the existing departments as a result.

In the Technical Services Department there were five DSOs that were responsible for carrying out vehicle maintenance, refuse collection, street cleaning, building maintenance, and highways/streetlighting/sewer maintenance works. The latter two DSOs were concerned with LGPLA 1980 work. The Education Department was the home of the Catering services DSO that undertook the school meals and the welfare meals contracts. Also located here was a school grounds maintenance DSO that was however soon amalgamated into the council's main grounds maintenance DSO in the Leisure Services Department. Finally the Chief Executive's Department was host to the Cleaning Services DSO, which ran the building cleaning contracts.

The council's committee structure was not overhauled in parallel with the departmental reorganisation. Oversight was still carried out by the relevant service committees, which considered departmental reports covering both client and contractor issues. Initially the chief officers saw no role for a single, authority-wide committee responsible for supervising and submitting all tenders. Indeed the previous year the council had considered and rejected a motion to establish such a committee on officer advice. The view was that the variety of the contracts to be let was too great to allow effective oversight by a single committee. Nevertheless, the existing arrangements were felt to be inadequate because members felt too far removed from the new contracting issues and also wanted to involve the staff. This was acknowledged in the July 1988 report:

> "...some method is needed for communicating between members and workpeople in regard to submitting tenders and progress of the Direct Services Organisation if successful once the "contract" has been let."

The local Joint Works Committee was considered but deemed unsuitable because the interests represented on it were too disparate to be able to deal with any particular area of contracting. The solution, albeit a temporary one, was the formation of a Contracts Consultative Panel as a special consultative sub-committee to the Policy and Resources Committee. It comprised a total of ten councillors and ten staff representatives (union and non-union) but these worked in fours, each foursome taking responsibility for one of five areas of work: building maintenance works, catering, building cleaning, parks, and sports facilities. Therefore the membership of the Panel rotated depending on the work or contract under consideration. Its terms of reference were widely drawn to allow it to act as:

> "...a forum for reference by the employees of any particular issues relating to restructuring, revised working practices, terms and conditions of employment and workforce levels...
> ...[and] a forum for discussion of the results of the tendering process in each case, and, where successful, to revise progress from time to time."

However all decisions on these matters lay with the Resources sub-committee of the Policy and Resources Committee. This lack of decision-making power, and a general lateness in the panel's consideration of the issues led to it being disbanded in 1991. In its place, a members-only Contracts Services sub-committee took reports from the various DSOs. This was a stronger and longer lasting arrangement.

1992 Reorganising to produce a "hard split"

The client/contractor arrangements of 1988 came under strain from several quarters in the new competitive environment. Firstly, although successful in winning contracts in the majority of cases, there was concern about the DSO's ability to achieve the financial returns on contracted work required under CCT. There was also concern about the effectiveness of client-side supervision, the legality of the client-side/contractor-side arrangements and the role of members in overseeing contracted services.

In July 1991 the council approved a plan to reorganise its departmental structure for the first time since the 1970s. Its declared purpose was "to produce a clearer and more effective organisation which was more responsive to member's policies, priorities and core values together with the changing external and legislative environment and which was able to address strategic issues more effectively". The principal features of the reorganisation were:

- the abolition of the Social Services, Technical Services and Housing, Health and Consumer Services (HHCS) Departments.
- the creation of a Housing and Social Services Department by merging the Social Services Department with the Housing Division of HHCS Department.
- the creation of an Environmental Services Department based on the

old Technical Services Department shorn of its five DSOs but joined to the environmental health and consumer services parts of the former HHCS Department.
– the creation of a Contract Services Department out of the five DSOs from the old Technical Services Department, joined by three DSOs from other departments dealing with grounds maintenance, catering services and building cleaning (but not leisure management).
– The remaining departments (Chief Executive's, Finance, Education, Leisure Services) were retained.

The creation of Contract Services marked the establishment of the hard split that had been rejected back in 1988. The council minutes spoke of the reasons for this change of heart:

> "It was felt that the present client/contractor split was not at a level appropriate to secure, in all cases, the objective and independent relationship that needed to exist between the Council as contractor and as client. Thus a separate department would clearly separate client interests from contractor interests, would achieve a single minded focus on competitiveness in price and service quality, clarify the accountability of management to achieve agreed 'profits' or rates of return, clarify the authority of management to negotiate for and acquire information technology, financial, legal and personnel support, attune democratic and financial controls of the Council to those requirements and build a staff team who could thrive on commercial challenges."

The role played by Contract Services is considered more fully in 8.3.4 below. Meanwhile, the client-side role was left to the remaining departments, particularly the new Environmental Services Department.

The committee structure had to change to reflect the departmental reorganisation, and the clearer separation of clients and contractors. The contractor role was overseen by an upgraded Contract Services sub-committee, which was renamed the Contracts Services Board to reflect the new status of contracted services. The Board also took reports from the Leisure Services DSO, which had remained a part of the Leisure Services Department.

After the departmental reorganisation the relevant service committees were now Environmental Services, Education, Leisure Services, Housing and Social Services, and Policy and Resources. These were now responsible for overseeing the client-side responsibilities of the council.

The move away from a hard split

The institution of a hard split along the lines of the blue-collar arrangements was never a serious prospect when preparations for the introduction of white-collar CCT got underway. Instead separate client and contractor units (often called purchasers and providers) were established within existing departments. The client units reported to the relevant service committee, while the providers were responsible to the Contract Services Board. It was to this type of arrangement that the council returned in the case of its blue-collar services at the beginning of 1997.

There were several reasons behind this. Contract Service's status as a freestanding department came under increasing financial strain over the years as the loss of some key contracts, in particular building maintenance, increased the burden of overhead costs on the remaining areas of work. The management structure became too lean to support a separate department. There was also concern that the division between clients and the contractor-side had gone too far, had become too confrontational, for the effective delivery of services. Therefore, at the beginning of 1997 following an internal review and a consultant's report Contract Services lost its independent status and was incorporated as a separate division into the Environmental Services Department.

This change has brought to an end the Council's experiment with a pure hard split between the client and contractor roles, but despite appearances this is only a partial reversion to the situation before 1992. Unlike then the council's blue-collar contracted services are all grouped together under one organisational umbrella to share overheads and management support. There is also still a real split between the Contract Services Division and its clients within Environmental Services. Contract Services reports separately and directly to the Director of Environmental Services and to the Contracts Services Board. Nevertheless with both sides being within the same department there is much greater scope for mutual co-operation. The Director of Environmental Services is currently reviewing arrangements within the department to foster greater co-operation between the two sides and this may lead to further changes.

8.3.3 The Contract Services Department/Division and the Contract Services Board

Despite its integration into the Environmental Services Department, the Contract Services Division remains the council's main provider of in-house blue-collar services and this section will consider more closely its operations.

Accountability

Contract Services is responsible to the Council's Contract Services Board, which has responsibility for the council's DSOs. Standing orders list the functions of the Board. These include overseeing the preparation and submission of any DSO bid under CCT legislation, the approval of DSO business plans, the monitoring of DSO performance and "operational management responsibility" for the Contract Services Department. It is also responsible for consulting and negotiating with relevant trade unions and staff representatives over terms and conditions of employment, redundancies, early retirements and disciplinary matters. The Board usually meet six times a year, and considers reports about the operational and financial performance of each contract. Contract Services also supplies statistical information to the Board including details on staff turnover, staff grievances and complaints from the public.

Objectives

Since 1992 the Board has set objectives for Contract Services (and the other DSOs) through 2-yearly service development plans. According to these, the purpose of Contract Services is to promote to the benefit of the local people the in-house provision of cost effective and quality based services through successful tendering, by exploiting the authority's resources and skills and reflecting its core values in a commercial and competitive environment. To these ends, the last declared set of objectives, approved in July 1996, covered the following matters:

"1. To deliver cost effective quality based services.
2. To work in partnership with clients to ensure best service.
3. To provide services within financial parameters to achieve required rates of return.
4. To improve and extend communications with clients, members and all users of DSO services to ensure smooth delivery and prompt payments.
5. Work to develop service provision to meet the future quality needs of clients and users.
6. Train and develop staff to bring added quality value to the delivery of services through "Investors in People" and other development programmes.
7. Work to ensure successful contract bidding through constant examination and review of all overhead and operational costs.
8. Improve inter-departmental and officer communication to achieve co-operative effort in service delivery.
9. To play a part in the focus of [*an environmental project*] through Local Agenda 21.
10. Encourage and support the voluntary sector where this does not conflict with the commercial priorities of the Board's services."

The eighth objective reflects the closer co-operation between the contractor-side and the client-side that was intended to follow from the integration of the Contract Services into the Environmental Services Department. The Head of Contract Services welcomed this softening of the client–contractor split. Where there were ambiguities in the service specification or other operational concerns, close co-operation between the two sides was very beneficial.

Management structure of the Contract Services Division

Day to day control is exercised by the Head of Contract Services who is responsible to the Director of Environmental Services. The Division is made up of a number of contract work sections.

Catering Services DSO

This has responsibility for running both the schools catering contract and the welfare catering contract. It is run by a contract manager, an area supervisor, a technical assistant and an administration officer. The DSO manager told me that this was "too tight" a structure to allow the frequency of site visits needed to run the contracts effectively (a view supported by the client catering manager, who attributed the contractor's deficiencies in operating these contracts to their being short-staffed).

Ground Maintenance DSO

This has responsibility for carrying out two area based contracts (parks and grass verges) and the trees maintenance contract. There is one contract manager, who is assisted on the ground by three senior charge-hands. There is no separate administrative support.

Cleansing DSO

This runs the refuse collection, street cleansing and other waste minimisation contracts. There is one contract manager, a refuse collection supervisor and two cleansing supervisors. This is again a lean management structure placing heavy demands: for example, the cleansing supervisors work four twelve-hour shifts each per week.

Car Parks and Estates Cleansing DSO

Originally two DSOs that were merged in order to cut costs. There is a contract manager, a car parks supervisor, and an estates cleansing supervisor.

These units are supported on the ground by a vehicle workshop and a stores section. Contract Services has its own administration and support staff, which number around thirty employees. Financial administrators deal with the trading accounts, payments and debt collection. There is also I.T support connected with purchasing and stock control. Finally the DSO has its own personnel officer and a couple of part-time staff share responsibility for the running of quality assurance systems.

The DSO manager enjoys a degree of financial autonomy, being empowered by standing orders to authorise purchases of up to £10,000. Purchases of up to £50,000 may be authorised by the Director of Environmental Services. The use of subcontractors is also permitted by standing orders provided that at least three tenders are obtained. In the case of very small jobs, this requirement is dispensed with.

Staff and industrial relations

A new staff structure was implemented on the formation of Contract Services in 1992. The contracts of employment for Contract Services manual employees were then governed by local agreements, with the result that pay and conditions tended to reflect ordinary commercial rates in the local area. The terms and conditions of Contract Services employees were therefore different from those of employees elsewhere in the authority and even varied amongst themselves depending on the contract worked. Although there had not been any problems regarding the law on equal pay for work of equal value, the potential for such a problem was recognised (see below).

Industrial relations have been good, although there had been problems in the early years when CCT was being introduced for the first time. The council pursues a consultative style of management to avoid problems, acting through the recognised trade unions (who are strongest in the Cleansing DSO) and through staff consultative committees for non-unionised staff. The management considers the unions to be active and vocal but not a problem.

A senior member of management explained that they were conscious that whenever bids were submitted there were invariably direct effects on employee terms and conditions. The preferred course of action when pricing in-house bids for CCT was to bring down costs by productivity improvements. The in-house bid for the second round refuse collection contract illustrated this point: costs being contained by reducing the number of collection rounds from eight to six per week, made possible by agreed productivity improvements. If possible the aim was to keep employees' "pay in the pocket" constant. Staff agreement to such changes was essential and required the widest consultation. These were the people who had to carry through any changes and deliver the service.

> "It's the only way ... the only way you an survive in the 90s; the modern management approach has got to be ... the democratic process. It works."

In the course of 1997 the council was consulting and developing plans for the harmonisation of the contractual terms and conditions of all its employees in the context of local needs and circumstances. It was recognised that Contract Services would need more time to implement any harmonisation, so that it could plan ahead for the increase in costs. These plans were not finalised in May 1997.

8.3.4   Tender evaluation

Tender evaluation is the most crucial part of any tendering process. Its utility in the implementation of council policies and priorities was examined earlier in 8.3.1. This Part is intended to provide a more general picture of Greenbrough's approach to this area.

The guide to tender evaluation

As part of its preparations for white collar CCT, a Guide to Tender Evaluation was produced in June 1995 to assist officers and members involved in this area. Prepared by the Corporate Legal Advisor, who has general responsibility for this area, its purpose is to encourage a uniform approach to the handling of CCT across the authority:

> "This document is designed to guide Officers and Members on the Council's processes, procedures and techniques for evaluating tenders in relation to contracts over the EU limit. It codifies practice to ensure compliance with statutory and organisational requirements and assists consistency of approach when evaluating tenders."

Responsibility for the conduct of CCT

The Council entrusts the conduct of tender evaluation procedures to the relevant service committees, purchasing panels and working groups. Committees have ultimate responsibility for awarding contracts. Purchasing panels are appointed by the relevant committee and include officers, councillors and service users. They are responsible for most of the key decisions in tender evaluation and for recommending a "preferred provider" to the committee for approval. Finally, the purchasing panels work closely with dedicated multi-disciplinary working groups throughout the entire process. These are officer groups appointed by the leading officers involved in the CCT tender with the approval of the Director responsible for the relevant service. They are informal and flexible in terms of membership and working methods, and report back to the relevant purchasing panel.

Contemporaneous documentation of all decisions

Particular emphasis is placed on the justification of decisions as they are made, and the careful recording of all assessments, evaluation results, calculations and meetings. The Public Service Contract Regulations do indeed require a high level of documentation but the Guide stresses it as a guiding principle in all tendering areas. In particular it provides the means to justify decisions taken in the face of a legal challenge whether from the Secretary of State, the District Auditor or an aggrieved contractor.

Benchmarking the cost of service provision

To be sure that the accepted tender allows for sufficient resources to carry out the service to the minimum of the specified requirements, officers will usually prepare a "minimum resources bid". This is in effect a dummy tender, prepared from first principles with the intention of meeting the minimum level of service with the most economical use of resources. It is intended to yield an indicative minimum contract price, which can later be used to:

- provide a cost benchmark to measure whether the tendered costs are reasonable
- identify "loss leader" tenders

- identify tenders that are insufficiently resourced to meet the minimum requirements of the specification.

To fulfil its purpose, the minimum resources bid must not be based simply on the current levels of service or on the in-house bid, but should be "demonstrably justifiable as a professional reasonable assessment of the resources and their costs which a competent contractor would allocate to the service". Greenbrough is a member of the Inter-Authority Group from which data about comparable costs can be obtained.

Evaluation models

Greenbrough makes use of formal evaluation models in relation to quality issues. Some of these are illustrated in the CCT case studies in 8.4. However the balancing of price against quality is not attempted in such a formalised manner. That is down to the judgement of the responsible officers and members.

8.3.5 Client units and contract management

The Council's service contracts are managed by client units, which report to the relevant departments and committees. They are not always located in the same department as the service clients. For example, the council has a single Client Catering Unit that manages the schools, welfare, leisure and civic catering services contracts, each one of which is the responsibility of a different department and committee. This section will profile the CCU as an illustration of the work of the client-side.

The CCU is staffed by two full-time posts (including the client catering officer) and two part-time posts. The cost of the client unit is 2.4% of the total catering budget, which is the lowest out of all the client units within the authority. Its contract management responsibilities are shown in Table 5 below:

The CCU acts as client agent for the departments, and reports on their behalf to the relevant committees. Being located in the Environmental Ser-

Table 5: Catering Contracts (1996)

Contract	Contractor	Client Department	Client Committee
Schools catering	DSO	Education	Education
Welfare catering	DSO	Housing & Social Services	Housing & Social Services
Leisure catering	Private	Leisure Services	Leisure Services
Civic catering	Private	Chief Executive's	Policy & Resources

vices Department, the unit is perceived as being independent of any particular client. Since the beginning of 1997 it has been joined in Environmental Services by the DSO, which runs two of its contracts. However a clear client–contractor split has been retained, because each reports separately to the Director of Environmental Services.

The relationship between client units and their client departments is governed by service level agreements. The CCU has a service level agreement with the Education Department under which it undertakes to carry out two full inspections of each school every year. These cover matters such as food quality, hygiene and customer satisfaction. The headteacher of each school is also surveyed at the end of every term, and survey questionnaires are regularly sent out to parents (twice in 1996).

Relations with contractors are governed by the terms of the service contracts. The client units report and are authorised to act on behalf of the Authorised Officer under the terms of contract. The CCU acts on behalf of the Director of Environmental Services, who is the Authorised Officer in respect of the catering contracts. In the event of a dispute with the contractor, the contracts provide for resolution by the Authorised Officer in the first instance, and then by independent arbitration the results of which are final and binding. For catering contracts, the Hotel and Catering International Administration Association will appoint an arbitrator for these purposes. It has never been necessary to call on its services.

Meetings between client unit and contractor are worked out informally, although the client unit will generally have the contractual right to demand an immediate meeting (eg – within two hours, where a catering outlet is open). The norm is for monthly meetings in the case of schools catering, and quarterly meetings in the case of welfare catering. The user panel is the forum for meetings regarding welfare catering. It brings together the head of the client unit, the contract manager and representatives of the main customers of the service (day centres and the meals-on-wheels service). There is no user panel for schools catering because of the sheer number of users (64 schools establishments). Therefore the client unit has to play a more active role as agent for the users.

The enforcement of contracts may take four forms. The more extreme sanctions are either terminating the contract or for the Council to carry out any necessary work itself and charge its costs to the contractor. More usual will be the issuing of rectification notices and/or default points. Rectification notices are issued to a contractor where there has been a redeemable omission or other failure in performance. The contractor is simply required to make good the situation within a set time. Default points are issued in respect of irredeemable failures. In a contract for the running of a leisure catering outlet default points are issued in respect of a number of matters including those shown in Table 6:

Default points are awarded according to a set scale that is calculated to reflect the Council's loss as the result of the default (penalty clauses being illegal). The contractor is then invoiced on a basis such as that shown in Table 7.

Table 6

Default points will be awarded for...	No.
Late opening	2
Over 15 minutes late opening	+4
Customer having to wait 10 minutes for service	2
Failure to maintain plant, equipment, machinery	3
Breach of health and safety requirements	4
Breach of council policy	2
Score of less than 80% (Food) on Client Inspection	10

Table 7

Default points incurred in any consecutive 4 week period	Amount to be invoiced to the contractor
1–4	£0
5–10	£10
11–15	£30
16–20	£50
21–25	£80
26–30	£100

In the event that the contractor incurs over 30 default points in any consecutive four weeks or 100+ in any twelve-month period, the Council has further rights including that to determine all or part of the contract.

Relations with contractors are kept as informal as possible. This approach is outlined in the Introduction to the Conditions of Tender for the leisure catering contracts:

> "The Council recognises that it has to have formal Contract Documentation and that it wishes to make clear that the emphasis is on partnership with both the Council and its Contractors working together to develop the service, to address any problems jointly and to provide the best possible service to customers."

The Chief Client Catering officer said that this flexibility was maintained in practice. He regarded his contracts as being open to negotiation from Day 1, with possible variations to the contract being discussed in the usual course of client–contractor meetings. The DSO manager took a similar view regarding his contracts, although indicating that relations between the DSO and the CCU were better than the norm. This would suggest that personal relations play an important role in the productivity of client–contractor discussions.

While client–contractor relations in catering services have been good they have not been trouble-free. Strong disagreements have arisen when the client unit has imposed requirements that increase the contractor's costs. For example, the DSO protested to the client unit when beef was withdrawn from primary school menus as a result of the BSE or "mad cow" controversy in December 1995. In that case the client unit refused to come up with any extra money because the DSO had already received for that year an increase in its funding over the rate of inflation. It was expected to bear the increase in cost itself.

However the use of contractual sanctions has been rare. In fact the client catering officer has had to issue default points on only two occasions since 1993. One involved a deduction from the DSO on the schools catering contract for non-compliance with the specification. The other was a much larger deduction from an outside contractor on a leisure catering contract for improper food hygiene. In neither case was the deduction contested by the contractor. Likewise the arbitration provisions have not yet been called upon to settle disputes.

There are indeed examples of active co-operation between the two sides. For example, the Client Catering Unit was dissatisfied with the DSO's handling of the schools catering contract, in particular with the lack of marketing, inadequate surveying of customers, and the shortage of information sent to parents. These faults were having an impact on the uptake of school meals and in turn on the profitability of the DSO. The two sides agreed to the seconding of a client staff member to the DSO to assist in surveys and meal promotions with successful results. Both sides jointly reported on the progress of this cooperation to the Education Committee.

8.4   Case Studies of CCT Tenders

This Part to the Chapter consists of four case studies, which examine in detail the way in which the Council has carried out CCT tenders in different services.

8.4.1   Welfare catering

Within the defined activity of catering for schools and welfare, the council has responsibility for 64 school sites, a number of day centres and the provision of a meals-on-wheels service. This case study considers the second round of CCT the provision of welfare catering services during 1996–97.

Background

The Council decided at an early stage to let separate contracts for its catering operations for schools and for welfare. A 4-year contract for schools catering was put out to tender over 1989–90, commencing in September 1990. A 4-year contract for welfare catering was then tendered at the normal time, commencing in January 1992. The DSO won both contracts. By tendering the schools contract early, the Council ensured that school catering arrangements were in place before schemes for local management for schools took effect (schools would be bound by existing contractual arrangements). The separation of schools catering from welfare catering had other advantages for the Council. In particular, it kept contracts down to a manageable size and made allowance for the different age groups served by each. However the council was only in a position to do this because of the fortuitous circumstance that it owned kitchens away from school sites, because different contractors could not have shared school kitchens.

In 1994 the Education Committee exercised an option in the schools contract to extend the contract period by a year to the beginning of September 1995. This had a knock-on effect. The expiry date for the schools contract was now very close to the January 1996 expiry date for the welfare catering contract. To save the DSO from having to tender for two big contracts more or less in parallel, the Housing and Social Services Committee exercised a similar option in the welfare catering contract, extending it to January 1997 (and later again the following year to the end of March 1997).

The timetable for tendering

The Housing and Social Services Committee settled the timetable for the tendering process and the membership of the contract evaluation panel in September 1995. From then onwards the tender process developed as shown below:

- Approval of service specification in January 1996
- Advertisement of the contract in May 1996
- Approval of Select List of tenderers in September 1996
- Deadline for submission of tenders in November 1996
- Presentations by tenderers in December 1996
- Decision to award contract in January 1997
- Commencement of contract in April 1997

Selection of candidates for invitation to tender

There were six expressions of interest in carrying out the contract but only three (including the DSO) actually returned the pre-tender questionnaire. The committee was required by the CCT regime to invite tenders from three private sector firms as well as the DSO. Therefore they had no choice but to invite tenders from all of them, (even if, as was not the case here, one of them had been considered unsuitable). Even this course of action was still technically in breach of the law because one of the three was the DSO. The only alternative course of action would have been to readvertise the work, something that was probably pointless because there was no reason to suppose that there would have been a different outcome the second time around. In the end all three parties submitted tenders by the required deadline.

Evaluation of tenders

The committee approved evaluation criteria and methods in July 1996. They were to be "effective, transparent and auditable". A 3-stage procedure was adopted:

- the opening of tenders and a separate financial evaluation;
- a separate technical or quality evaluation carried out on each tender; and,
- a comparison of price against value for money and quality considerations.

Financial evaluation

The financial evaluation involved careful checking of the figures contained in each tender. The outcome was clear-cut. Of the three tenders received, the DSO tender was the cheapest and even represented a small saving on draft budgetary estimates for welfare catering services, as shown by Table 8:

Because the DSO submitted the lowest bid there was no requirement on the Council to consider the 1993 Competition Regulations, concerning the possible extraneous costs of awarding the contract to an outside contractor.

Quality evaluation

A set of evaluation criteria and a formal evaluation model had been agreed before the submission of tenders. Tenders were to be marked against twenty criteria, with each criterion ascribed a weighting of 5, 3, or 2 to reflect its importance. Tenders were then to be marked from 1 to 12 against each criterion on the following basis:

- fails to meet acceptable minimum standard: 1–3
- achieves acceptable minimum standard: 4–6
- complies fully with requirements: 7–9
- proposals exceed requirements: 10–12
- 2, 5, 8 and 11 to be used as mid-range marks.

The service specification had been revised for the new contract, and contained higher quality standards than the previous specification. Therefore a mark of

Table 8

Bid	Difference over lowest price (£)
DSO	0
Tenderer A	+ 157,017
Tenderer B	+ 301,481

7–9 ("complies fully") was considered indicative of a very high level of quality. Anything higher risked being considered undesirable or economically disadvantageous.

Marking was carried out by members of the contract working group, led by the client catering officer. After they had been marked, a weighted score was calculated for each criterion (by multiplying the weighting and the mark) and overall, with each tender's final score being considered as a percentage score from all possible weighted marks. Tenders were required to pass a quality threshold set at 60%. The results of the quality evaluation are shown in Table 9.

The scores can be better appreciated by reference to the evaluation report, prepared for consideration by the evaluation panel (see below). Taking the first criterion "Understanding" as an example, this criterion refers to a general understanding of the specification. Both Tenderer A and the DSO fully met the required standard (8 points), but Tenderer B only managed to comply with the minimum acceptable standard (5 points). The evaluator's comments are reproduced below:

Table 9: Quality Evaluation

Criterion	Weight W	Tender A Mark	Score W	DSO bid Mark	Score W	Tender B Mark	Score
Understanding	5	8	40	8	40	5	25
Compliance	5	8	40	10	50	8	40
References	2	5	10	8	16	5	10
Site reference	3	5	15	8	24	5	15
Management	3	10	30	8	24	5	15
Staffing and TUPE	3	10	30	5	15	8	24
Tech. Experience	3	10	30	8	24	5	15
Approach	5	10	50	8	40	5	25
Quality control	5	8	40	8	40	2	10
Method of operation	3	8	24	8	24	8	24
Menus	5	10	50	8	40	5	25
Portions	5	8	40	8	40	10	50
Customer needs	5	10	50	5	25	3	15
Healthy eating	5	5	25	8	40	5	25
Purchasing policy	3	8	24	8	24	5	15
Transition plan	5	8	40	10	50	5	25
"Green issues"	5	5	25	8	40	5	25
Marketing	5	10	50	5	25	8	40
TOTAL SCORE			613		581		423
PERCENTAGE SCORE			**68%**		**65%**		**47%**

Chapter Eight

"[Tenderer A]
1. This company have a thorough understanding of welfare catering. All aspects of the specification have been addressed with the exception of a few minor points that will need to be addressed at the presentation stage.
2. Currently puddings are purchased in multi-portion packs and are divided into a single portion prior to delivery. [A has] chosen to serve individual sweets which increases their price to the Authority by approx. 20p per meal. Why they should select this method is questionable as the present system is very successful.
3. [A has] looked ahead regarding the way in which customers can select a better meal using the DECARPO system [a more environmentally friendly system employing reusable containers] and would envisage the system being introduced to the contract within a year. They have also outlined a more extensive frozen home delivery to those recipients who are able to reheat their own food. The benefits of this system are numerous, giving an individual much greater control over menu choice and when they would wish to eat.

[DSO]
1. A very detailed tender has been submitted by [DSO] covering every aspect of the specification in detail. As the incumbent contractor they have a good knowledge of what is required and have based their menus etc on what is offered now. Bearing in mind that the current menu was drawn up under the various price restrictions within the present contract, I would like to have seen an improvement in their menu selection, ie. less casseroles/stews and more whole meat dishes, such as chicken breast and other alternatives such as lamb korma.
2. [DSO] have stated that they would wish to continue to provide a menu that is compiled in conjunction with the customers and Clients requirements. It is a concern that due to the low initial cost of their tendered menu it is unlikely that there will be any room for manoeuvre. The majority of remaining dishes that are available in the [product range] are the higher priced items therefore giving Housing & Social Services little room for alternative selections without increasing the food cost.

[Tenderer B]
1. [B] have submitted a very basic tender submission with minimum information. Although they have covered most aspects of the specification requirements, detail such as where they intend to purchase their meals from is not included."

It should be explained that there is a close correlation between price and quality because the welfare catering service is based on pre-cooked frozen meals. Meals are bought, brought in and reheated before being served. Under this set-up there is no scope to improve the quality of a particular meal after it has been bought. The only option is to buy a different meal, something that is limited by the contract price. Frozen meals are bought-in from commercial suppliers and the better quality ranges of meal inevitably come at higher prices. Admittedly this relationship is not borne out in the scores for Tenderer B, but that is explained by peculiar factors relating to their bid.

Balancing price and quality

The next stage was to balance the factors of price and quality so that a "preferred provider" could be recommended to the Housing and Social Services Committee. The contract evaluation panel met for this purpose in November 1996. It was led by the client catering officer and included financial representatives and managers from the chief service users, namely the day centres and the meals-on-wheels service. There was a clear consensus in favour of the DSO bid. The client catering officer suggested that the real question for the panel to decide was whether the DSO was so far ahead of the field that they could dispense with the need to hear tenderer's presentations (which were scheduled for December). Of the three bids, the one submitted by Tenderer B was ruled out immediately: on both price and quality grounds it ran a clear third. The DSO bid was a lot cheaper than that of Tenderer A, and although scoring lower on quality grounds (by a margin of 3%) the difference was generally felt to be too small to justify the extra cost of accepting Tenderer A's bid. Other factors counted in its favour. It had cleared the quality threshold and had (to general surprise) been preferred by the panel at a food tasting session the previous day.

Having been led though and having agreed the results of the financial and quality evaluations, the remainder of the meeting was concerned with particular concerns of the service users, and points of detail to be negotiated with the preferred provider. Certain details still needed to be worked out with the DSO, but the Panel was agreed that the DSO should be recommended as the preferred provider without the need to hear presentations. This committee ratified the recommendation and the contract went ahead on time.

8.4.2 Revenue services tendering

Revenue services work, which forms part of the financial services defined activity, was put out to competitive tender in 1996–97 and was won by an external contractor. This case study examines the conduct of that tender from the perspective of the client-side, and focuses on the tender evaluation procedures.

Preparations for competition

Preparation for CCT involved the creation of a client–contractor split, the calculation of the specified proportion of the defined activity to be put out to competition, the selection of activities to be put forward to satisfy the specified proportion, and the drafting of a detailed specification.

The council's financial services were mainly based in the Finance and Corporate Services (FCS) Department, but other financial services staff (essentially financial administrators) could be found in most departments across the authority. The FCS Department underwent a division into client and provider sides in advance of CCT. The Client Unit was very small consisting of a client manager, an outside consultant and one other full-time post. This was out of around 140 financial service employees in the FCS and Housing departments (the other principal location of such employees). The client manager oversaw the CCT process supported by a purchasing panel with input from audit and corporate legal sections.

The council was required to submit a specified proportion of its financial services work to CCT by the 1 April 1997. The specified proportion was to be determined according to the formula "T − (A + B + C + D + E + F + G)", where T represented the total value of defined activity work carried out by or for the council, and A to G represented various credits that could be deducted from this amount. In addition, because CCT only applies where the council carries out work itself, the value of any externalised work could afterwards also be deducted from the specified proportion. The chief credit was A, which represented the greater of an amount equal to 65% of T or £300,000.

The calculation of T was a difficult process because financial services work was spread across various departments, all of which had to be counted towards the T value. Other difficulties arose in calculating the value of the credits. For example, Credit C covered the amount of financial services work undertaken by the authority on behalf of schools with a delegated budget. There are around fifty of these in the local authority area so the complexity of this task can be imagined. In the end formulaic assumptions had to be used, whose accuracy would be difficult to challenge. Basically, the council's existing financial management systems were not designed to cope with the mindset of the specified proportion formula.

The council's policy was to subject only the required minimum amount of financial service work (roughly 35% less the value of credits B to G) to CCT. Of the activities that were considered appropriate to face competition, the work carried out in the provision of revenue services satisfied the specified proportion and was considered to have a good chance of success because its favourable performance indicators (high collection rates, and low collection costs). A service specification was prepared in the last half of 1995. Because this was done before the days of D.O.E. Circular 5/96, no preliminary consultations took place with potential tenderers over the best form of contract packaging.

The contract would be for a 5-year period commencing from 1 April 1997. The provision of revenue services would cover the administration of billing, collection and recovery procedures and provision of an enquiries service in respect of Council Tax, the National Non-Domestic Rate and residual Community Charge. It would not include the provision of a Council Tax Benefits service or a cashiering service.

Advertising the contract and selecting contractors for invitation to tender

The contract was advertised in January 1996, with the specification being open to inspection from 26 January to 29 March. Copies were available on request for £100. Suitably qualified contractors with experience of large financial managed services contracts were asked to return a completed questionnaire and audited accounts by noon on the 2 April 1996.

The purpose of the council's questionnaire was to determine whether a particular firm was capable of carrying out the work and so was suitable to be invited to tender. By the 2 April deadline, the council had received eleven expressions of interest including its own revenue services provider unit. In order to select those firms that would be invited to tender for the contract, each member of the purchasing panel marked each contractor on the basis of its answers to the questionnaire. The responses were weighted under a number of headings, and contractors were accorded a score from 0–5 on each to produce an overall weighted mark. The assessment covered the matters discussed below.

Technical Ability (Weighting – 30%)

Contractors were asked to supply answers relating to their proposed operating location, specialisation in the provision of revenue services, and exposure to public sector work. A lot of thought was clearly expected even at this stage. For example, contractors were asked about their business plan for delivering the service if awarded the contract and how this would fit into their other business and market development plans. They were also asked whether they would be willing to set up a specialist department specifically for the council's work, and in relation to TUPE, whether they had experience of managed transfers of staff and assets from public sector organisations.

Staffing and Managers (Weighting – 5% each)

Contractors were asked to supply details of the number of staff they employed, indicating the numbers involved in managerial, supervisory and clerical roles, the length of time employees had been with them, and their recruitment and training procedures. Outline C.V.s were also requested in relation to the senior managers who would be responsible for the service.

References (Weighting – 5%)

Five technical references were requested relating to the full range of work for which the contractor wished to be considered.

Quality (Weighting – 15%)

Information was requested about the contractor's management systems for the allocation of work, the control of staff resources, supervision of work, and internal document control. In particular, contractors were asked whether they operated or proposed to operate a formal quality and/or environmental management system such as the ISO 9000 series or EMAS. Contractors were warned that the council might later carry out an on-site Quality Audit as part of the evaluation of any tender submitted.

Complaints/Customer Care (Weighting – 10%)

Contractors were asked to supply a copy of their written complaints procedure (or details of how they handled complaints). They were also warned that an effective approach to customer care would be critical. The questionnaire referred contractors to a customer care information pack and asked them to outline their approach to addressing general and specific customer needs.

Health and Safety (Weighting – 10%)

Contractors are asked seven standard questions relating to health and safety. Firms based outside the UK are asked to answer them by substituting where relevant the appropriate laws or codes of practice applicable within their domestic jurisdictions. The questionnaire requires contractors to name the person responsible for safety policy, to supply copies of their health and safety policy and completed risk assessments relating to the work types covered by the tender, and to provide details of the safety training undertaken by their staff. In addition, they are asked to give details of any safety related prosecutions or notices served on them by enforcing authorities, and to allow council officers reasonable access to premises, plant and equipment for the purposes of inspection.

Equal Opportunities (Weighting – 10%)

The questionnaire sets out the six questions approved by the Secretary of State in D.O.E. Circular 12/88 relating to council's duties under section 71 of the Race Relations Act 1976. Where contractors are located outside the UK, an additional question asks them to supply details of their experience in working under equivalent legislation which is designed to eliminate discrimination (especially racial discrimination) and promote equality of opportunity. In two further questions, contractors are asked whether they comply with the Sex Discrimination Act 1975 and the Equal Pay Act 1975, and whether they undertake to comply with the Disabled Persons Employment Act 1944.

Environmental Policies (Weighting – 10%)

The questionnaire draws contractors' attention to the council's Environmental Statement and asks whether they would be willing to work with the council to protect and improve the environment. Where the contractor already has an environmental policy or an environmental purchasing policy, it is asked to supply the council with a copy, and to detail the steps it has taken towards their implementation. A more general question (in that it covers contractors who have not yet formulated "green" policies) asks for details of any practical measures taken in the previous three years to improve the environment, reduce consumption of fuel and other natural resources or reduce pollution.

Deductions

The assessment model allowed for points to be deducted where a contractor's answers to the questionnaire revealed any of the following (to a maximum of 1 point per category below):

- relevant criminal offences committed by the contractor or any of its employees.
- complaints/disciplinary proceedings concerning the contractor or any employee that have been brought before a professional body.
- former client's refusal to pay an invoice.
- claim on the contractor's professional indemnity insurance.
- conflicts of interest.
- premature termination or non-renewal of a previous contract.

Insurance and pensions

The questionnaire asked contractors about their employers liability insurance, public liability insurance and professional indemnity insurance. Contractors were also asked about their company pension scheme, and whether they were prepared to vary it to meet the requirements of TUPE and match the Local Government Superannuating Scheme. On both insurance and pensions arrangements, contractors' arrangements were assessed on the simple basis of "acceptable/not acceptable".

Minimum scores were prescribed for each heading but there was no overall required score or quality threshold. The evaluation panel was looking to invite to tender between four and six providers (including the in-house team). It was hoped that this would ensure a reasonably competitive field without also extending invitations to clear also-rans, which would have been costly and time consuming to evaluate. In the event there was a big points gap between the top five and the rest and so those five were invited to tender.

Evaluation of tenders

Although five contractors (including the in-house team) were invited to tender, only three actually submitted tenders by the required date. The tenders were then evaluated on the basis of price and quality. These evaluations were conducted separately from one another, and the tenders were divided up accordingly into financial and non-financial documents.

The financial documents were evaluated on normal commercial criteria. The in-house bid was the most expensive of the three. The outside bids involved the introduction of new information technology systems that enabled them to forecast lower costs further into the contract period. The in-house provider did not have the same commercial freedom. It could not commit the council to spend money on additional I.T. systems, and consequently could not offer the same cost savings in the future.

An Evaluation Pack made up of the remaining non-price documents, such as method statements, was then given to each member of the evaluation panel for the Quality evaluation. Method statements require tenderers to describe the procedures and resources they will use to meet particular sections of the specification. There were 23 method statements in this case. Contractors were required to submit their statements according to a set format (not through the submission of standard procedure manuals) in order to facilitate tender evaluation. Each member of the panel was also supplied with a number of evidence schedules. These are papers relating to particular method statements that consist of a list of "evidences" whose presence may go towards showing compliance with the specification. The idea was for evaluators to tick off the key items of evidence from the evidence schedule as they arose on the method statement.

For example, contractors were asked to complete a method statement on "Environmental Issues". The corresponding evidence schedule reminded evaluators to look for, and tick off, the following points:

"1. Firm commitment to an environmental policy.
2. Proposals and timescale for introduction of Environmental Management Audit systems.
3. Training of staff on Council policy and general environmental management issues.
4. Direct effects of purchasing procedures and operating methods recognised. Environmental Purchasing Plan.
5. Indirect effects where operations impact on others eg – if operating from Civic Offices, clear awareness of responsibility to support EMAS initiatives of other providers/occupants.
6. Evidence of environmental commitment outside this contract."

In another method statement contractors were asked to outline their proposed handling of "Customer Care and Inquiries [inc. Special Needs]". The matching evidence schedule reminded evaluators to look out for things such as "customer focused service delivery", "staff taking ownership of inquiries/problems" and "telephone answering response and manner".

The maximum points available for any one method statement was 5, which would indicate a high degree of excellence. There was also a quality threshold of sorts in that a minimum mark of 2 was expected for each method statement. Failure to attain this would not have been fatal but would have been a serious problem. In the event, all the tenders got through the quality threshold, although not by a great margin and of the three in-house bid was the clear winner.

The success of all three bids in overcoming the quality threshold meant that the more expensive in-house bid could be eliminated on cost grounds.

The two remaining tenderers were invited to give a presentation and answer questions. The outcome of this clinched the decision because one of the tenderers was considered to be offering an off the shelf service based on the general requirements of its existing customers, rather than one geared to the specific needs of the council.

Outcome

The contract started on time on 1 April 1997. The successful contractor runs the contract from the Civic Offices using the council's existing I.T. support, to which it will add new elements in due course. There were no redundancies and the 28 council employees all transferred over to the new contractor under TUPE. The contractor is hoping to win further contracts, which it would operate from the Civic Offices using the existing staff. The additional I.T. would allow this expansion in workload to take place without increasing the number of staff. If there are no new contracts then the additional I.T. will result in up to 10 redundancies by the third year of the contract with the council. Meanwhile the remainder of the financial services function is the subject of a management review by outside consultants, which is expected to result in major changes. If the council is required to put further financial services work out to tender (as seemed possible under the Beresford Review in the last months of the Conservative government) then the most likely candidate is payroll services, for which there is already a partly written specification.

The client unit view was that the exercise had benefited the council by forcing it to concentrate on the financial efficiency of the services. There was a feeling of self-assurance amongst officers about the efficiency of their services that exposure to the market had shown to be misplaced. This had been the case despite good performance indicators for the in-house service.

8.4.3   CCT for Legal Services: 1995–96

Greenbrough was required to subject the specified proportion of its legal services to competition by 1 April 1996.

Background

As the government's plans for white-collar CCT began to be released for consultation from 1991 onwards, the Council took note and began its own preparations. The provision of legal services was clearly one of the areas intended to be subject to CCT. Time and cost measurement were introduced in 1992, as were trial service level agreements. A client–contractor split for legal services was established in 1994. "Legal Services" was the contractor or in-house provider, whilst the client role was performed by a new post of Corporate Legal Advisor. Her section had responsibility for the progress of the CCT tender.

Testing the market

To assist the Council in the task of selecting the work that was to go towards satisfying the specified proportion, the Corporate Legal Advisor carried out a market testing exercise based on fifteen common categories of local authority legal work. Forty-five law firms that had previously written to the Council expressing an interest in working for it were contacted and asked to outline their prices. Participants were also asked whether they would prefer the work to be tendered as a single contract package or split into two or more, and about their preferred contract lengths. There were thirty replies out of which the majority expressed a preference for a single contract. Clearly there was a large potential market for the authority to tap.

Internal clients of legal services were also consulted about the service they currently received and the service that they wanted in the future. The main result was a demand that a specialised knowledge of child care law should be a priority in the new contracted service.

Contract packaging

The Council decided to package the work in a single contract, as most respondents to the market testing had preferred. The amount of work that was to be put out to tender remained to be decided. The Policy and Resources Committee considered five options. These ranged from a "minimum" option of tendering no more than the specified proportion, to a "maximum" option of tendering the lot except for obviously core functions such as corporate advice. The other three options fell between these two and involved splitting responsibilities for child care work between client and contractor. This was considered undesirable and they were all rejected. In the end the Committee chose the maximum option and CCT went ahead on that basis.

Process and outcome of CCT

The competitive response was initially good. Fifteen firms returned the pre-tender questionnaire and of these seven were invited to tender. However only the in-house team actually submitted a bid and they were awarded the contract.

Trouble soon followed. The DOE suspected anti-competitive behaviour from the lack of competitive response and asked the Council for an explanation. It was in fact one of twenty local authorities that the DOE had decided to investigate on those grounds and at that time. The Corporate Legal Adviser described the situation as "very embarrassing".

The circumstances of this challenge illustrate the practical application of the enforcement provisions of the LGA 1988. The DOE will take up complaints and/or suspicions about a local authority's conduct of CCT on an informal basis before setting in motion the formal sanctions mechanism by issuing a Notice requesting further information under s.13 of the 1988 Act.

It also illustrates the benefit of clearly documented and contemporaneous justification of decisions throughout a tendering process. The Corporate Legal Advisor was able to respond to the DOE by sending a detailed case file, which documented the entire process. The DOE commented later on the helpfulness of this response.

The "official" response was supported by informal political contacts to the Minister in charge. This included a letter from an involved council member known to the Minister, in which the correspondent assured him that although a Liberal Democrat, he was to the right of the party and would never have allowed anti-competitive conduct to occur.

In the end, the DOE accepted the Council's explanation of events and matters did not proceed any further.

8.4.4   Construction and property services

Following the departmental reorganisation of 1992, the Council's construction and property (C&P) services work was placed in the Environmental Services Department. The largest part was in a C&P Division made up of four sections: Architects, Repairs and Maintenance, Valuation, and Building Control. The remainder was located in the Engineers Division, either in the Highways/Major Works Section or the Structural Engineers Section. No separation of client and contractor roles occurred, despite the implementation at that time of a client–contractor split in respect of blue-collar services: perhaps in retrospect, a missed opportunity.

While consultations about the precise form of CCT proceeded at national level from 1992 to 1994, the Council brought in management consultants to train its white-collar staff for operations in a business environment. This covered areas such as trading accounts, business spreadsheets, market intelligence, and SWOT analysis (standing for "Strengths, Weaknesses, Opportunities, Threats"). However this failed to capture the imagination of the staff on the ground, as one manager observed:

> "It was all very much an academic exercise. There was nobody who felt involved or interested or wanting to apply themselves to it."

The period was one of uncertainty for the staff. The final shape of the CCT regime was of course still unresolved, and in this climate the Council's own preparations seemed unfocussed.

> "There was an enormous amount of frustration beginning to build up. They knew it was inevitable, [that is the staff generally], and that something had to be done but they couldn't see anything happening and they were getting very edgy and disillusioned with everything and just wanted something to start happening."

Things did start to happen in 1994 (see Chapter 3). The legal regime for CCT in C&P services was approved by Parliament in November of that year.[3] The implementation date for CCT was 1 April 1996, and there was suddenly a great deal of work to do in a very short time.

Preparation for CCT

Greenbrough decided to tender its CPS work in a single five-year contract starting 1 April 1996. The deadline for the submission of tenders would be the end of September 1995. To be ready for this decisions and action were needed in a number of areas including:

- the proportion of CPS work to be put out to tender.
- the selection of work to meet the required proportion.
- the separation of client and contractor roles.
- the commissioning of a service specification and evaluation model.

(I) The proportion of CPS work to be put out to tender

The legislation required a specified proportion of CPS work to be subject to CCT. This was determined in accordance with the statutory formula "T – (A + B + C + D + E + F)" where "T" was the total value of defined activity work and A–F represented deductible credits. Staff calculated the total value of CPS work carried out in the previous financial year, which together with the value of all externalised work produced the value of "T". Of the available credits, the chief was Credit A, which permitted 35% of the defined work to be carried out free of competition. The Council did not want to go through with competition in this area at all, and resolved to meet no more than the minimum requirements of the legislation. The end result was an approximate division of the work between 65% that would be competed for and 35% that would be competition free.

(II) The selection of work to go out to competition

In order to satisfy the specified proportion, work had to be selected from both the C&P and the Engineering Divisions, and decisions on this fell to the divisional managers. They selected for tender a varied package including elements of architectural work, surveying, chemical and electrical engineering, valuation, structural engineering, highways and major works, a selection that was largely guided by ease of defining and separating out the work. The basis on which this was done varied from area to area. For example, it was found easier to tender architectural work on a project by project basis, whereas valuation work was easier to define on a functional basis.

The related task of determining what work was to be included within the competition-free allowance was guided by different considerations. Obviously client-side functions such as framing corporate policy and related

---

3 S.I 1994 Nos. 2888 and 3166.

advice made up no more than 20% of the defined activity. The Council could have settled on that, decided to maximise the work put out to competition and established a clean separation of client and contractor roles. However it was keen to retain (and continue to attract) sufficient in-house expertise to be able to deal on an equal basis with the staff of an outside contractor, if that was to be the outcome of CCT. This meant making full use of the 35% competition free allowance by topping up the pure client-side functions with practical work. That way the existing staff could continue to practice their professional skills and the Council could continue to attract high calibre new recruits to its in-house team by offering a varied package of work. This was perhaps an understandable response given that the Council wanted to preserve a viable in-house capacity. However it can also be seen as a short-term and highly defensive response to a situation which it had not given itself sufficient time to think through strategically. It only made sense on the presumption that the in-house provider would lose and that the Council would be dealing in future with an outside contractor. Therefore all of the distinctions between client and contractor roles were blurred in the overriding goal of maximising the use of the competition free allowance.

(III)   Separating client and contractor roles

This followed on from the decision to subject the minimum 65% (not counting other credits) of CPS work to competition. C&P Division employees were divided between the contractor and client sides on a pro rata basis, roughly 65:35. When it became clear that this division did not satisfy the specified proportion, the structural engineers and some of the highways/major works staff from the Engineers Division joined the in-house provider unit. The methods used to place staff on either side of the divide varied. In some cases managers simply told staff where to go with minimal consultation. In another the staff were asked to state a preference confidentially with written reasons. In that case at least, all the staff's wishes were accommodated. The client-side was generally seen as a safer bet in terms of job security, but most employees preferred the work offered on the provider side.

So far what had occurred was a "soft" split in that the existing management structures had not yet changed. This was in fact only the beginning of what needed to be done for the council to be ready for CCT. New management structures had to be created for the client unit and the in-house provider. As this happened, the character of the client–contractor split "hardened".

(IV)   Commissioning the service specification and evaluation model

The newly created client side faced the task of drafting the service specification and contract documentation, and choosing a tender evaluation model and evaluation criteria. A client-side officer directly responsible to the Director of Environmental Services managed this task.

Preparation of the in-house bid

While the client unit was going about its task, the (also newly created) contractor side, on which this case study will now concentrate, had to prepare and submit a viable bid. Because of the short time scale, all of these tasks were being carried out in parallel. The manager of the in-house provider unit was given a free hand in preparing the in-house bid. When he was appointed at the beginning of March 1995 he faced a difficult task. It was to take over a new organisation of around fifty staff, establish a new management structure, and supervise the preparation and submission of a bid that had to be successful if the in-house provider was to avoid closure. This all had to be done in the space of seven months up to the end of September 1995.

The manager had been appointed following a brief and unsuccessful attempt to run the organisation as a three-man partnership. The Council took one direct measure to assist their new appointee. He believed that he lacked experience of financial management, so the Council agreed to fund a consultant from outside the authority to help him look after that area. In all other respects he was left to his own devices. The first task was to establish an internal management structure. In his own words, he had in the beginning "fifty staff and no posts". Positions had to be created (starting with the most senior and working down), job descriptions prepared and applications considered. In doing this, the Council's Equal Opportunities Policy had to be followed, throwing applications open to staff on the client-side and people outside the authority. This was a time consuming process and the last position was only filled after the closing date for the submission of tenders.

An accurate understanding of the costs of providing the service was considered essential. If the in-house provider won the contract it had to be able to carry out the work for the price it had put forward. Costs fell into two broad categories: the cost of staff doing the work, and overhead costs. Working out the cost of the former involved every member of staff in identifying the different work tasks that were being carried out, together with the staff grade responsible for each and the time taken to complete it. Overhead costs had to be worked out by the authority's Finance and Corporate Services Department. The time that this took was the cause of considerable frustration. In the end an agreeable figure for overhead costs was reached. It was lower than before, and while still considered to be above comparable market rates, it at least "bore some resemblance to reality".

A complicating factor was uncertainty over the final content of the service specification. A member of staff was seconded to the client unit to assist in preparing the specification. Bits of drafts were produced throughout the tendering period, and the final version was only ready two weeks before the tender submission date. This made planning the tender very difficult as the presence or absence of particular points in the specification made a crucial difference to the ultimate price of the tender.

Consultations with internal customers of CPS played an important role in the preparations for the bid. A questionnaire was sent out to all customers to ascertain their views on the current level and quality of service. The balance of the responses was critical and this information proved useful in framing the bid.

The in-house team had to prepare and submit its bid on the same basis as any other tenderer. They in fact received little help from the client during the tendering process. The chief client unit officer was very strict about maintaining a level playing field between the in-house provider and other tenderers. This meant that they had only the service specification (or rather bits of it as they became available) and the remaining contract documentation to work on. They knew that they would be evaluated on quality and price but were not told which quality evaluation model would be used or what the different criteria and their relative weightings would be. Nor were they allowed to know against whom they were competing.

When questioned about the strengths and weaknesses of the in-house bid, the manager said that it was easier to think of their weaknesses. Among these he listed his staff's inexperience of business operations and culture, their lack of experience in operating trading accounts, the unit's inability to spread overhead costs over a wider range of work and clients, and inability to submit a loss leader bid. Their real strength, he said, was focus: they had nowhere else to go. Other tenderers were perhaps not as dedicated to the local authority as their client because they had other work, clients and therefore different priorities. They also believed they had a greater knowledge of what the work involved. This posed a dilemma because they could see shortcomings in the service specification and had to make a determined effort to put this knowledge to one side and bid strictly according to the specification as it stood (as would any other tenderer). As it turned out both they and the client-side were wrong about the future workload. Some areas of work did not materialise but other unexpected areas took their place.

The manager based the in-house bid on two particular policy decisions. The first concerned the balance they should strike in attempting to win the contract. They knew that evaluation would take place on quality and price and that there was a minimum quality score. The choice lay between bidding on the basis of high quality or low price. They experimented by testing different bids against a number of possible evaluation models and price–quality weightings. The conclusion was that however well they may do on quality, it would not make an enormous difference to the final price. The manager took the strategic decision that, subject to meeting the quality threshold, they should bid to win by submitting the lowest price. This lay behind his concern to drive down the overhead costs attributed to the unit by the Finance Department.

The second policy decision was however on a quality issue. The contract terms required the contractor to operate an environmental management system or to have a realistic plan to bring about such a system within the duration of the contract. This was a direct product of the Council's environmental policies. They decided to be among the first tranche of Council services to gain EMAS accreditation in the hope that this would give them an edge if the tender evaluation turned out to be a close race. Four out of the provider's seven works sections did achieve EMAS accreditation before the closing date for the submission of tenders.

The award of the contract

The Council received twenty-one applications to be included on the Select List. Six were invited to tender (including the in-house provider). The contract was awarded in-house. They were told that they had won on both quality and price but no further details were given to them.

Performing the contract after CCT

The CPS business unit is a typical example of the white-collar business units operating within the authority. It performs the contract through around 50 staff plus financial services support staff who maintain the trading account. As is the case for the blue-collar DSO, employees work under different terms and conditions to the rest of the Council. Disciplinary procedures are the same but in other areas the business unit applies council policies without necessarily following the detail of its procedures. For example, where the equal opportunities policy requires staff to attend certain courses the business unit sends such staff as can be spared who then pass on what they may have learned to their colleagues.

The unit has strained to achieve operational autonomy. For example, it resisted a Council moratorium on the recruitment of new staff, imposed to contain costs. The unit, which had just lost a key manager and needed an immediate replacement, said simply that the moratorium did not apply to them. It was argued that the post had to be filled for the unit to meet the terms of its contract with the authority. If the authority wanted to cut the costs of the unit it should go about it by reducing the amount of work that it commissioned from them. The business unit manager explained the reasons for his stance in the following terms:

> "We are still council employees. We still have to comply with the Council's policies and want to. We still want to be part of the Council. But we are running a business and have to operate and compete with the private sector. In four years time I will have to tender again so I can't go soft. We have to be allowed to manage the business properly. That means that we have got to be given some sort of freedom within the overall responsibilities of achieving the policies to run the business. I would like to see that set out."

To this end he was drafting a Management Handbook for all the council's business units, which would provide guidelines on areas in which business units could follow different procedures to the rest of the council, while still following the overall policies. It was due to go before the Directors in the first half of the year, and then on into the council committee cycle for approval.

Relations between the provider unit and the client agent had been beset by some "teething problems" since winning the contract. The client had been pleased that they had won but had not understood (or had reason to) what the contractor side had gone through in order to win. They had expected things to carry on as before and were resentful when the contractor insisted on negotiating a price for work that was not in the service specification. Such disagreements tended to be about the standard of service required. The client saw the contractor's stance as being "cute and clever". The contractor saw it as a straightforward question of survival. They had tailored their prices according to what was in the specification and could not afford to do extra work for nothing. In doing this they were acting in a thoroughly commercial manner, something they had confirmed through their own market intelligence. The client-side had since gone through their own reorganisation and so had a better idea of what the contractor staff had experienced and what was needed in future to survive. The manager described this in the following terms:

> "...to maintain that hard split ... and when I say "hard" I don't mean its unfriendly but its firm and clearly defined. They have come to terms with that now and understand it, so it feels much more of a partnership, and a contract only works if you are working in partnership. If you start getting out the rulebook and specification every day you will be in trouble. The client gets a lousy service and the contractor makes no money and ceases to exist."

The manager said that the customers were the most important consideration when debating the advantages and disadvantages of CCT, and customer feedback since the outcome of CCT showed that the service had "enormously" improved. They were getting a better service for less cost.

Staff morale was, in his view, very high because they had won the work after redesigning their own working methods. He emphasised that the preparation of the tender had been largely a bottom-up process. He had professional experience in only one of the fields of CPS work and so as manager relied heavily on his staff to make the appropriate arrangements in the remaining fields. He did not possess the knowledge to dictate the work methods they should use. He summed up the manager's job as "make a profit and keep the customers happy". Carrying out the work was down to the others and the way in which they had done it was a credit to them.

Looking to the future, he feared things going "slack" and back to the way they had been before. It was possible that the Council would not go through competitive tendering again (if, as has now happened, the Conservatives were to lose the general election). He doubted how effective a purely internal renegotiation of the contract could be if competitive tendering did not take place. It might work, but only if there was a genuine and believable threat of competition in reserve.

On the subject of competition, he felt that in-house providers were at a disadvantage compared to their private sector rivals. Competitors from the private sector enjoyed greater flexibility to spread costs across a variety of work and customers, and in being able to submit loss-leader bids. Some of the other competitors the in-house team had beaten could, in his view, have effectively "bought" the contract had they really wanted. The solution was for in-house providers to have greater freedom to trade, including trading in the private sector. At present they did carry out work for some other public bodies and charities but were limited by the current state of the law while the Council's own attitude towards external trading was ambivalent.

8.5   Summary and Conclusions

1. Greenbrough covers a prosperous and suburban local area. It is a unitary local authority that is responsible for the whole range of local services and defined activities. In political terms, Greenbrough was once strongly Conservative but has since the mid-1980s been controlled by the Liberal Democrats. It is among those local authorities that have had the maximum exposure to CCT. In particular, it has been in the forefront of white-collar CCT.
2. Before the passage of the LGA 1988, Greenbrough had considered voluntary contracting out of services but had not gone down that road in any significant way.
3. CCT has increased the amount of work that is contracted out, but the majority of work is still being performed in-house. Of the twelve blue-collar defined activities (including for this purpose all LGPLA 1980 work) a total of four were being carried out by private contractors in May 1997. A private contractor has also won the housing management contract, but of the remaining white-collar services, where only a proportion of the defined activity is required to face competition, only the provision of revenue services has been captured from the in-house providers.
4. The council has followed a policy of supporting in-house providers where they offer best value. In almost all cases in-house bids have been made for defined activity contracts, although certain areas have in the light of experience been abandoned to external providers.
5. The council has been careful to comply with the CCT regime. It has done the same with the European rules on public procurement. Conscious efforts have been made to harmonise tender evaluation procedures across departments. Particular emphasis has been placed on the documentation of decisions relating to tendering matters as they are made, so as to leave an audit trail of key decisions. This has been done to protect the council from complaints of anti-competitive behaviour, and has assumed great importance in the light of the council's practice of pursuing its own policy agenda through the contracting process
6. The council has attached high importance to the achievement of its core values and corporate policies. It has a particular commitment to environmental protection and quality assured management of services. The fulfillment of these goals has been systematically built into

the tendering process, through service specifications, contract conditions and the tender evaluation procedures. CCT has been able to accommodate the achievement of these goals.

7. CCT has resulted in significant organisational change. This has been driven by conflicting pressures. On the one hand, the anti-competitive conduct provisions of CCT have dictated the separation of client and contractor roles. On the other hand there has been, initially a desire to minimise disruption, and latterly a preference in the light of experience for greater co-operation between clients and contractors. There have been three departmental reorganisations in the course of the Council's experience with blue-collar CCT. The initial response in 1988-89 was to avoid any radical disruption by carrying out a client–contractor split within the affected departments. In 1992 there was a more radical separation of client and contractor roles with most defined activities being amalgamated within a free standing Contract Services Department under its own Director, and with the remaining departments concentrating on the client role. In the light of experience and to foster greater client–contractor co-operation, this hard split was softened in 1997 by ending Contract Services' status as a separate department and integrating it as a separate division of the Environmental Services Department.

8. The council has also had to experiment with its committee structure. This has been motivated by the need to ensure a separation of client and contractor roles, and to meet demands from council members for continued accountability of services. At first the existing pre-CCT committee structure was retained, with the client and the contractor sides in each department reporting to the same committee. An ad hoc consultative committee was also created to consider workforce concerns. Neither arrangement was satisfactory, and when Contract Services was created in 1992, a Contract Services Board was created at the same time. Contract Services reported directly to this, leaving the remaining committees free to concentrate on client responsibilities. This arrangement has not altered. Where services have been contracted out, the council has generally ensured through contractual conditions that information about service performance is reported to the Contracts Services Board.

9. The organisational arrangements for white-collar CCT have reflected the council's earlier experiences with blue-collar CCT. At the departmental level, there has been a soft split of client and contractor roles, with the creation of separate provider units and client units located within the same department under a single chief officer. However there is a hard split at committee level, with the provider units reporting to the Contract Services Board and the client units reporting to the relevant service committee.

10. The council has responded to the challenge of competition by creating in-house service providers with a large measure of operational autonomy. Contract Services is the council's main blue-collar service

provider. It has its own management and support services. The precise extent of operational autonomy is as yet unsettled.

11. Council staff working for Contract Services and the other in-house provider units are employed on different terms and conditions to the rest of the council staff. This reflects the commercial environment in which they work. There are also differences between the terms and conditions of council staff working in different defined activities.

12. In conclusion, CCT has led to significant changes in the provision of services regardless of whether work has remained in-house or has been contracted out. The notion of clients and providers, the use of service specifications, and the rigorous evaluation of proposals for service provision are all deeply embedded in the culture of the organisation.

Part four

Summary and Conclusions

Chapter 9
Summary and Conclusions

CHAPTER NINE

SUMMARY AND CONCLUSIONS

Part 1 of this book considered the legal framework of CCT. This, it will be recalled, was based around the LGA 1988, which applied to most local authority blue-collar services (see Chapter 1). Modified CCT provisions governed local authority professional services (see Chapter 2), and construction and maintenance work, which was covered by the rules of the LGPLA 1980 as amended by the two later statutes (see Chapter 3).

The CCT regime consisted of a number of requirements and prohibitions relating to the methodology of competitive tendering. CCT was about the means not the ends of local authority procurement. As such, while it could seek to drive down costs and improve efficiency it did not necessarily prevent local authorities from directing their procurement of work and services towards their own chosen political goals. The single exception to this lay in the field of social policy, which continues to be constrained by the ban on non-commercial considerations contained in Part II of the LGA 1988 (which is not actually a part of CCT as such). This point was illustrated by the case studies.

The chief problem for local authorities lay in the arbitrariness of CCT and in particular, the provisions against anti-competitive conduct on the part of local authorities. This was a general and ill-defined power, policed by a Secretary of State and backed by strong enforcement powers. Because the courts proved reluctant to interfere with the exercise of discretion by the Secretary of State, the prohibition of anti-competitive conduct made the conduct of tendering by an authority wanting to do its own thing, the legal equivalent of traversing a minefield.

Part 2 of the book went on to consider a number of salient aspects of CCT. This included its inter-action with EC public procurement law (see Chapter 4) and the Transfer of Undertakings Regulations (see Chapter 6), and the in-roads on local authority discretion in contract tendering matters resulting from Part II of the LGA 1988 and the aforementioned ban on anti-competitive conduct (see Chapter 5).

So much is the background to the research findings presented in Part 3, which lies at the centre of this book. The purpose of the research was to examine the effects of CCT on the delivery of services by local authorities. It sought to do this by examining the experiences of two case study local authorities, identified by the pseudonyms of Resbrough BC and Greenbrough BC. They were selected, in part, because they offered contrasts in size, range of functions and political character. Resbrough is a small, lower tier district council with a longstanding non-political tradition in its local politics, while Greenbrough is a large, unitary authority now dominated by the Liberal Democrats, having previously been a Conservative safe borough.

This research study has not attempted to assess the financial implications of CCT for the two authorities. Clearly this was an important matter. The reduction of local authority costs and improved efficiency were two of the principal reasons behind the government's championing of CCT. There were two reasons for missing out this assessment. First was the fear that investigation into financially sensitive areas might put off local authorities from agreeing to become case studies or hinder their co-operation in other areas. Second was the consideration that the financial effects of CCT have been the subject of other research studies, most recently the Austin Mayhead report for the DOE "CCT and Local Authority Blue-Collar Services'" (1997).[1] This indicated annual cost savings of 9% in the second round of CCT, following on from 6.5% savings achieved in the first round, while at the same time the quality of services had either been maintained or improved for the majority of local authorities. Although these matters were not tackled directly in the present research there was no indication or evidence that suggested the experience of the case study authorities differed from the general experience of local authorities, as shown by the Austin Mayhead report.

Instead this research has looked at the changes within the organisation of the case study councils and their practice in relation to delivering the services covered by CCT. From this, the following conclusions have been drawn.

1. The extension of competitive tendering would not have happened without the element of compulsion

Neither council had shown much in the way of an ideological commitment to the voluntary contracting out of services before the era of compulsion. Greenbrough's previous Conservative administration had considered contracting out a number of its services in the early 1980s but had not gone ahead with it. Its reaction to the 1985 Consultation Paper was that CCT should only be used against councils that were identified by the Audit Commission as high spenders. Hostility to central government coercion persisted when the Liberal Democrats took control from 1986 onwards. Nor did the Liberals take further steps to voluntarily contract out services. Resbrough, controlled by Resident's Associations (although probably Conservative leaning) throughout this period, showed a similar pattern.

Of course, both councils faced financial constraints and potential capacity shortages. Resbrough was far more vulnerable in this respect than Greenbrough because of its small size. Therefore the possibility that either council might have contracted out some services at some later date cannot be ruled out. However it is likely that this would have come later rather than sooner and on a much smaller scale. Changing the status quo, especially in circumstances where jobs are to be put under threat, is a difficult task to carry through and requires firm political will and leadership. It is doubtful that

---

[1] This and further research studies for the DOE are cited in the bibliography. See also the study by Rao and Young for the Joseph Rowntree Foundation.

either council possessed these qualities. Legal compulsion from central government (even if unwelcome) supplied the necessary excuse.

In conclusion, it is unlikely from their track records or political outlook that either council would have implemented voluntarily, competitive tendering on anything like the scale that has been seen with CCT. The element of compulsion was crucial.

2. Direct service providers have survived the onset of outside competition

Despite early fears for the survival of local authority DSOs, in the case study authorities direct service provision has survived the onset of competition, although each in a different manner.

Resbrough organised most of its direct service providers into a single DSO in preparation for CCT. This took a battering over the period 1989–92, losing contracts to competition from the local county council's DSO as well as to private contractors. However it always managed to retain the refuse collection contract and this ensured its survival, although as a niche rather than a general provider of local authority services.

Greenbrough underwent several reorganisations of its direct service provision, but whether as a number of specialist DSOs (1988–92) or as a single Contract Services Department (1992 onwards), it bested outside competitors more often than not. Unlike Resbrough, although a significant part of service provision has been contracted out, the majority is still directly provided.

3. CCT has led to significant organisational changes

This has occurred on both a departmental and a committee level. The impetus for change has been the CCT regime's implied requirement for some degree of client–contractor separation backed up by the threat of sanction by the Secretary of State for anti-competitive conduct.

Resbrough moved early towards a full separation of the two roles, establishing a free standing DSO in 1988. It was anxious to avoid any perception of a conflict of interest and so appears to have been motivated to fulfil both the letter and the spirit of the CCT regime in this respect. When a lack of success in early CCT tenders undermined the DSO's position, it was reconstituted as a division of the council's Community Services Department. Even after such a demotion, the DSO remained in a separate department to all of the client units responsible for managing its contracts. Ironically it may have been easier for Resbrough to retain its hard split because its lack of competitive success has meant that it carried out so few contracts in-house. Nevertheless, if some early critics doubted that small local authorities had the staff resources to operate separate client and contractor organisational structures, then Resbrough's experience disproves this.

Greenbrough was also motivated by the prospect of being challenged for anti-competitive conduct. To minimise disruption, the split was carried out within the existing departmental structures: an example of a "soft split". Continuing concern about the legality of the soft split and the need to maximise operational efficiency by combining management structures and overheads into a single in-house contractor led to the amalgamation of most of the DSOs in a single free-standing Contract Services Department in 1992. This development was a full organisational separation: an example of a "hard split". However, operational requirements again led to change. The loss of some key contracts meant that the continuing workload could ill-support separate departmental status. The council was also keen to foster greater co-operation between contractors and clients to improve service quality and further its policy goals. Following the 1993 Competition Regulations, with their minimalist prescription on client–contractor separation, the way was clear for the council to return to a softer split. This was achieved in 1997, when Contract Services was brought within the council's Environmental Services Department. It retained a separate divisional status but shared the department with the client-side of many of its big contracts.

Neither authority has moved towards the creation of a dedicated contract management department. Such a step was considered by Resbrough in 1993, but eventually rejected in favour of an inter-departmental working group. Had that gone through it would have resulted in the most radical of splits possible.

Greenbrough has been in the front of the implementation timetable for professional services CCT. These services have been organised to face competition on the basis of a soft split between client and contractor roles. These preparations for professional services CCT influenced the move back to a soft split in the blue-collar services.

The separation of client and contractor roles in the departments had consequences for the committee structures of both authorities. In order to maintain accountability, each established new committees to oversee their DSOs. Members of the service committees responsible for overseeing the client–side of contracts did not participate in these new committees, so ensuring a client–contractor split at committee level as well. The remaining service committees have looked after the client–side of contracts.

4. CCT has forced councils to develop new skills and methods in their service provision

Competition has forced direct service providers to become more commercial in their outlook. The two authorities have both shared similar experiences in this regard:

- close supervision of DSO trading accounts
- identification of support service costs through the creation of internal trading accounts
- greater autonomy of decision-making for DSOs

- different terms and conditions of employment for DSO employees from the rest of authority

This has enabled DSOs to constrain their costs. In turn this has enabled them to submit competitive bids and, just as importantly, meet the required financial objectives for the duration of contracts. The success of DSOs in the face of competition can be attributed to their commercialisation.

On the client-side, both authorities have developed specialist contract management units within the existing departmental structures. There has not been any movement towards a single contracts management department, although Resbrough had considered and rejected such a move in 1993. This has made both authorities more focused on service outcomes, through the development of service specifications, flexible contractual terms (to allow variations of the contract or specification where needed) and contract monitoring. However this has not translated into the systematic use of market research into customer preferences, although this has been undertaken on an ad hoc basis.

5. CCT has highlighted the tension, inherent in the provision of public services, between the achievement of service quality and the constraint of costs

Competitive tendering has forced authorities to properly assess the pricing and quality of bids and to strike a reasoned balance between them. These issues have always been relevant to service provision but the stringent financial climate and CCT have made them more transparent. Both authorities have adopted tender evaluation formats that permit the separate treatment in tender evaluation of price and quality.

Resbrough has a more informal approach with different officers being allocated responsibility for technical matters (including quality) and corporate implications (including treatment of extraneous financial costs). Its approach has tended to be one of identifying the lowest priced bid for acceptance provided it is considered to be financially and technically viable.

Greenbrough has a more formalised and rigorous approach to quality matters. Tender evaluation models are used to measure the quality of tenders against agreed and mathematically weighted criteria. The results can then be used alongside the price of tenders in making the final decision. Even so, the balance struck between price and quality is not predetermined, but remains a matter of judgement. The evidence of the case study is that the price of a tender is the predominant factor so long as a quality threshold has been attained.

Finally, it should be noted that both authorities have official policies that appear supportive of direct service provision: "wherever possible within the constraints of the legislation (Resbrough); "wherever it offers best value" (Greenbrough). However the retention of in-house service provision would appear in practice to be less important than either price or quality of service, only playing a role where other factors are evenly balanced.

6. CCT has not prevented local authorities from pursuing their own political priorities in service provision except in the case of social policy, which is limited by Part II of the LGA 1988

Although CCT was a highly prescriptive legal regime, the most important prescriptions were negative in character such as the requirement not to award work in-house in preference to a lower priced outside bid without good reason (defined as anti-competitive conduct). This left authorities with some room for manoeuvre where they could put forward positive policies for services that were clearly stated and built into the contract documentation. In these situations they could validly argue that they have good reason for passing over a lower priced outside tender if they so chose. In this context, the EC public procurement rules provided a useful framework. Of course, this was not a watertight defence – the courts have shown themselves to be very reluctant to question the exercise of the Secretary of State's discretion under CCT. However this uncertainty did not necessarily deter a determined authority from implementing its policy agenda.

Of the two authorities, Greenbrough has shown the greater boldness in this area. It is the more political of the two case study authorities and has a distinct pro-environmental policy agenda. This has been systematically built into all parts of its contract documentation and tender evaluation procedures. Because outside contractors know in advance what they are getting into and appear to bid on the basis of equality with the in-house providers, Greenbrough has escaped being sanctioned for anti-competitive conduct.

Resbrough has taken a different political approach. It has opted for a quiet, value for money efficiency in its service provision, basically seeking to find the lowest priced, viable contractor. It has striven to play by the rules of the CCT regime. The one digression from this, the rejection of a lower priced bid for the refuse collection service in 1989, concerned what the members of the council considered to be their flagship service. Councillors were loath to lose the local political credit for the service. They have been less "committed" to most other in-house services.

In terms of imposing policy goals through competitive tendering, the big exception is social policy goals, which are excluded as non-commercial considerations by Part II of the LGA 1988.

Implications for the future

The evidence from general research into the effects of CCT is that it has brought about cost savings without affecting service quality. The evidence of the case studies is that the culture of specifying service requirements and competition to win work and achieve value for money is now deeply embedded. It is also clear that CCT can be used to serve local authority political goals, although some authorities may be unwilling or too cautious to take this route for fear of falling foul of the anti-competitiveness provisions. This suggests that the CCT regime may have served its original purpose in stimulating change and improved efficiency in local authorities and that while compulsory competition should remain, some of the detailed prescriptiveness of CCT should now be relaxed. This should encourage or facilitate local authorities in taking a more strategic approach to service delivery, without running an unduly significant risk of local authorities reverting to inefficient practices.

APPENDIX AND BIBLIOGRAPHY

Appendix 1 Research Methodology for Case Studies
Appendix 2 Recent Developments
Bibliography

Appendix One

Research Methodology for Case Studies

The local authorities chosen for these case studies asked not to be identified by name and so are referred to throughout by the pseudonyms of Resbrough and Greenbrough. The purpose of presenting these case studies is to consider in detail how the subject authorities have fulfilled their obligations under the CCT legislation and the effect that this has had on the "culture" of the authorities. The published research on CCT has tended to focus on the broad picture, examining common issues across representative samples of local authorities.[1] In approaching the study of these questions through case studies of individual local authorities it is possible to gain a far richer insight; something which, it is hoped will offset any disadvantages flowing from the narrower scope of inquiry.

The reporting of two case studies should also allow the comparison and contrast of their approaches to CCT: the two authorities share certain social and economic characteristics, but are in terms of size, range of function and local politics noticeably different.

Each case study has been researched through two principal methods.

(1) Documentary Research

This involved the study of official council policy statements and strategies, the minutes of council meetings and committees, confidential background reports to council meetings and committees, the minutes of meetings and reports prepared for officers of the council and related correspondence.

(2) Interviews

Ten interviews were conducted in total, five in relation to each case study authority. Interviews were conducted face to face and on a semi-structured basis. They lasted between forty-five minutes and one hour. In each case a senior council officer with overall responsibility for the conduct of CCT was interviewed. The remaining interviewees included the manager of the principal blue-collar Direct Service Organisation for each authority, and other managers representative of other aspects of CCT whether in a corporate, contractor or client role.

The case study authorities reserved the right to withhold approval for any part of the case study. This has not been exercised.

---

1 Research studies are listed in the Bibliography: see in particular under Audit Commission and Department of the Environment; see also the book by Lyons and Johnson, which profiles Wolverhampton MBC's experience of CCT, and Rao and Young (which is similar in character to the present research).

Appendix Two

Recent Developments

This Appendix will briefly examine the developments in the law covering the provision of local authority services since the Labour Party's victory in the general election of 1997 that ended eighteen years of Conservative rule. This period has seen the implementation of Labour's election manifesto commitment to abolish CCT and replace it with a duty of best value ("BV"). There has also been a revision the Acquired Rights Directive that will require some modification of the TUPE Regulations by 2001.

The Commitment to Abolish CCT

The Labour Party, which had consistently opposed CCT, reaffirmed its intention to abolish it in the 1995 Policy Paper on local government "Renewing Democracy, Rebuilding Communities". This document spoke of replacing CCT with a new system designed to obtain best quality services and value for money based on the publication of annual Community Plans for each council. These proposals formed part of the 1997 general election manifesto.

The Replacement: the Principles of Best Value

Following its election victory, the new Labour government confirmed its election pledge to abolish CCT and replace it with a duty of best value but indicated that it was not to be an early legislative priority. In the meantime it published twelve principles of best value which it saw as underpinning the prospective new regime. They are reproduced below:

> "1. The duty of best value is one that local authorities will owe to local people, both as taxpayers and as the customers of local authority services. Performance plans should support the process of local accountability to the electorate.
> 2. Achieving Best Value is not just about economy and efficiency, but also about effectiveness and the quality of local services – the setting of targets and performance against these should therefore underpin the new regime.
> 3. The duty should apply to a wider range of services than those now covered by CCT...
> 4. There is no presumption that services must be privatised, and once the regime is in place there will be no general requirements for councils to put their services out to tender, but there is no reason why services should be delivered directly if other more efficient means are available. What matters is what works.
> 5. Competition will continue to be an important management tool, a test of

best value and an important feature in performance plans. But it will not be the only management tool and is not in itself enough to demonstrate that Best Value is being achieved.
6. Central government will continue to set the basic framework for service provision, which will in some areas as now include national standards.
7. Detailed local targets should have regard to any national targets, and to performance indicators and targets set by the Audit Commission in order to support comparative competition between authorities and groups of authorities.
8. Both national and local targets should be built on the performance information that is in any case needed by good managers.
9. Auditors should confirm the integrity and comparability of performance information.
10. Auditors will report publicly on whether Best Value has been achieved, and should contribute constructively to plans for remedial action. This will include agreeing measurable targets for improvement and reporting on progress against an agreed plan.
11. There should be provision for intervention at the direction of the Secretary of State on the advice of the Audit Commission when an authority has failed to take agreed remedial action, or has failed to achieve realistic targets for improvement.
12. The form of intervention should be appropriate to the nature of failure. Where an authority has made limited use of competition, and as an exception to the usual rule, intervention may include a requirement that a service or services should be put to competition. Intervention might also take the form of a requirement that an authority should accept external management support, and may relate either to specific services, or to the core management of the council."

The twelve principles of best value were to play a dual role. Firstly they were to inform the conduct of competitive tendering by local authorities under the modified CCT regime that the government consciously chose to keep in place for a transitional period. The government wanted to retain a tight control over public spending and was not prepared to abolish CCT until a fully worked out replacement was to hand. Secondly they were to underpin the consultation process and local authority pilot projects that were to proceed the enactment of any BV legislation.

The Transitional CCT regime

The form of the transitional CCT regime was announced in November 1997 and was given effect through secondary legislation.[1] The changes were intended to provide local authorities with a breathing space (within the statutory framework) to pursue voluntary competitive tendering and new partner-

---

1   S.I. 1997 Nos. 2648–2649, 2732–2734, 2746–2748 and 2756.

ships with the private sector, to simplify the tendering process by repealing many prescriptive provisions and to encourage quality considerations and other innovative approaches to service delivery. The principal changes are outlined below in the order in which they appear in Parts 1 and 2 of the main text.

Blue-collar CCT (Chapter 1)

The blue-collar CCT regime was amended in the following ways:

1. The general de minimis exemption for work falling within blue collar defined activities was raised from £100,000 to £150,000 per annum.[2]
2. The small schools exemption was abolished and replaced with a general exemption from CCT in respect of all LMS schools.[3]
3. The prescription of minimum and maximum contract periods was revoked, as were the requirements contained in the 1993 Competition Regulations prescribing minimum time limits for CCT procedures and prescribing the conduct of the financial evaluation of tenders (treatment of allowable and prospective costs).[4]

White-collar CCT (Chapter 2)

The white collar CCT regime outlined in Chapter 2 of this book was also amended in a number of ways.

1. The requirement for local authorities to prepare Statements of Support Service Costs was revoked.[5]
2. The timetable for the implementation of CCT for white-collar services was adjusted.
3. The formula for calculating the specified proportion of functional work carried out in each defined activity (the value of work subject to CCT requirements in each financial year) was retained in its post Beresford Review form.[6] However changes were made to the definition of credits available under that formula, chiefly the expansion of the credit for voluntary competitive tendering: work awarded in-house following a qualifying VCT exercise after 1 October 1997 now counted towards the credit at 125% of its value. The credit relating to work carried out for LMS schools was also removed, this reflecting the general exemption of work carried out for LMS schools from the CCT regime.

---

2   S.I. 1997 No. 2746.
3   S.I. 1997 No. 2748.
4   S.I. 1997 No. 2747.
5   ibid.
6   S.I. 1997 No. 2732.

CCT under the 1980 Act (Chapter 3)

The CCT regime for construction and maintenance work outlined in Chapter 3 of the book was amended to exempt work relating to LMS schools from competition.[7]

European Public Procurement Law (Chapter 4)

The European public procurement regime outlined in Chapter 4 remains relevant to both compulsory and voluntary competitive tendering.

Local discretion and the tendering process (Chapter 5)

Part II of the LGA 1988 (prohibition of non-commercial considerations) has remained in force but future changes to allow appropriate workforce matters to be taken into account have been promised subject to consultations. The necessary enabling powers have been enacted through section 19 of the Local Government Act 1999, which enables the Secretary of State to amend the list of non-commercial considerations contained in the 1988 Act. Regarding anti-competitive conduct, the revocation of most of the 1993 Competition Regulations considerably enhanced local authority discretion in the tendering process, especially in relation to the financial evaluation of tenders. However the prescribed framework for the client-contractor split in organisational arrangements for interim CCT remained, as did the power to issue guidance of a mandatory nature. The Secretary of State issued new guidance to local authorities under those powers through DETR Circular 16/97 (replacing DOE Circular 5/96) indicating that anti-competitive conduct could be avoided by the following:

- ensuring that the competition process is undertaken, and is seen to be undertaken, in an open and transparent manner;
- consulting service users and potential service providers on the level and standard of services to be provided;
- securing services which are economic, effective and efficient, in which considerations of price and quality are properly balanced;
- seeing that all competing bids are objectively evaluated; and,
- acting fairly between potential contractors to ensure that tendering practice does not advantage any one potential supplier or suppliers.

These guiding principles do not differ greatly from those they replaced. The requirement to consult the potential market was retained for example. Perhaps the chief difference is the more explicit support for the evaluation of competing bids in terms of quality. The guidance makes it clear that nothing

---

7   S.I. 1997 No.2756.

in the principles contradicts the general fiduciary duty of a local authority towards its council taxpayers.

TUPE (Chapter 6)

The Acquired Rights Directive has been amended by Council Directive 98/50.[8] The revised directive enacts most of the recent case law of the ECJ regarding the definition of a transfer of an undertaking and other matters. It also requires member states to adopt measures to ensure that the transferor informs the transferee of all rights and obligations that will transfer (so far as they are known at the time of the transfer). Significantly, member states will have the discretion to provide for the transfer of employee's rights under occupational pension schemes. This is something that the UK is likely to implement. The directive was effective from 17 July 1998 and the member states have 3 years to carry out the necessary implementation measures. The revision of TUPE is the subject of on-going consultations.

Consultations and Pilot Projects on Best Value

Following the announcement of the principles of best value, the DETR invited local authorities to submit bids to participate in a 2–3 year pilot authority programme starting in April 1998. The purpose of the pilot programme was to test elements of the best value framework and assess the extent to which improvements in service quality flowed from the new approach. Authorities that gained approval for pilot status were granted exemptions from CCT. Meanwhile the DETR published a Green Paper "Modernising Local Government – Improving Local Services through Best Value" for consultation in March 1998. It was one of a number of green papers covering the new government's wider modernisation agenda for the public services. This agenda included measures such as the introduction of directly elected mayors, a new duty for local authorities to promote the social, economic and environmental well-being of their areas, a new ethical framework for local government and changes to end crude and universal capping of local expenditure. The government's proposals were published in July 1998 as a DETR White Paper "Modern Local Government – In Touch with the People". The proposed framework for the new Best Value regime was outlined in Chapter 7 of the White Paper. It formed the basis for a Local Government Bill that was introduced in the following Parliamentary session and became the Local Government Act 1999.

The Local Government Act 1999

The CCT legislation (but not Part II nor section 33 of the LGA 1988) is abolished by section 21 of the 1999 Act, with effect from 2 January 2000.

---

8   O.J. L201/88.

Part I of the 1999 Act replaces CCT with a new duty of best value. It is essentially framework legislation and much will depend on the regulations and guidance issued under it. The following is intended to be no more than a brief outline of the new regime. For a more detailed treatment, reference should be made to other local government law works and local government web sites.

The duty of BV applies to the bodies specified by section 1 or otherwise designated by the Secretary of State under section 2. It applies to a similar range of bodies as those covered by CCT. The duty, as defined in section 3(1), is one to make arrangements to secure continuous improvement in the way in which a BV authority's functions are exercised having regard to a combination of economy, efficiency and effectiveness. In order to satisfy the duty of best value, an authority will be required:

- to consult widely with local stakeholders on the implementation of BV (section 3),
- meet performance standards set by the Secretary of State (section 4),
- carry out a rolling programme of fundamental reviews covering every function of the authority (section 5), and
- publish every year a Performance Plan reporting on its progress and specifying priorities and performance targets for the year ahead (section 6).

The Performance Plan will be audited by the authority's auditor to ensure its conformity with the Act (section 7). The auditor's report will be published and its recommendations will be reflected in subsequent Performance Plans (section 9). The Audit Commission also has the power to carry out a BV Inspection of an authority's compliance with the Act (section 10). This allows for a closer scrutiny of an authority's performance under BV. Inspections can be instigated by the Secretary of State or on the Audit Commission's own initiative. The auditor's report under section 7 may recommend that an Inspection is carried out or that enforcement action is taken by the Secretary of State. The audit and inspection powers therefore provide the principal means of oversight under BV. This contrasts with the situation under CCT, where this role was undertaken by the Secretary of State. The enforcement provisions of BV are contained in section 15 and empower the Secretary of State to act where he is satisfied that an authority is failing to comply with the Act. The enforcement powers are wider than those provided under CCT. They include the power to direct an authority to take any action the Secretary of State considers necessary or expedient and the power to take over the management of any function. The Secretary of State has further powers to modify or exclude the application of any other enactment where he considers that it interferes with the achievement of BV by authorities (section 16).

The Act does not apply to Scotland because local government matters there have been devolved to the Scottish Parliament. BV principles are currently being applied in Scotland outside of any legislative framework. Wales has a more limited scheme of devolution than Scotland and there the

National Assembly for Wales exercises most of the powers held in England by the Secretary of State. The post-1997 devolution settlement has therefore brought a variable geometry to the BV regime, which means that BV has the potential to develop in markedly different ways in England, Wales and Scotland.

Bibliography

This bibliography includes sources cited in the text.

General Reference Works

"The Encyclopedia of Local Government Law" published by Sweet & Maxwell. 4 volume looseleaf work (updated).

"The Encyclopedia of Employment Law" published by Sweet & Maxwell. 4 volume looseleaf work (updated)

"Cross on Local Government Law" edited by Stephen Bailey and published by Sweet and Maxwell (updated).

Also the following journals –
LA Law
Law Society Gazette
Local Government Chronicle
Local Policy Studies
Industrial Law Journal
Municipal Journal
Public Procurement Law Review
Solicitors Journal

Other Works

Ascher K "The Politics of Privatisation – Contracting out Public Services" – part of Public Policy and Politics series (Series editors Colin Fudge and Robin Hambleton). Published by Macmillan 1987.

Association of Metropolitan Authorities (AMA) –
Model Contract Compliance Questionnaire.

Audit Commission –
"Competitiveness and Contracting Out of Local Authorities' Services": Occasional Paper: 1987.
"Building Maintenance Direct Labour Organisations: A Management Handbook": 1988.
"The Competitive Council": Management Paper: March 1988.
"Competition Advice to Auditors: Signposts to Anti-Competitiveness": December 1988.
"Preparing For Compulsory Competition": Occasional Paper: January 1989.
"Management Buy-Outs: Public Interest or Private Gain": Management Paper: January 1990.
"Realising the Benefits of Competition: The Client Role for Contracted Services": 1993.

Bowers J., Jeffries S., Napier B. & Younson F. "Transfer of Undertakings" published by Sweet and Maxwell (1998)

Byrne T. "Local Government in Britain"

Cabinet Office – White Paper
"The Citizen's Charter – Raising the Standard" Cm 1599 (1991)

Cassell C. and Symon G. "Qualitative Methods in Organizational Research – A Practical Guide" SAGE Publications 1994.

Chartered Institute of Public Finance and Accountancy (CIPFA) –
Code of Practice (as updated)
& Papers by Competition Joint Committee –
"Compulsory Competition and the Litter Code": December 1991.
"Compulsory Competition and the Separation of Duties": December 1991.
"LMS and Compulsory Competition – An Occasional Paper": May 1993.

Cirell S.D and Bennett J. –
"Compulsory Competitive Tendering. Law and Practice" published by Longman 1990. 2 volume looseleaf work (updated).
"Competitive Tendering for Professional Services" published by FT Law & Tax 1994. 2 volume looseleaf work (updated).
And further published Articles including –
"Tendering without confidentiality – A handicap on councils': Law Society Gazette: 6 September 1989.
"Evaluating tenders without proper guidelines": Law Society's Gazette: 19 October 1989.
"Management Buy-Outs of Local Authority Services": Solicitors Journal, 27 April 1990.
"Circular problems for competitive tendering": Law Society's Gazette 15 June 1990.
"Defining roles in local government": Law Society's Gazette: 16 January 1991.
"The Litter Code – Further Burdens on Local Authorities under CCT": Solicitors Journal, 12 April 1991.
"Packaging CCT contracts": Law Society's Gazette 3 July 1991.
"LAWDACS – CCT by Another Name?": Solicitors Journal, 29 November 1991.
"CCT and the Transfer of Undertakings Regulations": Solicitors Journal, 31 July 1992.
"The Inter-relationship of EC Public Procurement and Competitive Tendering in the UK": Public Procurement Law Review No.4
"Flesh on the Bones – An Examination of the Latest CCT Regulations": LA Law 26 May 1993.
"This Flawed Guidance": Municipal Journal, 8 October 1993
"Choosing the Company Route": Local Government Chronicle, 7 January 1994.

Deakin S. & Morris G.S. "Labour Law" published by Butterworths 2nd Edition, 1998

Department of the Environment: Consultation Papers –
"Competition in the Provision of Local Services" (1985)
"Competing for Quality" (1991)

Department of the Environment: Local Government Research Programme Reports –
"Analysis of Local Authority CCT Markets" by Ernst & Young [1995].
"CCT: The Private Sector View" by BMRB International Ltd. (1995)
"CCT and Local Authority Blue-Collar Services" by Austin Mayhead & Co. (1997)
"CCT and Local Government – Annual Reports" 1993–97.
"CCT Factsheet" (various)

Digings L. and Bennett J. "EC Public Procurement Law and Practice" published by FT Law & Tax. 2 volume looseleaf work (updated).

Elias and Bowers "The Transfer of Undertakings: The Legal Pitfalls": 1994.

Escott & Whitfield "The Gender Impact of CCT" published by the Equal Opportunities Commission, 1995

Ewing K.D. "Swimming with the Tide: Employment Protection and the Implementation of European Labour Law" (1993) ILJ 22

Ewing K.D. and McColgan A. "Law at work" 2nd Edition (UNISON).

Farnham D. and Horton S. (editors) "Managing the New Public Services" published by Macmillan 1993.

Fenwick J. and Harrop (University of Northumbria) "The Privatisation of Local Public Services in the United Kingdom". Paper for conference on "Subsidiarity and the role of Public Administration" at University of Bologna in September 1995.

Hepple R. "Workers Rights in Mergers and Take-overs: The EEC Proposals" (1976) ILJ 197; also (1977) ILJ 106 and (1982) ILJ 10, 29.

HM Treasury White Paper –
"Competing for Quality – Buying Better Public Services" Cm 1730 (1991)

House of Lords Select Committee on The European Communities, Session 1995–6, 5th Report "Transfer of Undertakings: Acquired Rights" (HL Paper 38) HMSO.

ICE Conditions of Contract 5th Edition

Konig K. (Post-Graduate School of Administrative Sciences, Speyer) "Privatisation and the role of Public Administration in Germany". Paper for Bologna Conference (see Fenwick and Harrop, above).

Local Government Chronicle Privatisation Surveys 1983–87 (various editions)

Local Government Management Board (LGMB): various publications, including –
CCT Information Service Survey Reports (periodical)
"Guidance on the Assessment of Quality in the Application of CCT to Blue-Collar 'Front Line' Services" (November 1995).
"Guidance on the Assessment of Quality in the Application of CCT to White-Collar and Professional Services" (1995)
"Contract Documents"
"Quality in the Balance" (1995)

Loughlin M., Gelfand M.D., Young K., eds "Half a Century of Municipal Decline 1935–1985" (1985) London: George Allen & Unwin.

Loughlin M. "Central – Local Government Relations", in Jowell J. and Oliver D. "The Changing Constitution" 3rd edition (1994) Oxford: Clarendon Press.

Loughlin M. "Legality and Locality. The Role of Law in Central – Local Government Relations" (1996) Oxford: Clarendon Press.

Lyons M.T and Johnson A. "Preparing the Winning Bid – A Handbook for Competitive Tendering" Charles Knight Publishing, Croydon 1992.

McCall & Simmons "Issues in participant observation. A text and reader." (Addison Wesley Publishing Co.)

Napier B. "CCT, Market Testing and Employment Rights": 1993.

Painter J. "Compulsory Competitive Tendering in Local Government: The First Round" Public Administration (Summer 1991)

Rao N. "Managing Change: Councillors and the New Local Government" (1993) York: Joseph Rowntree Foundation

Rao N. and Young K. "Competition, Contracts and Change: The Local Authority Experience of CCT" (1995) Joseph Rowntree Foundation.

Szymanski S. & Jones T. "The Cost Savings from CCT of Refuse Collection Services", London Business School, 1993

Sparke A. "The Compulsory Competitive Tendering Guide" published by Butterworths 1993 (2nd Edition – 1995).

Stewart J. "The Future of Local Government – The Changing Organisation and Management of Local Authorities" (1991) Macmillan

Stewart J. & Stoker G. eds "Local Government in the 1990s" (1995) London: Macmillan.

Stoker G. "The Politics of Local Government" – part of Public Policy and Politics series (Series editors Fudge C. and Hambleton R.). Published by Macmillan 1987.

Travers T. "The Politics of Local Government Finance" (1986) London: Allen and Unwin Ltd.

Walker B. "Competing for Building Maintenance – Direct Labour Organisations and Compulsory Competitive Tendering" (HMSO 1993)

Walsh K. "Competitive Tendering for Local Authority Services – Initial Experiences", (1991) London HMSO.

Walsh K. & Davies H. "Competition and Service – The Impact of the Local Government Act 1988" (HMSO 1992)

Walsh K. "Public Services and Market Mechanisms – Competition, Contracting and the New Public Management" (1995) Basingstoke: Macmillan Press.

Weiss F. "Public Procurement in European Community Law" – part of European Community Law Series (Series Editor – Lasok D.). Published by the Athlone Press. London and Atlantic Highlands, NJ

Willett C. ed "Public Sector Reform and The Citizen's Charter" (1996) London: Blackstone Press Ltd

Yates E. "Local Authorities and Outside Organisations" published by Sweet & Maxwell 1996.

INDEX

Accounts and Audit (Amendment) Regulation 47–9
Acquired Rights Directive
  amendments 281
  background 135–8
  implementation 137–8
  nature of transfer 138–40
  nature of undertaking 140–6
  number of employees 143–4
  stable economic entity 141–2, 144–6
administrative guidance *see* circulars
advertising notices 20–1
aggregation rules 83–4
allowable costs 132, 209
allowances *see* specified proportion
anti-competitive conduct 21–2
  circulars 116–19
  forms 115–16
  Greenbrough case study 251–2, 267–8
  political goals 265
  Resbrough case study 195–6, 198
  Secretary of State's guidance 115–16
  service quality 122–4
  statutory framework 112–14
  tendering process 119–22
  TUPE 162–4
Audit Commission 42

barring orders 28–9
Beresford review 57–8
best value
  pilot projects 281
  principles 277–8
  statutory framework 281–2
  transition 278–9
blue collar CCT
  amendments, transitional 279
  background 3–5
  cross-boundary tendering 16–17
  disclosure requirements 23–4
  enforcement 27–9
  exemptions 12–16
  functional work 16–24
  Greenbrough case study 215–18, 239–44
  judicial review 29–35
  Resbrough case study 171–5
  Secretary of State's powers 8–9, 13–16, 30–4
  time limits 22–3
  works contracts 16–18

case studies *see* Greenbrough Borough Council; Resbrough Borough Council
circulars
  anti-competitive conduct 116–19
  non-compliance 115–16
  status 114–15
  tender evaluation 127–8, 130–1
  TUPE 162–4
Citizens' Charter 20, 38
client/contractor roles
  conclusions 267–8
  Greenbrough case study 260, 267–8
  Resbrough case study 180–1, 267
  tendering process 119–22
Common Product Classification (CPC) 80–2
'Competing for Quality' Consultation Paper 38–9
competition free allowances 65
Competition Regulations
  tender evaluation 130–3
  time limits 87
competition requirements 40–1
compulsion 266–7
Compulsory Competitive Tendering for Professional Services *see* white collar CCT
conclusions
  commercial outlook 268–9
  compulsion 266–7
  Direct Service Providers 267
  organisational changes 267–8
  political goals 270
  service quality 269
conditions order 28–9
consequences CCT
  commercial outlook 268–9
  financial 265–6
  political goals 270
  service quality 269
construction and maintenance CCT
  accounting provisions 70–1
  amendments, transitional 280
  definition 61–3
  disclosure requirements 72–3
  enforcement provisions 73–4
  exemptions 62–5
  financial provisions 71–2
  functional work 69–70
  statutory framework inadequacy 74
  works contracts 66–9

contract compliance *see* contract tendering
    issues . . .
contract management, Resbrough case study
    188–92
contract tendering issues
    background 103–5
    constitutional issues 112
    contract compliance
        background 105
        commercial considerations 111
        health and safety 110–11
        legality 105–12
        non-commercial considerations 105–11
        race relations 107–8
        sex/disability discrimination 108–10
    environmental considerations 111
    notice requirement 111–12
contracts of employment 154–6, 184–5
costs
    allowable 132, 209
    extraneous 124–6, 195–6, 200
    prospective 132
    Statement of Support Service Costs 42–3,
        47–9
CPC *see* Common Product Classification
cross-boundary tendering 16–17

de minimis exemptions 14, 49, 50–1, 63,
    83–4
defined activities
    blue collar CCT 6–13
    client/contractor overlap 40–1
    construction and maintenance CCT 61–5
    construction and property services 45
    exemptions 12–16, 47
    financial objectives 25
    financial services 45–6
    informational technology services 45–6
    legal services 44–5
    list 5–6
    new activities 9–13
    original seven 6–8
    overlap 6
    personnel services 46–7
    Secretary of State's powers
        creation 8–9
        exemption 13–16
    white collar CTT 44–7
defined authorities 5–6
Direct Service Organisations (DSOs)
    accounts requirements 24

consequences CCT 268–9
financial objectives 25
Greenbrough case study 228
Resbrough case study
    background 182
    business viability 202
    client-side relations 185–6
    council decision 209–10
    employee consultation 205–7
    employment contracts 184–5
    management structure 183
    operational autonomy 184
    quality management issues 185
    status 186
    trade sale 202–4
    transfer of undertakings law 152
Direct Service Providers, business viability
    267
disability discrimination 108–10
disclosure requirements
    DLOs 70
    DSOs 23–4, 26–7
discrimination
    disability 108–10
    grounds of nationality 93–5
    race 95, 107–8
    sex 108–10
discriminatory contract conditions 92–5
dismissal 158–61
'double envelope' tendering 43–4
DSOs *see* Direct Services Organisations
duty of best value regime 85–6
duty to give reasons 99

EC public procurement law
    advertising requirements 87
    application 80–4
    background 77–80
    discriminatory contract conditions 92–5
    enforcement 99–101
    financial thresholds 83–4
    implementation 79–80
    interaction CCT 84–5
    overlap CCT regime 80–4
    post-award requirements 99–100
    procedures 85–7
    purpose 77–8
    remedies 99–101
    selection of contractors 89–95
    Services Regulations 80–3
    status 84–5

tender evaluation 96–8
time limits 86–7
Works Regulations 80
EC rules *see* EC public procurement law
economic entity *see* stable economic entity
emergency work exemption 12, 64
employee rights *see* transfer of undertakings law
employment contracts 154–6, 184–5
enforcement
    construction and maintenance CCT 73–4
    EC public procedure law 99–101
    judicial review 29–34
    notices 27–9
    Secretary of State 27–9
    Transfer of Undertakings Regulations 162
exemptions
    blue collar CCT 12–16
    construction and maintenance CCT 62–5
    de minimis 14, 49, 50–1, 63, 83–4
    white collar CCT 47, 49
    see also specified proportion
extension contracts 64–5
extraneous costs 124–6, 195–6, 200

fettered discretion 108–9
Financial Objectives Specifications 25
functional work
    accounting provisions 70–1
    definition 16–17, 69
    disclosure 23–4, 72–3
    financial provisions 71–2
    implementation 18–20
    local authority companies 23
    phasing-in 18–20
    pre-conditions 20–2
    professional services 56–7
    specified proportion formula 49–56
    statutory requirements 20–2, 69–70
    time limits 22–3

Greenbrough Borough Council case study
    anti-competitive conduct 251–2
    'Authorised Officer' 226–7
    blue collar CCT 215–18, 239–44
    CCT
        in-house/contracted services 218–19
        overview 213–15
        timetable 214, 215
    Client Catering Unit 236–7
    client/contractor roles 227–31
    conclusions 259–61
    construction and property CCT
        background 252
        client/contractor roles 253–4
        contract performance 257–9
        in-house bid 255–6
        specified proportion 253–4
    contract management 236–9
    Contract Services Division 231–2
    corporate initiatives 220–7
    DSOs 228–9, 231–4
    environmental policy 221–2, 224, 226, 249
    financial services CCT
        criteria 246–8
        process 245–6
        specified proportion 244–5
        tender evaluation 248–50
    in-house provision 221
    legal services CCT
        anti-competitive conduct 251–2
        background 250–1
        process 250–1
    non-price considerations 223–4
    political goals
        conditions of contract 226–7
        conditions of tender 225
        service profile 225
        tender evaluation 223–4
    'preferred provider'
        selection 235
        welfare catering 244
    profile 213
    restructuring 228–31
    tender evaluation
        approach 234–6
        policy incorporation 223–4
    vision statement 220–1
    welfare catering CCT
        background 239–40
        evaluation 241–4
        'preferred provider' 244
        process 240
        timetable 240
        white collar CCT 244–52
grounds of ineligibility 89–90

hard split *see* organisational changes

incidental work exemption 12–13
information technology services 46

internal market, Resbrough case study 179–80
internal trading accounts 41–2
invitations to tender 21

judicial review
　enforcement 29–35
　tender evaluation 128–30

legal transfer 138–40, 149–51
LGA *see* Local Government Act 1988
local authority companies 23
Local Government Act 1988
　application 5–6
　competitive tendering rules 16–27
　enforcement
　　directions 28–9
　　judicial review 29–34
　　notices 27–9
　exemptions 12–16
　secondary legislation 8–9
　time limits 23–4
　white collar CCT 49–59
Local Government, Planning and Land Act 1980
　application 61–3
　CCT requirements 65
　competition condition 68–70
　enforcement provisions 73–4
　exemptions 63–5

Management Support Unit
　review contract management 188–92
　tender evaluation 187
MSU *see* Management Support Unit
municipal trading 16–17

non-commercial communications 95, 105–11
notices
　advertising 20–1
　contract award 98–9
　enforcement 27–9
　exclusion/rejection contractor 111–12
　Official Journal of the European Communities 88–9
　prior information 87–8

Official Journal of the European Communities (OEJC) 86–7, 98–9, 193
organisational changes
　conclusions 267–8
　DOE view 119–22
　Greenbrough case study 227–31, 260
　Resbrough case study 180–1
overlap of CCT/EC law 80–4

pensions 159–61
Performance Plan 282
political goals 223–4, 265, 270
prescribed amounts 67
procedures 85–7
professional services CCT *see* white collar CCT
proportionality principle 35
public procurement law *see* EC public procurement law
Public Services Contracts Regulations 1993 80–3
Public Works Contracts Regulations 1991 79–80
purposive interpretation
　Acquired Rights Directive 141–2
　TUPE 147–50

race relations 95, 107–8
rate of return 25
redundancy costs *see* extraneous costs
Resbrough Borough Council case study
　CCT
　　blue collar 171–5
　　implementation 169–70
　　overview 169–70
　　timetable 169–70
　　white collar 175
　client/contractor roles 180–1
　conclusions 210–12
　contract management
　　monitoring 190–1
　　MSU review 188–92
　　service specifications 189
　　working group 191–2
　contracted services 175–7
　corporate initiates 177–80
　DSO
　　background 182
　　business viability 202
　　client-side relations 185–6
　　council decision 209–10
　　employee consultation 205–7
　　employment contracts 184–5
　　management structure 183

operational autonomy 184
quality management issues 185
status 186
tender evaluation 207–8
trade sale 202–4
extraneous costs 195–6, 200
highways maintenance 202, 205
internal market 179–80
management structure 180–2
Management Support Unit 187, 188–92
profile 167–8
refuse collection CCT
councillors decision 198, 209–10
criteria 193–4, 205
extraneous costs 195–6
financial evaluation 195–6
process 193–5, 202–5
tender evaluation 195–7, 195–8, 207–9
service delivery 177–92
sports/leisure CCT
additional incentives 201
process 199
tender evaluation 199–201
tender evaluation
DSO trade sale 207–8
refuse collection 195–7
sports/leisure 199–201
TUPE effects 204
vision statement 177–8
voluntary contracting out 168, 168–9
research methodology 275
retention of identity test 146–52, 152–3
Ridley, Nicholas 4, 126

Secretary of State's powers
anti-competitive conduct definition 115–18
arbiter of breaches 30–3
defined activities 8–9, 13–16
enforcement 27–9
exercise of sanctions 33–4
selection of contractors
approved contractors 93
financial standing 82, 90–1
grounds of ineligibility 89–90
minimum standards 90
number of participants 93
requesting information 91–3
technical ability 91
service specifications 89
Services Regulations 80–3

sex discrimination 108–10
small schools exemption 14–15
soft split *see* organisational changes
Sparke, Andrew 26–7
specified proportion 49–56
allowances outside formula 54–6
Beresford review 58–9
credits 50–4
Greenbrough case study 218, 245, 253–4
pre-shrunk allowance 55–6
total value of work 50
splits, hard/soft 120–2, 180–1, 227–31, 260
SSSC *see* Statement of Support Service Costs
stable economic entity 141–2, 144–6
standing orders 103–4
Statement of Support Service Costs (SSSC) 42–3, 47–9

tender evaluation
'abnormally low' tenders 97–8
approaches 126–8, 130–1
Audit Commission 196
circulars 127–8, 130–1
Competition Regulations 130–3, 131–3
criteria 96
EC law 96–8
extraneous costs 124–6
government approach 126, 130–3
Greenbrough Borough Council 223–4
judicial review 128–30
most economically advantageous 96
non-commercial considerations 207
Resbrough case study
approach 186–8
DSO trade sale 207–8
refuse collection 195–8, 207–9
sports/leisure 199–201
tendering, cross-boundary 16–17
tendering process
advertising requirements 87
amendments, transitional 280–1
client/contractor roles 119–22
notice 87–9, 98–9
procedures, EC law 85–7
selection of contractors 89–92
service quality issues 122–4
time limits 86–7
tied accommodation exemption 14
time limits 22–3, 86–7
trade union rights 159, 161–2
transfer of undertakings

anti-competitive conduct 162–4
commercial venture 146–8
contracts of employment 154–6
dismissal 156–8
duty to inform 161–2
European case law 138–46
Greenbrough case study 250
nature of transfer 138–40, 149–51
nature of undertaking 140–6, 147–8
number of employees 143–4
pensions 159–61
protected employees 153–4
stable economic entity 144–6
statutory framework 136–8
trade union rights 159, 161–2
UK case law 147–51
see also Acquired Rights Directive
Transfer of Undertakings (Protection of Employment) Regulations 1981
  applicability
    circulars 162–4
    commercial venture 147–8
    government guidelines 151–2
    nature of transfer 149–51
    nature of undertaking 146–8
    transfer of ownership 149–50
  contact compliance 111
  effects
    collective agreements 159
    contracts of employment 154–6
    dismissal 156–8
    duty to inform 161–2
    objection to transfer 153–4
    pensions 159–61
    protected employees 153–4
    trade union rights 159, 161–2
  enforcement 162
  Greenbrough case study 250
  implementation 137–8
  Resbrough case study 204

specified proportion credit 53
statutory framework 138
see also Acquired Rights Directive
TUPE *see* Transfer of Undertakings (Protection of Employment) Regulations 1981
twin-hattedness 119–22

undertakings, nature 140–6

variation of employment contracts 155–6
voluntary competitive tendering 51, 168–9

white collar CCT
  accounting regime consistency 41–3
  amendments, transitional 279
  background 37–44
  Beresford review 57–9
  competition requirements 40–1
  consultation process 37–9
  defined activities 44–7
  exemptions 47, 49
  functional work 49–57
  Greenbrough case study 218–19, 244–52
  policy issues 39–40
  quality evaluation 43–4
  Resbrough case study 175
  research studies 41
  specified proportion 49–56
  Statement of Support Service Costs 42–3, 47–9
  works contracts 49
winter maintenance 65
works contracts
  definition 16–17, 66
  statutory authority 66–9
  statutory provisions 17–18, 49
  tendering procedures 66–8
Works Regulations 80

STUDIES IN LAW

1. R. Mullerson, M. Fitzmaurice and M. Andenas: *Constitutional Reform and International Law in Central and Eastern Europe.* 1997 ISBN 90-411-0526-3
2. A. J. Cygan: *The United Kingdom Parliament and European Union Legislation.* 1998
ISBN 90-411-9650-1
3. E. Guild (ed.): *The Legal Framework and Social Consequences of Free Movement of Persons in the European Union.* 1998 ISNB 90-411-1073-9; Pb 90-411-1090-9
4. M. Andenas and A. Turk (eds), *Delegated Legislation and the Role of Committees in the European Community.* 2000 ISBN 90-411-1275-8
5. M. F. Makeen: *Copyright in a Global Information Society: The Scope of Copyright Protection Under International, US, UK and French Law.* 2000 ISBN 90-411-9786-9
6. P. Gosling: *The Effects of Compulsory Competitive Tendering and European Law on Local Authorities.* 2001 ISBN 90-411-9825-3